THE PROVINCE OF THE CAT

A Journey to the Radical Heart of the Far North

George Gunn

Islands Book Trust

Utras Leabhraichean nan Eilean
LIVING HISTORY

Published in 2015 by the Islands Book Trust

www.theislandsbooktrust.com

ISBN: 978-1-907443-42-8

Text © George Gunn

Islands Book Trust, Laxay Hall, Laxay, Isle of Lewis HS2 9PJ
Tel: 01851 830316

Typeset by Erica Schwarz (www.schwarz-editorial.co.uk)
Cover design by Raspberry Creative Type
Front cover image courtesy of Roddy Ritchie
Printed and bound by Martins the Printers, Berwick upon Tweed

In memory of Mary Beith (1938–2012)

Acknowledgements to Creative Scotland; Light in the North; Bella Caledonia; The Mackay Country Community Trust; Strathnaver Museum

Contents

Often when I see these men play-acting: the unreality of their role was their security – even their own destinies were to them saga and folk-tale rather than a private matter; these were men under a spell, men who had been turned into birds or, even more likely, into some strange beast, and who bore their magic shapes with the same unflurried equanimity, magnanimity and dignity which we children had marvelled at in the beasts of fairy tale. Did they not suspect, moreover, with the wordless apprehension of animals, that if their magic shapes were to be stripped from them the fairy tale would be at an end and their security gone, too, while real life would begin with all its problems, perhaps in some town where there was neither Nature nor mirage, no link with folk-tale and the past, no ancient path to the far side of the mountains and down to the river gulleys and out beyond the grass plains, no landmarks from the sagas? – only a restless search for a sterile, deadening enjoyment.

— Halldór Laxness, *The Atom Station* 1948

Introduction

Caithness is a stage for giants. Set on the plateau of her flagstone floor she has her audience in the great stalls of the rest of Scotland to the south with the Northern and the Western isles hanging from the balcony of history, related and interested spectators as the epic play-opera of the Province of the Cat is acted out. Our script for this great production is chiselled from the very rocks beneath our feet and woven from the cold clean air we breathe and written in the blood of the countless people who have added to our story. The huge cathedral sky above us tells the world that the characters who inhabit these enacted fables are indeed giants for only giants can impress upon the audience of the rest of the world the need for truth. On this stage only giants can be seen.

For here is where the Atlantic clashes with the North Sea and their eternal struggle boils and rages daily in the tidal cauldron of the Pentland Firth. In Caithness the four winds seem to freely push and pull the land as much as they excite the sea. This fashions the mettle of the people which is forged from the hot blood meld of Norse and Celt which in turn colours the hair, the eye, the temper and psychology and supplies the people with their sturdy culture and their inclination for art and infuses the nature and quality of its manifestation.

It is how the people make art which interests me. What is behind the creativity, how do they survive the forces of history, the disasters and the slaughters and still cling to the concept of beauty? From the Neolithic to the Atomic age the making of beauty has been a constant. The stone work, the pottery, the poetry, the music, the painted variations of lived experience: are they all the products of dream or are they the optimistic artefacts and art forms of a durable people who grind their corn close to the indestructible temple-well of life?

To write a sustained account of your native place is, in many ways, to step out of your childhood and to leave it behind. Is it the case, as Hamish Henderson sardonically puts it at the end of his *Ballad of the Twelve Stations of My Youth* – 'From now, my boyhood's done.' Or is it, as I feel it is, more of a pilgrimage by a poet (me) through the narrative sea of prose, not my natural element, to fashion some meaning out of all this action, all these transitions, all these characters in these settings? The giants may be seen but is it necessary that they are understood? Caithness is a beautiful and unique place but most people do not know where it is. I am in search of the Caithness I see every day but also the Caithness deep inside of me. When I look over my shoulder I see that Caithness, those various Caithness's, following me.

Whatever the subject the main question which actually stalks me is this: what is the function of the writer? Is it to look at society, to report back? If so then what follows is an attempt at that. It is the irony of fiction that no-one will believe it if it is not true. That holds fast for history as well: no-one will believe it unless, somehow, you make it up. But I am not interested, particularly, in making it up. What I am concerned about is reporting back what I see and describing as best I can what I think it means. Telling the truth about what you see has been the responsibility of every artist in any and every age. This is a constant throughout history, so the historians tell us, and it does not make artists popular with their contemporary authorities. Of historians I cannot comment because I am not one. Although I would say that one other constant of history which is parallel to this is that all government at any time is authoritarian. So, as in the Pentland Firth, we have a perennial collision.

Scotland is a poetic nation. From the time of the first Celtic bards and the Norse skalds the story of Scotland's people has been told and expressed in poetry. Poetry is the form of the imagination: it flows from the heart to the tongue and possesses the collective energy of the tribe in a way no other literary art can match, for poetry is the song of the people's intellect, it is our signifier on the Earth and our codification for the hereafter.

Prose has had no corresponding function. The Scottish playwright George Byatt used to proclaim that 'poetry is the language of the theatre' and what he meant, I think, was that poetry spoken in a public space before a collection of people who shared a common cause was a medium which articulated discontent and facilitated enquiry. So powerful a medium in fact that governments have tried throughout history to control and regulate it. Prose, on the other hand, has had no similar constituency when it comes to a public function and has tended to be the clerical dictates of those twin controllers: church and state. Even when it is used in a defiant manifesto, such as The Declaration of Arbroath, it is still the barons, the powerful who are doing the talking and the writing. Is it that even such a seminal blast of Scottish self-determination is merely a case, artistically, of content dictating form? If so why then does a poet choose to write a book about Caithness, the northern half of the 'Province of the Cat' – Sutherland being the other – in prose?

To compound matters, as is probably obvious from this introduction, and as I have indicated, prose is not my natural medium. Even when I write a play it is not strictly prose. If dialogue can be described as prose then it is not good dialogue. Stage directions are simply words of instruction like signposts. But I have written this book in prose and that must be, surely, significant? Well, so be it: I have stepped out from the innocence of poetry into the worldly cynicism of prose. From here on in the language stands naked.

Chapter One

THE POINT OF CATS

It was during the coldest winter in one hundred years that I decided to abandon waiting. What I had been waiting for was the big song-story which would comprehensively replenish the hearts and minds of the people of the north of Scotland and me, but waiting is a flawed strategy. Morven, that mountain of song, and beside it Braemore of the tragic story, were unlikely to come to me. The thing I desired was never going to land in my lap. So it was I undertook to set off into memory, my own and others, to build the book-ship of remembering. For ten thousand years the land of Caithness and Sutherland has been lying 'out there', risen up, released from the pressure of glacial ice, waiting for the day of songs. This is an attempt to tell that story.

I grabbed what I could in material and ambition and set off down the old drove roads of the past, cold and icy as they were from the half remembered state of permafrost in which our history resides. My roads would lead to the future, I told myself, although I knew that the snowy indifference to our past was only matched by the 21st century's frosty indifference to our future.

I know that the geology and botany of the 'Province of the Cat' is fascinating, but they are not my primary concern: my desire is to interpret the history of the people as best I can, to record through my own eyes and from my reading and research, the human ecology of what lies north of Strath Fleet and Glen Oykel, west of Cape Wrath and east of Duncansby Head.

Nor do I make any claims to be a historian but as it is my intention to deal with the lives of people it would be as foolish to ignore their past as it would be reckless to predict their future. As a poet I know that the present is just a stopping off point to somewhere else and through my work as a playwright I have learned that any place is a stage where events can and do happen. What I feel emotionally about all of this is of no real import although I would hope some sense of connectedness comes through. All I can do is report what I see and be vain enough to think that these messages can add to 'the big song-story', which when attempted, can add subjectivity to the collective experience and can inform the reader in some unique way, or at least give a different flavour of telling to something rather less known than it should be.

Also I believe that myth and fable are as important to understanding a people's psychology as dates and events are in understanding their history and because what follows is a stravaig, or a wander through a landscape, I choose to read it as I please in the hope that such an idiosyncratic narrative will illuminate and entertain as much as it informs. In other words this is a personal guide to these rocks, bays and bogs and I will pull swatches of it out of my pocket like *Skidbladnir*, the folded ship of Norse mythology, in the same way as I may stumble over things I have never come across before and cannot explain. There is no authorised or definitive biography of anybody or anything and all I know with any certainty is that the 'Province of the Cat' has been subjected to so much history, invented as well as actual, that the people wear it in their eyes and keep it in the salt it in their blood. They keep their mythology in the corner of their smile.

All of that as the snow lay six feet deep and the temperature had never climbed above minus five for three weeks.

—

Caithness sits like a three cornered hat on the top of Scotland. Not many people, including a significant amount that live under its cathedral sky, understand this place. It is often referred to as 'the land beyond the Highlands', or 'the northern lowlands' or some such thing. Usually this is by people – politicians, tourist officers or time-share salespeople – whose ignorance is only matched by their false passions. These people confuse topography with culture. What Caithness may physically look like and what it actually is in human terms is a completely different thing.

Often I have heard local councillors declare with the certainty of zealots that Caithness has a 'proud Norse heritage' and that 'Gaelic was never spoken here', despite the fact that about two thirds of the place names in Caithness are Gaelic or a mixture of Gaelic and Norse, with the purely Norse place names being confined to the eastern and northern coasts. The very name 'Caithness' proclaims this duality with the Celtic 'Cat' alluding to the 'place of the Cat tribe' and the Norse 'ness' describing the 'point' which Caithness undoubtedly is, poking its sandstone snout defiantly into the North Sea: the point of cats.

This duality is further heightened, physically, by the titanic meeting in the Pentland Firth – the '*Péttlandsfjördr*' as the incoming Vikings called the 'firth of the Picts' – of the Atlantic Ocean to the west and the North Sea to the east. The racing tide-rips and the swirling whirlpools seem to articulate this dichotomy, this confusion. While the Pentland Firth, which marks the northern boundary of the 'Province of the Cat', and its beautiful, hypnotic and dangerous seascapes, is a result of nature the constructed confusion surrounding the cultural identity of Caithness is the result of the deliberate prejudice of humankind. This has been ongoing from the time of the first Norman colonists arrived in the north, to the demise of the Norse Earldom when Magnus died and Henry St Clair, through marriage, became Earl of Orkney, which then included Caithness. Henry was the first non-Norse, non-Celt to hold power. This process was begun during the reign of the Scottish King Malcolm Canmore and his virulently anti-Celtic wife, Queen Margaret. It was they who 'invited' the de St Clairs and other Norman barons into Scotland. This process of Normanisation was intensified in 1124 when their wayward son David, who had spent his youth in England under the tutelage of Henry I, became on the death of his brother Alexander, David I of Scotland.

The Gaelic word '*Gallaibh*', which means 'stranger, or among the stranger' – or, critically, in Gaelic it can mean something else entirely – and is how Caithness people are referred to in Gaelic, seems to activate a counter-productive anti-Gaelic sentiment in a few which is detrimental to understanding and is based on nothing but the calculated sectarian attempt to re-write history and cultivate stupidity. A people who are denied their history are all the more easily controlled, especially when they compound it out of ignorance. But ignorance is a disease that can be treated.

It is also the case that in denying the Celtic origins of the people of Caithness, their history and culture – including language – the anti-Gaelic zealots, whilst accepting the Normanisation as normal, overplay the Norse influence. Only where the ground could take a plough – and in the 10th century this was restricted to certain areas in from the coast – do we find strong evidence of Norse settlement. So much for the 'rape and pillage' of cartoon history. Also it is common practice for Anglo-Norse historians to debate the 'problem of the Picts' – where did they go? – in tones of academic impatience. The usual answer to 'where did they go?' is that they, along with their language, died or they were killed or were bred out by the Scandinavian settlers. The truth is more likely to be the opposite. If you want to know where the Picts are the answer is that they are not dead but are out in the fields driving tractors or Council lorries; working in hospitals or are on the deck of a fishing boat or a drilling rig. The native language of the pre-viking

Cat clan may have gone but it is the incoming Norse stock which has been absorbed, and this would have happened relatively quickly. The mighty Earl Sigurdson of the 11th century, Earl of Orkney, Caithness and Sutherland when the earldom was at its zenith, was himself three-quarters Celt. The same process absorbed the de St Clairs, or Sinclairs as they have become, but I doubt if the present Viscount with his cut glass accent and his Eton education would care to admit it.

I use the terms Celt and Pict in cross-fertilisation and in utility and unity because although undoubtedly the people of the ancient 'Province of the Cat', that distant Celtic kingdom, were Pictish and spoke a Celtic language there were seven other Pictish kingdoms in Scotland, or Alban as it was known, and undoubtedly there were other Pictish languages. That they were insular Celtic languages is almost certain but whether they were Brythonic or Goidelic in origin is unknown.

The pedantry which surrounds the language question in relation to the Picts is I think unhelpful. There were, of course, native people in the north of Scotland long before the Picts arrived from mainland Europe with their fertility goddesses, matrilineal ways and their horses. The language of these pre-Celtic people would have been absorbed in the P-Celtic (Brythonic), if that is what it was, of the Picts. Bilingualism would have been both common and necessary and it would have been strange indeed if the Picts from the 6th century, or even before, did not have trade and linguistic ties with their Irish cousins in Antrim. Indeed the name 'Atholl', which we encounter below, means 'new Ireland' and 'Strathearn', is the 'strath of the Irish'.

The first written record of the seven kingdoms of Alban is to be found in the *Historia Britonum*, as it is contained within the 'Chronicle of The Picts and the Scots', and this is no doubt based on some earlier oral sources. The story is that Cruithne, the legendary ancestor of the Picts, who divided Alban – which is the land, roughly, north of the Forth – into seven provinces, one for each of his seven sons to rule over. Contained in the *Historia* is a poem attributed to St Columba, or Colm Cille, of the 6th century, where we learn the names of these seven sons. This is a translation by the Reverend Angus Mackay of Westfield, Caithness, who died in 1911 and of whom we will learn a lot more later.

> Seven sons of Cruithne
> Divided Alba into seven divisions:
> Cait, Co, Cirig, warlike clans,
> Fib, Fidach, Fotla, Fortream.

From yet another source, the *De Situ Albanie*, compiled in the 12th century by Andrew, Bishop of Caithness, we learn that these seven names correspond geographically with the Mearns and Angus, Atholl and Gowrie, Strathearn and Monteith, Fife and Forthrene (which is Kinross and parts of Fife), Mar and Buchan, Moray and Ross, and finally, Caithness. Now Caithness is the only one of the seven provinces, or kingdoms, to be a singular name but Bishop Andrew does note that 'Cait', or the province of 'Caithness' is divided down the middle by a 'mons Mound' or 'The Ord' as we know it. His bishopric was contained within the same contours. This, I think it fair to assume, was the lie of the land of Alban, the northern half of Scotland, in the 9th century and how the Norsemen found it.

The physical area of Caithness is fifty kilometres from north to south and fifty kilometres from east to west which encompasses 1,844 square kilometres of hill, bog and good arable ground. It is an island in the sense that it has sea on two sides and a vast bog which joins or separates it from Sutherland depending on your point of view. It has never been and I suspect never will be much of a tourist haven. Despite the county's obvious and subtle natural beauties the native population has been reluctant to embrace this aspect of the travel and leisure industry with much enthusiasm. Caithnessians are welcoming and kind in the usual Highland manner but their instincts have always been to benefit from the labour of their own hands rather than depend upon the vagaries of a service industry. That was, at least, the pattern up to the 20th century with its two world wars and the coming of the nuclear age to the Far North. These cataclysmic events certainly broke a pattern and their consequences on Caithness have been profound. But still the people remain, if not in the numbers they once enjoyed.

The county's peak population was recorded in 1861 at 41,111. At the census of 2001 the population was 23,866. All of these things, as populations rise and fall, in the past, have been fluid, as no doubt they will be in the future. For example in 1992 the population was closer to 28,000. The modern decline is due, in many ways, to the fluctuating fortunes and inevitable population drop the decommissioning of the nuclear plant at Dounreay on the north coast has engendered. As the necessary workforce is reduced so the human drift to the south increases. There will be more to be said about this later. But who is to say that the population of Caithness might not increase in the future?

The general boundary of Caithness in the south is atop the mighty Ord of Caithness but centuries before it was generally agreed to be the Helmsdale River. In the west the traditional boundary between the land of the *Gallaibh* and that of the *Cataibh* was The Split Stone (or *Clach Sgoilte* in Gaelic) which sits to the east of Melvich and at the north end of Strath Halladale. Centuries before ancient Kataness stretched down as far as Dornoch in south-east Sutherland and included much of the wilds of Strathnaver to the north-west.

When one approaches from the south, as most visitors do, up the notorious A9 road, having driven through the gentle links land north of the Dornoch Firth, what confronts the visitor is The Ord, a formidable granite and sandstone edifice with cliffs of 400 feet plunging down into the Moray Firth to the east. From here you can get a feel for the shape of Caithness. To the west runs the chain of quartzite hills which form the Scarabens and fanning out beside them the dream-tors of Carn Mor, Smean, The Maidens Pap above Braemore and beyond that sits Caithness's claim to a mountain, the beautiful twin-peaked conical pyramid of Morven. To the north-west of Morven the land opens out into the glorious peat bog of The Flow, or 'e Flou' in Caithness Scots, or *Bog na Gaoithe* (bog of the wind) in Gaelic, which stretches to the far north coast of Sutherland and to distant Assynt in the west. From the top of The Ord the ancient Celtic clan lands lie open before the viewer. Here is the 'Province of the Cat', the home of the Cat people, the Picts, first so named in 296 AD as a result of the containment campaigns of the Roman Constantius Chlorus. He was neither the first nor the last Roman Emperor to be thwarted by the Picts and their inaccessible country. Here is a landscape rich in both real history and in dreams and myth.

Immediately to the north runs the Grey Coast, made so famous in the 20th century by the novelist Neil Gunn, which is a ragged sandstone and flagstone definition, cut with innumerable geos, inlets, gloups and blowholes and constantly pounded by the ever restless North Sea. If one lets the eye follow the land-line east from Noss Head lighthouse you can readily understand the sedimentary nature of the geology of Caithness, as what you see is a raised sea-bed, the Ocean of the Orcades, a shallow sea of the Devonian period, some 400 million years ago. On their flagstone bed the soils of Caithness form rich and fertile land and the low-lands of this far north part of the Highlands have for many centuries produced oats and barley in abundance. Evidence of this is the patchwork quilt of fields which stretches in an arc from Latheron in the south-east and as far north-west as Reay, beyond Thurso on the north coast, where the grass and barley parks meld into the open brown peat deer ranges of the Mackay Country.

It is a handsome, contrasting setting with the North Sea to the east, the Pentland Firth and Orkney to the north. To the west the more typical 'Highland' landscape of glen and loch and mountain, which is Strathnaver, rolls outwards from Strath Halladale to Cape Wrath, the 'turning point' of the Vikings, at the top of the Minch in the far north-west. Here the mighty Atlantic stretches endlessly beyond that, all the way to America. And above everything hangs that most impressive feature of the 'Province of the Cat', the cathedral dome of the infinite northern sky.

In Caithness, the point of cats, what is not seen is as important as is what is seen. What most visitors notice when they make their way down from The Ord, carefully navigating the savage hairpin bends on the Berriedale Braes and with some relief descending upon gentle Dunbeath, is a the absence of trees. It is only when the visitor is down upon the cliff-edged plateau which is Caithness that this becomes fully apparent. Calder, in his *History of Caithness* of 1887 puts it like this, 'The only tree that indicates congeniality with the soil is the common "bourtree", or elder, which thrives everywhere, and without any protection from the Northern blast.'

That is not to say that there are no trees at all in Caithness – there are, but like many other things in this deceptive place, they seem ill at ease. It is ironic that the elder, the 'bourtree' of Calder's time is not so frequent now, having suffered from land enclosure and agricultural 'improvement'. Some, like the deciduous plantation at Thurso East, are shaped into a frozen topiary of escape by the incessant salt-blast of the north-west wind. Or they can be found clinging onto unlikely places like the dwarf aspen on the cliff tops of Dunnet Head, relics of a more wooded past. Others huddle into regimented green log-pole pine squares, like Wellington's troops at Waterloo, better to defend themselves against the savageries of the weather.

These latter types are the result of late 20th century tax dodging, land-cash banking, where well-heeled individuals from the City of London or the media, in the 1980s and after, would 'invest' in huge plantations of Sitka spruce or some other quick growing variety, more often than not planted, and to its detriment, on the bogland of the

Flow Country which is one of the far north's unique attractions. After World War Two Caithness had, it was estimated, around 600 acres of woodland. Now, in the second decade of the 21st century, there are approximately 42,000 acres of forest in the county, if one combines publicly owned forestry with private.

Yet still the unexpected open-ness of the landscape of Caithness renders even this quantity of timber almost invisible. Mostly the native forest of Caithness – which was part of the great Caledonian pine forest – lies beneath your feet. Whether these appear as petrified stumps at low tide on Reiss or Dunnet beaches, or as what my father would call 'bog-fir' which was pieces of pine trees preserved in the peat bog and which we would inadvertently dig up when we cut peats on Dunnet Head every spring; the evidence of this post-glacial forest lingers like a ghost. My brother and I would respectfully lay these ancient relics out on the heather to dry in the sun and watch in amazement as they turned to dust. I did exactly the same thing once, as I worked on the shale-shakers on a semi-submersible drilling rig in the North Sea. This branch specimen came up, from a formation some ten thousand feet below the Earth's surface, on the mud returns. Is this not poetry?

The Caledonian pine forest succumbed to climate change, the encroachment of mankind and the insatiable hunger for fuel and agricultural land. However there is the legend of '*Dubh Giuthas*' which offers a more flamboyant and occult reason for the de-forestation of Caithness.

Many years ago, the legend has it, the woods in Caithness were so plentiful and luxurious that the King of Norway was worried that his timber trade would suffer. So being a good early medieval monopolist he had to hatch a plan to maintain his dominance. Simple – burn all the trees in Caithness. This was not as easy as it sounds. The King of Norway knew that all he had to do was to burn all the trees at once, creating such a furnace that nothing could survive, but this was not easy. As is the way of the Viking Kings and our modern London City bankers – he resorted to witchcraft. Or at least he subjected his daughter so to do. At the time of which we speak there was a famous 'Black School' of witches in the Western Isles where all kinds of sorceries were being taught. By whom, unfortunately, we do not know. To this 'school' the King of Norway sent his beloved daughter to study for a whole year. After this the King sent a ship for his daughter and had her transported to Caithness. In her demonised and scholarly maiden's mitt she clasped a huge flaming torch and floated, as is the way of witches, over Caithness sending down bolts of all consuming fire from the heavens. The Caithness folk called her '*Dubh Giuthas*', or 'Black fir', because every time they saw her she was blackened with smoke.

Fortunately there was a 'wise man', and I put this in inverted commas because then like now they are extremely rare, who lived in Strath Kildonan. He asked the people to gather up all the female animals in the county plus a single offspring and to take them to Kildonan. This they did. When the 'wise man' thought that '*Dubh Giuthas*' was coming he separated all the young from their mothers. This set up such a cacophony of lowing and bellowing and boagling that the fiery Princess of Norway grew totally confused and fell to the ground in a frenzy. There she was unceremoniously shot through with an arrow and killed. So ended the immolationary terror of '*Dubh Giuthas*'.

Whatever variety of legend you prefer, natural or fantastic, the result is still the same: Caithness has few trees. What is true for trees is also true of history. Caithness has very little in the way of recorded history. Of course the place is quite simply bursting at the seams with history but it is of historians I sing: the intellectuals and the scribes of both great events and minutiae. The county has not been blessed like Orkney to the north with an historian of the calibre of William Thompson; nor has she an equal of the Rev Angus Mackay who charted his beloved Strathnaver to the west. All I do is walk through the place and let the place do the talking.

What we do have is the *Sketch of the Civil and Traditional History of Caithness from the Tenth Century* by James Traill Calder published in Wick in 1887. This is a problematic tome to say the least. One could forgive Calder his clunking Victorian prose style which dances off the page like team of Clydesdale horse if it were not for his sickening reverence for the Sinclair Earls of Caithness who, without exception, were violent land grabbing robber barons who added nothing to the 'civil and traditional history of Caithness' other than a collection of imposing towered castle keeps, a list of battles, a trail of blood and a systematic and deliberate destruction of the cultural heritage of the county. But as we will learn, in this they were not alone.

As for Calder's claim to 'sketch' a history of Caithness from the 10th century this is almost impossible other than to cite, as he does, the mentioning, short and brief, the northern mainland has in the *Orkneyinga Saga* or in the writings of the Icelander Thormod Torfeson who wrote, as Torfaeus, a history of Orkney in Latin in Denmark in 1690. Calder also quotes from Sir Robert Gordon of Gordonston (1580–1650) whose *Genealogical History of the Earls of Sutherland* he uses as an information source, with the caveat that 'Sir Robert … with all his industry and research, cannot be considered an impartial historian.'

This is the understatement of the age. Sir Robert was an out and out propagandist for the House of Gordon, chief chronicler of its past, major architect of its future and director of operations in its perennial hunger for other people's land and as such was an anti-historian in as much as he did away with other people's history. In 1611 he became, in effect, the 'Earl' of Sutherland as his brother Alexander, the sitting Earl, was subject to 'diverse diseases and infections of the body' and was sent off to the continent for the good of his health. The health of the 'Province of the Cat' did not improve much under Sir Robert

Gordon's tutelage for he was, as the Reverend Angus Mackay accurately noted, 'a crafty and cunning fellow.'

He also shared King James VI's racist attitude towards the Gaels. It is unclear who influenced the other the most but what is certain is that there was royal approval of Sir Robert's invasion of Caithness, on some dubious pretext of the burning of corn fields at Sandside near Reay, not long after he has his reins on Sutherland. Local legend has it that it was a Gordon agent who did the burning. Whatever the cause the episode was fanned by Sir Robert into a full scale military operation against the Earl of Caithness whose lands, as was natural for a Gordon, he desired. This was sanctioned by King James who wrote:

> because of the Godless and beastly behaviour of the said Earl (of Caithness), the country is come to that estate as not only our subjects of the more civil disposition are oppressed and enforced to leave it, but likewise so evil disordered as no part of the Highlands or remotest islands of that our kingdom were ever more barbarous.

The Earl of Caithness fled to Orkney as the Gordon forces, with a cannon from Edinburgh, pillaged and blasted and burned their way across the county consigning to the flames of eternity 'the entire muniments of the ancient earldom, charters dating back to the time when a Norwegian king had authorised the Sinclair expedition to Greenland.' As Iain Grimble notes in his *Clans and Chiefs*, 'It cannot be proved that Sir Robert destroyed them all, but it is a virtual certainty. From the saga period to the 17th century the history of Caithness is almost an entire blank and this vacuum is probably the most formidable achievement of his destructive genius.'

Previous to this act of vandalism Sir Robert Gordon had written a letter of advice to his nephew who in due course would become the next Earl of Sutherland. In it he states quite categorically his attitude to the native culture and how the young Earl could profit by it, 'Use your diligence to take away the relics of the Irish barbarity which as yet remains in your country, to wit, the Irish language and the habit. Purge your country, piece by piece from that uncivil kind of clothes, such as plaids, mantles, trews and blue bonnets. Make severe acts against those that shall wear them.' One of the 'severe acts' was to destroy any thing that could contradict his own 'Genealogical History'. These methods were let loose upon the whole of the Highlands after 1746. The violent acts of fire and sword used by the Gordons in Caithness in the early 17th century were just a rehearsal for the immediate future. The point of this text is to say this: you did not win. We, the natives, are still here.

So legend has it that *Dubh Giuthas* burned our trees and so it is that the Gordons burned our history. The continuity of human inhabitation remains for everyone with eyes to see. But as I have said, in Caithness, it is often difficult to distinguish between reality and a mirage. There are the ghostly microlith flints of Mesolithic hunter gatherers found in the sands at Freswick which suggests these early nomads followed the herds as the ice retreated ever north. Then came the Neolithics who put a spade or an antler into the ground and left evidence of their hearths and little houses in places such as Yarrows where the power of the past draws you almost physically into the ground. All over the county stand their stone circles and mysterious stone lines like poems in stone which articulate their curiosity, knowledge and generosity. We, too, can join with our antecedents of 4000 BC and gaze up to the heavens and participate in the dance of the cosmos. Even more impressive are the many burial cairns which rise up across the Caithness flatlands like swollen bellies pregnant with the reverence the builders gave to the lives of their ancestors.

At the Grey Cairns of Camster, near Lybster, it is physically possible to crawl, if you so desire, into the long cairn and touch both the stone and the process of death. This is no mere memorial: this is a flagstone memory machine. There is nothing macabre about it. In fact it is the very opposite. Here it is actually possible to gently lay one's hands on the stone masonry of love. The blood beats through your own hand in the same way as it did in the hand which laid that stone on its neighbour as it once did in the person whose charred remains were put into the clay beakers, after the bodies had been brought down from their place of public and sacred exhibition and ritualistically burned, then respectfully positioned onto a shelf in the burial cairn. What places such as Camster and Yarrows offer the 21st century human is a sense of proportion; the notion that it is possible to get beyond the cliché of human existence and all the mystical mumbo jumbo which urbanites bestow on things they cannot or will not understand.

So my advice is not to go to these sites on your own. Go with someone you love, or at least like. Look at the hollow bowl of the Hill of Yarrows with its stone journey from the Stone Age to the Brochs; admire the enduring architecture of the three cairns of Camster, older than the Pyramids of Giza; then look at yourself and the person you are with and if a pattern does not emerge then go again and again until it does. It will. If you crawl into the timeless centre of the Camster cairns you will not crawl out the same person.

The people who built the Grey Cairns were farmers, primitive ones by modern standards, but successful nonetheless. It is difficult to credit how humanity managed to get from the simple field systems which operated before, during and after the Middle Ages to the great hi-tech lumps of technology we call combine harvesters. It is ironic, is it not, that you can sit in the cab of a super-tractor where the app on your computer can tell you exactly where you are but you have, because of your education, no idea where you actually are. This is called progress?

In the late 18th century the physical prospect of Caithness was of a wide open, treeless expanse of fenceless land with patches of cultivation here and there, mainly oats and potatoes, with pasture land and heathery heath surrounding all. The main artery of agriculture runs along the river straths from Wick in the south-east, through

Watten and Halkirk, to Thurso in the north-west. But this regulated field system with attendant farm steadings and houses is, like many other things, illusory.

Agriculture, although certainly advanced since the Iron Age, had stood still in Caithness from Viking times up until the beginning of the 19th century. Both in arable acreage and in the structure of division and rental Earl Thorfinn Sigurdson would have easily recognised the layout and structure of the fifty or so 'estates' which made up Caithness prior to 1800. The effects of the Industrial Revolution and the unstoppable mania for 'improvement' changed all that. This is not to say that the previous, old system was not efficient because it evidently was. But as Bob Dylan sang, 'money don't talk, it swears.'

Under the rather eccentric stewardship of Sir John Sinclair of Ulbster (born in Thurso in 1754) Caithness willingly embraced these changes, these 'improvements', so that the common land was enclosed and the old structure of pennyland, tack, wadset and townland was replaced by larger farms with either flagstone fences or drystone walls denoting boundaries with the humble cottar or small tenant evicted in the process. For many poverty and emigration was the result. Not even the adoption of the potato, which appeared in Caithness around the middle of the 18th century as the staple diet of the poor, could prevent hunger and death.

Even as the 19th century wore on there was only one farm of 600 acres in the county and most holdings were of less than thirty acres. By 1890 when the appropriation of arable ground had run its course things, farm-wise, had expanded so that over 50% of all cultivated ground was in the hands of seventeen tenants and they, principally, came under the ownership of either a sept of the Sinclairs of Ulbster or the Dunbars of Hempriggs. It is still the case today that large farms like those in the south of Scotland or in England are a rarity in Caithness and a only a handful can boast an acreage over 1,000. The result of the Common Agricultural Policy of the

European Union has dealt both security and crisis in equal measure to the modern farming community. The mixed arable farm of my grandfather's time, between the wars, where a farmer could grow the feed for his own stock – and his family – is a thing of farming museums. Yet an agricultural crisis threatens to outweigh security as the 21st century progresses.

Despite its modern machinery and husbandry, its drains and hybrid crops and animals, it is as if the carpet of fields which is the farming heartland of the Point of Cats could be rolled up and set in a corner to reveal the real landscape hidden beneath. If you listen hard the voice of truth comes from the Camster cairns, not from the computerised cab of a tractor the size of a tank. When you travel through the barley fields and cattle-green parks of Caithness you realise that the only plough which leaves a lasting impression on the face of the landscape is time. At that moment the concept of ownership seems as bizarre and anti-human as if we were all stripped of memory or instinct.

If you walk out on an early spring morning when the ground seems to sing its way free of winter's sleep, with the skylarks peppering the air and the curlews crying and the shochads – as lapwings are called in Caithness – whistling and lambs dancing in their gangs what you inhabit is the emotional blood symmetry of the ones who erected the elliptical stone circle at Achavanich or the geometrical puzzle of the Hill O Many Stanes. The violent acts of powerful men melt into the salt air. In Caithness the past follows you like a friendly stone dog, and yet with each step comes the realisation that it is the land which will endure and that it is a step forward into how the future will work, where the idea of owning a field or a river will be considered as ridiculous as owning the wind or the tide. As I walk through this landscape it is a step we all take.

Just as the actual culture of Caithness springs from two cultural realities – the Celt and the Norse – so does she equally temper her people from two physical realities: the land and the sea. The land provided the sustenance of life and the sea a means of travel and communication. Up until the herring boom of the 19th century fishing at sea was an uncommon practice for most *Gallaibhs* and when it was undertaken it was a local and domestic enterprise. The sea, however, from the earliest times was the easiest and quickest way to transport goods and people.

Up until 1800 the roads in the north, where they existed at all, were little better than rough tracks which virtually disappeared in wet weather. The movement of livestock south for the markets at Dingwall or Crieff, which was impossible by sea, was the responsibility of the drovers, and their chosen roads were the natural highways south such as the straths of Halladale, Kildonan and Naver which offered grazing for their beasts as they went along. Even the forerunner of the modern A9, the main road North, until late in the 20th century, followed a spectacular and precipitous route hugging close to the clifftops of the Grey Coast.

As agricultural techniques improved trade increased as a result and although in 1655, the writer Thomas Tucker noted, that Thurso had only one vessel of thirty tons while Wick had none, this did not hinder, as history has shown, that the seas around Caithness saw a substantial increase in commercial shipping. As this traffic, as time went on, was ever more destined for America the use of the Pentland Firth as a short cut to the Atlantic and a fair wind became popular. The Sinclairs, up until John 'the improver', may have stood still but technology did not.

But it was never easy. The narrow channel which separates or joins Caithness to Orkney (again, depending upon your point of view) is where the North Sea and the Atlantic meet. From Dunnet Head in the west to the Pentland Skerries north of Duncansby Head in the east is a distance of some seventeen miles and at its narrowest point, with the island of Stroma in the middle, the firth is between six and seven miles wide, depending on which headland you start from. The result is ferocious tidal races – the second fastest in the world – with huge volumes of water passing both north and south of Stroma and east and west of the lumps of rock which are the Pentland Skerries. With tides of up to sixteen knots having been recorded here and with other tidal obstacles such as 'The Men o Mey' and 'The Bores o Duncansby' skippers of sailing vessels felt it prudent to take on a local pilot to ensure a safe passage. The northern shore of Caithness is littered with the wrecks of ships that did not fare so well or felt no need to heed local advice.

The sea also affects the psychology of those who work on it and live beside it in a different way, I would suggest, than those who live on and work the land. Whether the sea is female or male or whether the 'earth' is our 'mother' I will leave to others to decide but one thing which is apparent throughout the folklore of the sea and of the coasts is the importance put on superstition, on bad luck and good. With a field you can rely on its physical properties remaining the same, more or less. The seasons dictate what you can achieve in it and what you can expect from it. With a field it is possible to mark the passing of time – a day, a week, a month, a year: these are the perennial patterns. With the sea, and particularly the Pentland Firth, there are no such certainties. With a timetable one can predict the tides but that is as far as any reasonable seafarer would go. The Pentland Firth is treacherous at any time of day and in any weather. This generates a certain modesty in those who work it. There is also a more resigned, even sardonic, quality discernable in the nature of the fisherman as opposed to the farmer. Those who go to sea will never use two words instead of one. Seldom, if ever, do you hear of a sailor or fisherman boasting of their skill. Everyone who works the sea knows that the great hill of water you just missed last time out will, more than likely, be waiting for you the next time. In this the spirituality, or belief system, of sea-folk is close to the concept of 'fate' as described in the saga literature of the Norse. It is as if an individual's destiny is predetermined, cannot be escaped, so the importance of ritual, of ceremony takes on a sharper edge than the more relaxed rituals of those whose totems are cattle and barley.

While all respect the land there are few who do not fear the sea. Some may even love the sea but each person has an individual relationship with it. This relationship is predicated with many taboos, both ancient and modern. One must never whistle while at sea because this expresses dissatisfaction with the spirit of the winds. Neither must you mention by name a salmon, a pig or a hare. On the way to the fishing grounds you must never give anything away because you will give away the 'good luck' of the boat. No one should go to sea on a Friday. A boat launched under a waxing moon was a lucky boat, especially if she slanted a little to the right when entering the water. If you saw a minister on the way to the boat you turned around and went home again. The list goes on and on but in so doing the individual can at least assert some control over what is all powerful and if you forget then the sea will remind you.

The rational mind will never compensate for the cruelty and mystery of the sea. One way to both quantify and qualify uncertainty is through story.

Stroma, the island in the stream (Straumey, in the Norse), is the only island Caithness lays claim to and it sits slap bang in the middle of the Pentland Firth. At the north end can be found 'The Swelkie', a tidal whirlpool which in the past has seen the end of many a poor vessel but has a legend attached to it which can draw us right down to the beginning of time and of how the sea was made salt. What 'The Swelkie' offers us is a door into understanding how mythology works.

The story goes that there once was a King of Denmark called Frode, whose name means 'prosperity' and who was the great-grandson of Odin, chief of all the gods. During the time when Frode was king the world was filled with peace and harmony for this was 'the golden age' when there was no crime. As you might expect this did not last.

Now Frode had acquired a huge millstone called Grotte which no one could move but which possessed the property of being capable of producing whatever was demanded of it.

So Frode employed the services of two giantesses called Fenja and Menja who were strong enough to set Grotte in motion. He put them to work and instructed them to mill gold, peace and fortune for himself. Unfortunately Frode had the tragic flaw of all kings – he was unreasonable – and he gave Fenja and Menja no period of rest longer than that taken by the cuckoo. This did not please the two giantesses and legend has it that as they took turns at Grotte the quernstone they sang the 'Song of the Mill' which conjured up warriors with which they planned to fight for their freedom from King Frode.

Eventually along came a sea-king called Mysing and he killed King Frode and took to himself the wealth created by Grotte and the labour of Fenja and Menja and, as the saga writer has it, 'This ended the peace of Frode'. King Mysing then sailed north-west to Caithness and took Grotte the millstone and Fenja and Menja with him on his ship and instructed them to grind salt. This they did and at midnight, as they approached Stroma, they asked Mysing if he had enough salt. He told them to continue, which they did until there was so much salt on board that eventually Mysing's ship sank into 'The Swelkie' and the sea poured in through the eye of Grotte the millstone and all sank from sight beneath the foam. To this day Fenja and Menja still turn the quernstone and that is how the sea is salty and how 'the golden age' ended. The Swelkie still whirls as testament to human imperfection and the power of nature.

It's as good a story about creation and morality as I've ever heard. Many cultures have myths concerning millstones and the potency of the quernstone as a symbol of mystery, renewal and change unites both the theosophy of the sea and the land and is prevalent throughout Caithness folklore. In many ways the perpetual motion of the Pentland Firth fulfils the properties and action of a millstone and it is appropriate that this story originates from Stroma: that part of Caithness which is surrounded by the grinding of two oceans.

As this dichotomy of land and the sea moulded the mettle of the people as well as defining the contours of the county it may be beneficial here to consider a little the supposed dichotomy of *Caitibh* and *Gallaibh*, Gael and Gall, Norse and Celt, Highland and Lowland. Mainly these distinctions are both notional and recent and are the product of self-interest and political prejudice, as opposed to being in any way an accurate reflection of custom and history. The cultural meld of Caithness is one of her greatest riches but the modern tendency to say that this is one thing at the expense of the other has to be challenged because in the past these distinctions were unremarkable. This is not to say that everything was harmonious all of the time but it is worthwhile remembering that historically, in the main, what cultural and political divisions occurred were the results of interference from without as opposed to schisms within.

In his book *The Kingdom of the Scots* G.W.S. Barrow has this:

Neither the chronicle or the record of the 12th or 13th century do we hear anything equivalent to the 'Highland Line' of later time. Indeed, the very term 'Highlands' and 'Lowlands' have no place in the considerable body of written evidence surviving from before 1300. 'Ye hielans and ye lawlans, oh whaur hae ye been?' The plain answer is that they do not seem to be have been anywhere; in those terms, they had simply not entered the minds of men. We commonly think of this highland-lowland dichotomy as being rooted deep in the history of Scotland, as being, indeed, imposed upon the history by the mere facts of physical geography. Yet it seems to have left no trace in the reasonably plentiful record of two formative centuries.

The 'lawlans' Professor Barrow is referring to here are, of course, the southern Lowlands, known to the Gaels as '*Galldachd*'. Their own Highlands are referred to as '*Ghàidhealtachd*'. In fact Gaelic does not have words which mean 'Highland' and 'Lowland', as they are called in the present time. Caithness is predominantly 'lawlans' geographically but that is the result of geology not culture or history. The term 'Alba', as Gaelic speaking Scotland was known, was also the term referred to by the Gaels as to the whole of Scotland. Certainly in his poems the 17th century Bard of Keppoch, Iain Lom, talks of 'Alba' as being from 'Orkney to Tweed'. 'Alba' must not be confused with the older Pictish realm of 'Alban' referred to earlier. Indeed the fluidity of place names and what constitutes identity is further compounded by the reference to the Hebrides as *Innse Gall* in which the *'Gall'* are Norse. Although Gaels would call a man from the Lowlands a *'Gall'* or *'Gallach'*, they would also consider him to be an *'Albannach'*, that is someone who comes from Scotland. As is clear (if anything in this matter is) – it all depends where you are standing.

As John MacInnes in his essay 'The Gaelic Perception of the Lowlands' points out:

A more important source of misunderstanding, however, exists in the semantic range of the name 'Gall'. Originally denoting a 'Gaul' (from France), the word was applied successively to Norsemen, Anglo-Normans and English, and that does not exhaust its meanings. At an early stage it developed the general connotation of 'foreigner'.

This idea of *'Gall'*, of the foreign, was used in the Gaelic adjective *'Gallda'* which would have been applied to all things foreign whether they are animal breeds, clothes, food or whatever was brought into the north from the south or further afield. But as Professor MacInnes insists 'as a specific term "*Gall*" means "Lowland Scot", not "Englishman" and not "foreigner".'

Culturally the reality is of the synthesis of the *'Gall'* and the 'Gael' into the *'Gallghaidheal'*, which is the union of Norse and Celt, and which took place over a couple of centuries from the first refugee Norse settlers in Caithness, Sutherland and the Western Isles in the

9th century and results in the population of the present day. This led to the formation of the clans, if we trace it, most notably to Clan Donald, the Lords of the Isles, who claim as their founder Somhairle (in the Gaelic), or Sumarlidhi (in Norse), or Somerled as he is known in English, or 'Summer traveller' as it means literally.

No less is the claim of the Macleod's to Norse ancestry as found in the work of the Macleod bard Mary Macleod when she celebrates her chief as coming from 'a line of kings who laid the Isle of Man under tribute … (a) stately race, seed of Olver and Ochraidh; from the city of Bergen did your first title spring'.

What sprung from direct measures to suppress Celtic culture, which arguably began with the Anglicisation process when Malcolm Canmore marries Margaret, Hungarian born but daughter of an English prince, was tension. The main arc of this tension in both the *Gaidhealtachd* and the *Galldachd* was this straining of the traditional loyalty to the king of the Scots.

The rise of the House of Stuart tested this to breaking point and in 1609 James IV demanded that all Highland chiefs sign the Statutes of Iona which put down in black and white the range and scope of the prejudices against a group of people who spoke a particular language and lived in a certain way. Chief among the so called 'statutes' were the planting of Protestant ministers in Highland parishes; limitations on the bearing and use of arms; the education of chiefs' heirs in Lowland schools where they 'may be found able sufficiently to speik, reid and wryte Englische'; the prohibition of traditional hospitality and strong drink; the prohibition on the protection of fugitives; the outlawing of bards and other bearers of traditional culture.

This was extirpative legislation by a solely Scottish government and although it was an attack on Celtic culture it was aimed at turning the Highland clans away from Catholicism and towards Protestantism. In the wake of Culloden in 1746 and the subsequent passing by a British government of the Act of Proscription worse was to follow. The Statutes of Iona were compounded by making 'forbade … any part of whatsoever of what peculiarity belongs to the Highland garb…'. The 'peculiarity' included prayers, assembly, music and language. The penalties for breeching this 'Act' were a minimum of six months in jail and for a second offence transportation to a penal colony, usually in the Caribbean. It seems that for the *Gaidhealtachd* the veracity of Alasdair mac Mhaighstir Alasdair's phrase '*Mìorun mór nan Gall*', which translates, roughly, as 'the great ill will and hostility of the Lowlanders' had found its tragic fulfilment.

In 1751 Alexander Macdonald, as Alasdair mac Mhaighstir Alasdair was also known, published his famous book of poems *Ais-eiridh na Sean Chànoin Albannaich* (The Resurrection of the Ancient Scottish Language) which was a noble attempt to restore and refurbish Gaelic culture and tradition. Although the preface to this work was in English, addressed to the English speaking world in general and in particular to the 'inhabitants of the Lowlands of Scotland, who have always shared with (the Gaels) the honour of every action, and are now first invited to a participation of their reputation for arts', the authorities in 'the lawlans' thought so much of Alasdair mac Mhaighstir Alasdair's sentiments that they ordered the common hangman to have the book burned at the Cross in Edinburgh. Similar flames would envelop the thatched roofs of countless townships throughout the 'Province of the Cat' in the following century.

In spite of this Alasdair mac Mhaighstir Alasdair's son Ranald, in 1776 – well into the Hanoverian period and also writing in English – made a further attempt to place the Gaelic language in a broader context, 'The Gaelic language', he wrote, 'was once the mother tongue of the principal states of Europe. It was in particular, and for a considerable length of time, the only language spoken by our ancestors, the ancient Caledonians.' Shortly after these words were written one group of people who spoke that 'mother tongue' and who were direct descendants of 'the ancient Caledonians' and who had even fought with the British government in the '45, were feeling the full genocidal effects of '*Mìorun mór nan Gall*'. These were the Mackays and the Gunns of Strathnaver and Kildonan in the 'Province of the Cat'.

Politically the Mackays are often referred to as 'Whigs' but they should never be compared or confused with their English name sakes for, if anything, they were associated with the 'Whiggamores', the Covenanting Presbyterian rebels of the 17th century. The political history of the Clan Mackay indicates that for a Celt, siding with the British Crown and government, for however noble a reason, will always end in disaster.

The third main contributory factor to the decline of the Gaelic language was the passing of the Education Act of 1872. This made school attendance compulsory and where there was, notionally, provision for teaching in Gaelic through the voluntary system up to this time there was no provision for Gaelic whatsoever under the terms of the 1872 Act. After this education in the English language became like a greasy spliced rope choking native literacy out of the Gaelic speaking population. The 'hostility of the lowlanders' had been actualised into a State sponsored policy of cultural suppression.

In Caithness and Sutherland the main agents of this suppression and overt hostility to the Celtic half of the collective identity was officered over time by the various holders of the Earldoms of Caithness and Sutherland: that is the Sinclairs in the north and, latterly, the Gordons in the south east. Far from being 'the back of beyond' as many Scottish historians would have it, or '*Cul-fraoin*' as it is in Gaelic, the 'Province of the Cat' was always an important strategic area, protecting Scotland's 'back door' militarily. During 1745–46 the Sinclairs and the Gordons kept their inherent Catholicism very quiet but both houses were very busy in the period afterwards when traditional clan chiefs were translated into landowners and money became the main faith.

This latter metamorphosis, probably more than anything else, proved to be the undoing of the Clan Mackay and others and the making of the Gordons. The proud Chief of the descendants of the 'sea bright' Pictish Clan Morgan, unconquered by either Norse or Scot, who claimed kinship with the Mac Eth Pictish Mormears of Moray, who were expelled from these lands in the 12th century for supporting the Mac Eth against Malcolm IV, to settle in Strathnaver; this Chief would see his Mackay clansmen reduced to landless rag-bound refugees and emigrants by the 19th century's close. These people, more than any other, felt the true benefit of 'improvement' and 'progress' wrapped up in the dodgy title claims, eviction notices and solicitors letters which are the parchment traces of '*Mìorun mór nan Gall*', 'the great ill will and hostility of the Lowlanders'.

Where the Gordon Earls led the Sinclair lairds followed and Caithness, despite propaganda to the contrary, suffered more than its fair share of this human clearance. The empty parishes of Latheron, Reay, Halkirk and Skinnet stand in silent witness to that, their Gaelic speaking populations forcibly removed, all traces of their existence extinguished. It must be remembered also that both the Gordons and the Sinclairs were from without the 'Province of the Cat', being Norman in origin, feudal in social attitude and hostile to the culture and language of the indigenous people by instinct and design.

What I wish to convey here is a sense of the mental map of the Far North and in this language is the key. The attention to Gaelic, and its detractors, only reflects its importance in the psychological development of the nature of the native people and their cultural expressiveness. As the course of history flows the political map gets drawn and re-drawn so the only real and accurate guide to a people's actuality is the cultural map or the poetic map. This is what fashions the landscape of the imagination and gives meaning to the physical landscape. The plateau of Caithness, defined within its cliff-lipped coasts and its dream-bog hinterland, is to me the primary stage upon which 'the story and the fable', as Edwin Muir called them, are composed and acted out. This landscape, of itself, perhaps is not as dramatic as the heroic mountain-scape of Assynt or as tragic as the rugged dales and lochs of the 'moine' of Strathnaver, but it holds within it the poetic history of its people, their legend and the map of the future. And upon it they act out the tragedy of their history.

As I have alluded to before, the cultural richness of Caithness is one of her strengths and so far this has been unsung. The Norse language, or 'Norn' as it sometimes called, can be found echoing in that other vibrant language of the Far North – Caithness Scots. I will discuss this robust language in another chapter but suffice to say here what it is not – it is not a dialect of English. It is the Caithness dialect of Scots with variations within it, differing from the west to the east of the county as one would expect from a language which has been spoken, in one form or another, for five hundred years.

In addition to this it is well to remember that Norse, or Norn, was spoken on the eastern and northern coasts of Caithness for around four hundred years from the first Viking settlers to its decline in 1206 when the last Norse Earl, Harald Maddadarson, died and the Earldom passed from Norse to Norman. In 1379 Henry St Clair, after much feuding, wrangling and a fortuitous marriage, emerged as the first non-Norse Earl of Orkney and in 1455 his descendant Walter Sinclair became the first Sinclair Earl of Caithness. Prior to all this, in 1266, after the Battle of Largs and the subsequent Treaty of Perth, both the Hebrides and Caithness became part of Scotland. The rise of the Scots tongue followed this assimilation.

Caithness Scots was the language of the cottar and the peasant, the merchant and trader of the eastern portion. In the west Gaelic was the common tongue of the same. The Sinclairs would have conversed in Norman-French. All these influences echo into the modern day. They furnish the land I walk upon.

Today the common language of the people is the usual urban mixture of American and English mostly morphed from TV and film. Like spoken Gaelic in the Western Isles Caithness Scots now mainly resides upon the tongue of the elderly and is relegated to the country districts but unlike Gaelic there is no media stimulus. As the 21st century grinds on it is difficult to say what will become of it for, again unlike Gaelic, there is no campaign to save it, promote it or use it as a means of education. What little literature there is in it is usually of the 'Kailyard School', which is sentimental and nostalgic, and of local circulation. If there is an 'historical sense' in this material, as T.S. Eliot defined it in 'Tradition and the Individual Talent', there is also an abundance of the 'temporal', but this acts in opposition to the 'timeless', therefore it is difficult to speak of a literary tradition because there is so little of this harmony in evidence. Only absences. It was spoken. It goes, with the teeth, into the earth.

This is not to say that the language is parochial. It is only the random nature of history coupled with modern notions of class, which themselves are the product of external hierarchies, which would allow it to be perceived as such. Although in reality an island tongue, separated from Orkney and Moray and Buchan by sea, Caithness Scots is part of that family of dialects of Scots which make up the language of Barbour, Dunbar and Henryson and latterly Burns and was once, like Gaelic, the language of aristocrats.

The 'tradition' Caithness Scots inhabits is the oral tradition of the commonality and that, by its very nature, is of the here and now. Timelessness is subsumed by more immediate diurnal considerations. It is not the language of the Kirk or the schoolroom but it does thrive in the playground and the pub. In conflict often with an urban environment it currently exists in opposition to Standard English which is the official language of authority. However Caithness Scots is a resilient entity and what it lacks in refinement it compensates for in endurance. Its longevity is proof of that. As 'the Point of Cats' lives through its most recent radical change – the decommissioning of Dounreay with the loss of up to 2,000 jobs (this will be looked at in a further chapter) – who is to say that, like Gaelic, Caithness Scots will not have a renaissance?

So the snow has gone and the ice has melted and all across the 'Province of the Cat' the words, music and people are coming out of the ground. This is the springtime of their telling and before me as I go the road opens up.

Chapter Two

THE COAST OF WIDOWS

1.

The north coast of Caithness is defined by Dunnet Head to the west and Duncansby Head to the east. Between these two sandstone certainties flows and surges the nautical uncertainty which is the Pentland Firth. Dunnet and Canisbay are the two low lying sea-beat parishes which bear the brunt of this 'wild and open sea', as the Roman historian Tacitus described it in 83 AD. For me and for many who live along this sea-way, from the crofting township of Brough to the tourist magnet of John O Groats, this is 'the Coast of Widows'.

My mother was the district nurse and midwife for the Dunnet area and in her Highland Health Board Mini Cooper – a wooden floored Ford Popular before that – she patrolled the back roads and by ways of her salt drenched 'district' with myself or my brother riding shotgun with a shovel in the winter if the snow was bad. The crofters would call her 'the blue angel' because of her blue standard issue uniform – and latterly because of her blue rinsed hair – and would, in age old recognition of a service freely given, stuff the car boot with cod bigger than me, lobsters, crabs or whatever they had and could give. So it was the district nurse's two boys had the best of nourishment which was just as well because my lasting memory of those growing years in the early 1960s was of always being hungry – not because we were ill fed, far from it, but because our natures and the wide open spaces we had at our disposal meant that we never stayed still and were hardly indoors, even in bad weather.

It was on these nursing 'rounds' of my mother's that I got to know the inside of the croft houses on the Coast of Widows and in a typical kitchen come living room, decked out in ship's fittings and mirrors – which again was not unusual along this coast where almost all the men had a direct relationship with the sea, either on the merchant marine or from wrecks – an ould crofter wife told me why it was called the Coast of Widows.

"Weel, hids lek iss Choarge. Thurs three kinds oh feeshurmen along iss coast. Thurs inshore feeshurmen, thurs ootshore feeshurmen an thurs drooned feeshurmen! Now ee hev id."

And I remember the teller of the tale rolling her head back and laughing heartily, all missing teeth and the smell of pandrops.

"Dinna bay tellan ay loon ay lek oh aat, Chessag", my mother would say, half laughing herself and pulling me to her for some kind of unspoken protection.

And Chessag would reply, "Uch, fur why noh? Hids ay truth."

"Aats as mebbe. But dinna bay takan aat bandages off afore Ah come back til ee on Tuesday."

And with that we would be off once more, down the road to Skarfskerry, or to Mey, or up to Barrock, or wherever it was she was needed and would go, no questions asked, all heart and giving.

It was not always duty and work for my mother, but as a district nurse and midwife she was on call twenty-four hours a day. Illness, incident and new human arrival keep an open clock. So it was one early February, which is the worst time for snow, but at this particular time there was none. Nevertheless, when the phone rang at half past five in the morning my mother picked it up. When she put it down she picked up two other things: her nurse's bag and me. It may not have been snowing at that particular time but I was brought along, with shovel, just in case. So off we set to Skarfskerry in the pitch black.

What had happened was that a crofter 'mannie' had taken 'a turn'. In Caithness parlance 'a turn' can mean anything from a brain tumour to a cardiac arrest, or a grazed knee. Eventually we got to the croft house. Correspondingly at this time the regular doctor, Doctor Sutherland, was off 'on holidays'. 'Holidays' were not a thing my mother, and her colleague along the coast at John O Groats, Jessie Budge, had much experience of. The thing was that when crofters or fishermen – and often they were both – took ill or were injured in some way, and it had to be serious before these people lifted a phone, it was 'ay nurse' they phoned, not 'ay doctor'. The nurse then phones the doctor and so it went on and in the early 1960s phones, you have to understand, were rare.

In this instance my mother phoned the locum, a Doctor Mackay, from Strathy which was over thirty miles away. Now it is only fair to report that my mother had a 'thing' about doctors: they were either very good or very bad and in my experience she did not broker a middle way about this. One also has to remember that in the 1940s, when my mother was starting out on her medical career, for a woman to become a doctor was if not impossible, then unthinkable, or at least unusual. I know I am biased and that the 'tunnel of years' heightens some experience at the expense of others, but to my mind my mother was the best doctor I have come across and the population of the 'Coast of Widows' agreed. I suppose, also, her tragic flaw was that she was such a harsh critic when it came to doctors that she was, as a consequence, not sentimental in any way. She was meritocratic in all things and although sometimes grumpy was as loyal as was necessary in her defence of her medical 'betters'. On the other hand this only stretched to their ability to do their job: after all, there were lives at stake.

To summarise: she had not a high opinion of our local doctor although she liked him as a person. Of Doctor Mackay she held a high opinion of his gifts as a doctor but as a human being she thought, and he was, a disaster. For example no one was very sure as to how many wives he had and what continent they were on, or even if the 'wife' who resided in Strathy was actually his wife. He was also an alcoholic and was known as 'Doctor Drams'. He had a habit of dressing like an aristocrat in tweeds and to add to his panache he used to drive a huge pink car, which I seem to remember as being a Rolls Royce but maybe it wasn't – but whatever it was it was certainly pink. This was one man of medicine that no-one could fail to recognise. The people of Reay, Strathy and the North Coast of Sutherland certainly recognised him as a sincere practitioner as to their medical needs and whatever his habit of driving when most grown men should be sleeping or his tendency to have his boot full of fish, fowl and game acquired by less than legal means, they never raised a word against 'Doctor Drams'.

So we ended up, my mother and myself at the Skarfskerry croft and we went in. In the scullery, on the flagstone floor, was Willie Manson, dead I thought, or as near dead as was advisable. Bessag, his wife of many years, was in a state of shock, so seeing the situation, my mother attended to her, sat her down and calmed her a little. Then she knelt down over Willie. Suddenly in strode 'Doctor Drams', all moustache, plus fours and cravat. He looked at Willie, then at Bessag.

"A large whisky, if you please, Mrs Manson!"

"For goodness sake, Doctor," exclaimed my mother, "you're not giving the man strong drink in his condition!"

"Not at all, Nurse Gunn, it's for me!"

My mother for a brief moment was silent, then she conceded that indeed it was a cold morning and a long way from Strathy. Bessag got the doctor his dram and then they went about their work. After a time there was a sign of breathing and when the ambulance duly arrived a crofter's life had been saved.

This incident, however comical or tragic, or poorly remembered or related, offers, I think, a window into the lives and character of the people of the north coast of Caithness. They do not panic and as James Miller puts it in his book *A Wild and Open Sea*: 'They are intelligent, friendly people, intolerant of fools, steady but still quick to laugh, resourceful and thrifty. A quiet enthusiasm is preferred to a loud voice.'

They have always been fishermen who farmed. They have had to deal with the often harsh realities, moods and tempers of the Pentland Firth and to wrestle subsistence from it and from the peaty soil of the Coast of Widows. They are a people of few words but they are shrewd and for all their forgiveness and kindness they have long memories. All these qualities ensure survival in this beautiful but demanding place. We only have ten thousand years as evidence.

Or at least that is how it used to be. Since the mid-1980s when the full extent of Margaret Thatcher's government's ideological commitment to the 'property owning democracy' began to take effect, one by one the old croft houses succumbed to prices unheard of in the north of Scotland, but mere fractions of those attained by the sellers in the south, who now became buyers in the north. With them came a significant cultural change. It is often quoted as a cliché but up to this time the indigenous population of the Coast of Widows had a tangential relationship with the concept of 'ownership'. Instinctively, if maybe not intellectually, they would have agreed with the French anarchist philosopher John Pierre Proudhon, when he exclaimed in 1840 that 'property is theft'. If one can ignore the inbuilt irony of such a statement, then its truth for the crofting-fishing population of the north coast and all the 'sea-beat parishes' of Caithness has been that from 1979 until the present time the native population of these places has drastically declined, to be replaced by a moneyed but aging influx, mainly from England. Except not replaced entirely.

For generations the people worked the land in order to live. Whether they had a title to it or rented it from a laird their relationship to that land was one of husbandry – you looked after the land because it looked after you. The idea that these few croft parks or that peedie hoose could be viewed as capital, something of value, a commodity to be bought and sold, was an alien concept to them as it was throughout the Highlands and Islands. They saw themselves as custodians of the land. The ground they worked they held in trust for the future generations. The idea that you could own it was as foreign to the generations who preceded World War One and saw out World War Two as was the idea that you could own the sea, which they also worked. Now it appears that the sea also can be owned.

The extent of the powers enjoyed by the Crown Estate and the Commissioners who exercise that power is only being fully realised in the 21st century now that the Pentland Firth is being harnessed for its tidal energy as opposed to its lobsters. Power lies, as exemplified by the Norse god Thor, in energy.

It is not so much a way of life that has passed as a way of being. When Dunnet Primary School closed in the 1970s a central light in the community went out. No longer could the people of the parish have something which they could rely on to bring them together. When the children went to other schools such as Castletown and Crossroads it was more than their laughter that went with them. Let me state; this was no perfect paradise – far from it – but the extinguishing of a social locus, coupled with incoming residents who had a completely different set of economic, social, cultural and political attitudes, frameworks and references, brought a new kind of silence to the community. Peat cutting died away. Tattie picking went the same way. Fields were sold off for housing. The village became a collection of individuals whose reasons for being there were financial and aesthetical; not hereditary or because of subsistence. In a matter of a decade no-one knew anyone else. This internalisation, this 'bourgoisification', made this silence, to those who were born to the sound of the surf and the corncrakes cry, the most deafening racket of all. It is still loud.

2.

It is springtime on these craggy and salt blasted sets of cliffs, which run and dip from the eastern side of Dunnet Head on the Atlantic entrance to the Pentland Firth and slope up to the eastern wall of Duncansby Head, which guards the Firth's fearsome and skerry strewn North Sea approaches. One of the north's great annual natural acts of renewal is well under way: the return from the ocean of the thousands of seabirds to nest and breed on these beautiful yet pitiless cliffs.

Every year since the ice retreated and the sandstone and flagstone plateau of Caithness rose up out of the Ocean of the Orcades countless pairs of Puffins, Kittiwakes, Guillemots, Razorbills and now, that most recent arrival, the Fulmar have made the vital pilgrimage from the deeps of the North Atlantic to find a peaty hump to burrow in or a ledge on which to make a nest and lay an egg. As spring leads into summer the noise from these breeding colonies increases as does the wind-blown smell from their pervasive guano. As a child this marked for me the reality of the coming summer. Looking down onto the brilliantly coloured, never still, colonies of seabirds – all motion, noise and purpose – from the cliff top beside Dunnet Head lighthouse, was to enter into a fabulous and foreign world of feathers, air and dreaming.

In each species of bird is held a particularity of the sea. That laconic sea-parrot, the Puffin, shares the shape and submarine habits of its more dowdy auk-cousins, the Guillemot and the Razorbill – decked out like waiters or for a night at the opera – their short torpedo-like bodies which make them so perfectly adapted for their true element which is the sea. Bairnlike I wondered at their ability to fly – their wings appeared too short, the effort needed to stay in the air seemed unsustainable. Only when I saw them under water did I learn the purpose of their construction, which allows them to dive and swim and hunt for sand-eels. In this they are a work of sublime design. They spend eighty percent of their lives on the open ocean. The land is not their element. They are birds of the water.

The Kittiwake is a child of both air and water for this bird exists just above the surface of the sea. Here it fulfils its compact with evolution and with gull-like persistence melds both to its meaning. The cry of the Kittiwake is its acoustic signature and the cliff ledges where it chooses to breed are always the colony's loudest and most colourful with their flashing yellow beaks and white and blue-grey plumage and their sheer numbers, restlessness and volume. For a short season they fasten their manic life onto the solitary and sombre headlands of Caithness with a mixture of droppings and seaweed which serves as a nest.

The most successful of the avian inhabitants of these springtime cliffs, and the most recent in historic time, is the Fulmar. So named by the Norse because of the nasty smelling and toxic vomit the bird ejects if you get too close to its nesting young – this 'foul maa' – the Fulmar, is the master of the air. Nothing in human engineering can replicate the perfection of a Fulmar for catching whatever thermal or down or updraft of wind that there is in it. With its stocky frame, thin narrow wings and debonair escallop fan shell shaped tail feathers this bird can cross oceans and it is easy to see that the Fulmar is no seagull but of the albatross family, the petrels. When you sit on a cliff top in early summer and watch the effortless figure eight manoeuvring of this ocean traveller is to be hypnotised by the natural beauty of their shock white head, their egg yolk and green knobbly beak and their slate grey plumage. So close do they come by if you are still, that to look into the dark pool and ochre-yellow eye of a Fulmar is to feel the pull and the grace of existence. It seems often to not be so much a bird but an organisation of air and feathers, a benign messenger from the spirit world.

If the Fulmar is air and light then the Great Arctic Skua, or Bonxie, is darkness and malevolence. This spring and summer visitor is a bruising pirate, a hijacker of other birds' food, a mugger and a murderer: a flashing shadow. There is refreshingly nothing beautiful about this bird, except its ability in flight. It is a large stocky bird, dappled brown in colour with white markings on the end of its powerful wings. A Bonxie can achieve great speed and can accelerate upwards as well as down and change direction, going back the way it came, in mid-flight – a sight which has to be seen to be believed. For sheer manoeuvrability no other bird can match it. The favourite tactic of this fearless thief when confronted by a Gannet – which is much bigger than a Skua – is to grab the Gannet's wing with its powerful beak and tip it off course so that the gannet falls into the sea. The Bonxie will there attack it mercilessly until the Gannet regurgitates its catch or, often, it will kill it. If the Gannet is wise and jettisons its food in mid-flight, so be it – the Bonxie will catch it as it falls. They nest on Hoy on Orkney – and now on Stroma, as I found – and if you walk up near the Loch of Grutfea or Suifea Lochs on Hoy the best tactic is to put a hat on the end of a stick and hold it above your head as the Bonxies are fiercely territorial and will dive bomb you remorselessly. Many are the unsuspecting hill walkers who have ended up face down in the peatbog, terrorised by the Bonxie. Needless to say, I am very fond of this rogue bird.

The Coast of Widows is the southern extent of the Bonxies' breeding ground and it is fascinating to see them circumnavigate the equally impressive Black Backed Gulls which patrol the cliff tops on the same scavenging mission of no good as the Skua. But whereas the Bonxie is like a stealth fighter jet, the Black Backed Gull is similar to a B-52 bomber, with the wingspan of a mature male reaching five feet and its ability to achieve maximum output from the minimum of effort is one of nature's triumphs. The Black Backed Gull is a native and the Bonxie is a summer raider, so in the air above our cliffs is acted out the bird equivalent of the ancient conflict between the Pict and the Viking. Unlike the humans of history these two equally matched predators manage to give each other enough space in order to co-exist, albeit uneasily.

When August comes and the birds leave the cliffs there is a silence and an emptiness to the world that for a few weeks is hard to bear. The headlands do not look unoccupied or naked, so much as bereft. All that remains is the white guano stain of their breeding season and as the weeks pass and autumn turns to winter it turns dark as if some secret grief is transforming it into sandstone.

When the 'King of the Firth' – the north-west wind – is blowing I like to sit on top of what the Ordnance Survey map calls a 'souterrain', but in fact is a Neolithic burial mound, just a few hundred yards on a cliff top from the spectacular setting of the farm at Ham, which itself stretches back to Norse times and before. Viking Earls were laid to rest here but their burial mounds have disappeared. Most mornings in April the sea hammers the Coast of Widows. To the east the village of Skarfskerry is strung out across its promontory like a row of broken teeth. From Skarfskerry there used to be a ferry which braved the 'Men o Mey' and crossed over to Brimms on Hoy. The Ferry House can still be seen much as it was in the 18th century.

Usually, out in the Firth, with its bow and all its hi-tech engineering nose to the wind, you can spot a tanker heading west. From time to time it will disappear from sight only to be lifted back into view by the sea-swell. It is easy to see why at Ham James Bremner, that fine 19th century engineer and harbour builder, felt so much despair as he watched his flagstone harbour being beaten into rubble by the sea before his very eyes. Time, by the tide, is measured by the hour and the minute. Sitting a-top this beautiful mound to the dead, with its doorway pointing south to the winter solstice, you can feel that real time and the tide of human affairs along this coast is measured in a much deeper span.

The sea off St John's Point is a swirling, boiling swatch of breaking waves and white water: these are the 'Men o Mey'. This tide-rip stretches north to South Walls and west of Stroma. A ship entering into the Firth from the west when the tide is on the ebb will find the 'Men o Mey' to be like a wall of water, a natural barrier of bad tempered salt wave and energy. Like most things which impress, no one is really certain what causes The 'Men o Mey' – they just are. But what they are is a sickle like sweep of water which stretches out from St John's Point and begin their dangerous dance just after high water and as this turns into the ebb tide they grow in stature, ferocity and distance, stretching well out from the Caithness shore into the Pentland Firth, spreading their turbulence south from Tor Ness on Hoy. When the tide is flowing against the prevailing wind and sea-swell the waves created as a result can cause great damage to shipping, tearing off everything not welded fast to the deck. In 1969, when the Longhope lifeboat was lost on the 17th of March, the then lifeboat secretary Dr Sydney Peace wrote of the conditions in the Firth, 'I am not surprised that men reported waves of sixty feet in height that night in that place.'

Some six miles east of St John's Point is the Ness of Duncansby, off which another formidable tide race begins. The 'Bores o Duncansby', although not as violent as the 'Men o Mey' nonetheless have a severity all of their own and begin before high water and extend out into the Firth towards the Pentland Skerries. After a time the tide flow turns anti-clockwise until it is pointing north-west as it does so the sea off the Ness of Duncansby seems to boil as white water breaks and foams even on a beautiful calm day. When the wind blows in from the east, in opposition to the flood tide, the Bores can put fear into the hearts of the bravest of sailors. Many times have I seen happy and summer clad tourists waving and smiling from the deck of the passenger ferry from John O Groats to Burwick only to be clutching the rails and sharing their breakfast with the gulls and fish with the vessel no more than ten yards from the pier.

From the time when the Phoenicians passed through the Pentland Firth to the present day all manner of shipping in all sorts of ways have found grief and tragedy where the Atlantic Ocean and the North Sea meet. The Firth may be only seventeen miles in length from Dunnet Head to the Pentland Skerries, and roughly six and a half miles wide from Burwick on South Ronaldsay to Duncansby Head, but the tides which sweep back and forth twice a day can produce currents which can exceed ten knots and literally become a river in the sea. Before the days of steam engines most mariners preferred to take the safe route west between Orkney and Shetland using the Fair Isle as their turning point. Now, every year on average, over 6,000 vessels navigate through the Pentland Firth and no matter how sophisticated the craft no skipper worth his salt dares take the Firth for granted. W. Bremner and D.G. Sinclair of The Caithness Field Club published a list of all the wrecks in and around the Pentland Firth between 1830 and 1981 and it comes to some 450 vessels, with the peak being reached by 1850. Steam engines, better navigation aids such as lighthouses began to ease the toll. But if you go to the Muckle or Peedie Pentland Skerries you will see on the eastern side the russet oxidising steel carcass of a modern ship, deposited well up on the rocks, a hotel for shags.

The first mention of this Northerly land and sea came from Pythias, a sea-going mathematician and astronomer, around 400 BC. He was sent out into the unknown to find and promote trade by the merchants of the Greek colony of Marseilles. He describes 'Britain' as being three cornered, a bit like the shape of a battle axe. More detail was added to Pythias by the map-maker Ptolemy of Alexandria, who flourished circa 140 AD, and who completed a geography of the known world in eight books which were so highly thought of they were used constantly up until the Renaissance. Ptolemy offered a well thought out, if a not somewhat squint, view of the north of Europe as his longitudes were calculated from a point in the Canary Islands, then the most westerly point of the known world, but he reckoned them to be 2½° West of Cape St Vincent when in fact they are 9°. Due to this some countries are thrown out of place. Scotland, according to Ptolemy, veers off at a right angle somewhere around the Kyle of Lochalsh. He called the people living in Caithness the 'Cornavii': the people of the horn. This derives from a Celtic root word which has 'Corn' in Gaelic and 'cornu' in Latin, both meaning 'horn'. So we have Cornwall in England and Cornouaillais in Brittany. Ptolemy also gave names to the headlands – Tarvedum or Orkas is reckoned to be Holborn Head or Dunnet Head; Virvedrum is taken to mean Duncansby and Verubium is assumed to mean Red Head on Stroma, off which Thorfinn and Rognvald had a mighty sea battle in 1040. Calder in his *History of Caithness* has Verubium as the Ord of Caithness. Whatever the veracity in placing the modern names alongside Ptolemy's classic nomenclatures the fact is that both Roman and Greek civilizations realised that there was a settled population in these regions and felt it important to map the coasts and islands in order to further the possibility of trade. Conquest, in the more southerly impregnations of the Romans and the subsequent arrival of the Norse from the west, came later.

From the *Irish Annals* we learn of 'Innsi Orc' which could mean Orkney – the islands of pigs (in Gaelic 'orc'), or mammals, or whales – or indeed, as some think, refers to the 'Province of the Cat' which, because of the topography offered by the deep inland cut of the Dornoch Firth in the east and the natural boundary line of Strath Oykel in the south of Sutherland and the physical barrier of the mountains of Assynt to the west, has all the features of an island to those who were young to the art of geography. In Gaelic the Pentland Firth was known as *Caol Arcach*, or the Sound of Orkney (*Arcaibh*).

It was the Norse, who keeping the Celtic prefix, called them Orkney, because of what they knew. Similarly they called the Pentland Firth 'Petlands Fiordir', the Picts Fiord. By such groping, approximation and amalgamation does knowledge form and come to be, through necessity, experience and time.

Much has been made of George Mackay Brown's phrase 'fishermen with ploughs', by which he described the crofters who worked the other side of the Pentland Firth in Rackwick, on his beloved Hoy. A more apt description for the people who worked the land between Dunnet and Duncansby would be 'crofters with boats'. For unlike the heathery hills of Hoy the ground which sits atop this northern plateau is, mainly, good growing ground with a dark, yielding soil. So as it is with the cliffs and the birds, the springtime, or the Voar as it is called in Norse, is the time when this land is seen at its best.

From March and throughout until April ends skein after skein of wild geese fly across the ever lightening sky to the north – to Iceland and Greenland – to signal spring's awakening. The fields retreat backwards from the cliffs in a greening pattern of grass and breather corn pushing through the dark brown earth, drawing up the green from the ground to mark out fields of barley beside those of grass or sileage or hay. It's as if the season is pulling the ground up towards the eastern horizon and the light.

The air is full of the bleating kazoo sounds of the newborn as the lambing and the calving season reaches its height. Field after field is full of staggering, jumping but delicate lambs. The new calves, never straying very far from their mothers, run gingerly along, allowing their sleek new skins all the more opportunity to embrace the fresh but still invigorating air and the deceptive sunlight. From Brough to Skarfskerry, from Mey to John O Groats, the season of spring unfolds itself along the Coast of Widows like a green flag.

The orchestra of the air is full of the sound of land birds, so different to those of the sea. The Curlew, or whaup as we know them, has a strangely melancholic call, both laconic and trilling, as if it is falling through a hole in time. Skylarks, on the other hand, with their polkadot warbling, signal to us on the ground sweet coded messages about meaning and space. *Shochads*, as Lapwings are called in Caithness, bring their tumbling joy to these flat open spaces; their flashing black and white displays – as if a pair of ill-matched gloves are dancing – coupled with the surging rise and gentle fall of their calling, which sounds like a note from a pipe reed, only in reverse, always fills the human breast with anticipation of the coming summer. The 19th century seer, James MacRourie of Reay, claimed to have come by the gift of second sight by listening to *Shochads*. The *Shochad* has no philosophy, occult or mainstream, other than the celebration of itself. No bird is so graceful, so comic or so welcome.

The cliffs of Caithness are one of its principal natural wonders, sculpted by the wind, the sea and geology, as if an artist has made a million attempts to express pure form. None are more sculptural than the Stacks of Duncansby which lie to the east of Duncansby Head and they have become the stars of an endless parade of postcards and photographs. Often portrayed as looking like witches hats the stacks are actually beautiful examples of the sedimentary nature of the local geology and of erosion. I have often thought of the stacks as being like two beautiful women and a child frozen in the middle of some unfolding drama, as if they were escaping over the sea to Norway only to have been becalmed in stone in mid-action, their gestures and dialogue petrified in rock and liquefied in the sea; or more melodramatically, swallowed by the baleful yawning roars of countless generations of grey seals which swim beneath their feet. The blizzard of seabirds which surround them in spring and early summer seem to both mourn and torment them, to support and to chastise them, to free them and to ensnare them. The cliffs behind the stacks appear to be equally frozen in pursuit and stretch off to the south east a serried rank of stone keels; a fleet in perennial chase but confined to the spot for eternity. If you sit on the cliff top long enough it would be easy enough to imagine this stony tragedy springing to life like a giant production of Japanese Kabuki theatre, all symbol and grace, deep meaning and timelessness. As I wait for the drama to unfold – which it does, endlessly – a pair of ravens perform their sinister ballet in front of me. These birds are so black they seem to possess their own gravity; light disappears into them. They hover and swoop over the cliff tops like two dense pockets of night. I swear, I saw one of the women move. The child raised a hand.

Sannick beach is one of the hidden jewels of the world, never mind Caithness. Barely a quarter of a mile long it lies to the east of Duncansby Ness and west of the lighthouse. Its sand is shell white and tucked under a protecting shoulder of green terraced dunes and no matter that it faces north east it seems to be sheltered from the wind as much as you ever can be on this coast. The brilliant white sand stretches out into the small bay for some distance and on a sunny day the combination of the clear water and the shell sand gives this corner of John O Groats a distinctly Mediterranean flavour, with the colour being more defined, as if the northern dimension, the cooler temperatures, keeps everything more heightened. This quality of the light, this clarity, attracts many artists to the north east corner of Caithness. There is a bigness and openness to the light which is a result of the rising sunlight reflecting off the sea, adding to its intensity and as the day progresses, with nothing physical for the best part of one hundred miles or more to the west for the light to bounce off, it just pours over the land like honey and there is no haze to it as whatever heat is generated on the ground rises unobstructed into the vastness of the sky. On Duncansby Head, on a good day, you can feel that you can see to the other side of tomorrow.

From Sannick beach, at certain times of the day, just off-shore, when the tide is in and flowing, is one of the best places to see the Bores of Duncansby, one of the two main tidal streams in the Firth.

With the Pentland Skerries to the north east, South Ronaldsay to the north and Stroma and Swona to the west, with the sound of the surf washing upon the shore and the sea boiling, it would be a hard soul who, finding themselves here, with the skylarks chirping in the blue spring sky, did not feel amongst the very most blessed in all the world. And always the spectacular light in which everything appears more real, more primary and more essential. It is as if the very place is saying, 'This, foolish human, is why Nature gave you senses!' The seals and the shell and eider ducks who call Sannick beach their home need no such telling.

John O Groats epitomises everything that is wrong with Scottish tourism. John O Groats is a brand and as such is owned, not by the people of Groats but a property company, Natural Retreats, which trades on the physical distance of the place from Land's End in Cornwall. For this reason it becomes apparent to the many thousands of visitors who flock to the place each summer that nobody loves John O Groats; which is a tragedy because it is one of the most beautiful places in Scotland. Guide books constantly refer to John O Groats as 'tacky', 'ugly' and 'with nothing there'. The slowly decaying hotel does, in some ways, justify these remarks and the jumble of buildings which make up the tourist centre and the various craft shops are not the most aesthetically pleasing. Although as I write the hotel is in the process of being transformed, which is good, but Natural Retreats are also building a small village of tourist pods which display all the charm of a prison camp. Contrast this to the sheer physical wonder of the Pentland Firth and the wildlife it supports, of Stroma and Orkney beyond, of Duncansby Head and the Stacks, of Sannick Beach, the snow-white sands and the world famous Groatie Buckie – the Trivia Arctica, Trivia Monacha or Cypria Europea, to give this humble cowrie shell (the home of a gastropod) its Sunday name – the treasured prize of countless childhood quests; all these add up to make John O Groats a special place. What John O Groats is, is a mess.

The nature of the tragedy is that the 21st century urban human is unable to communicate with the natural world – with their exterior reality – unless it is through some electronically provided interior translation or interpretation which must entertain and reward. They do not care much for the fact that John O Groats was and is a crofting township nor that the name of the place, so the story goes, came from a certain Johne Grote or Jon de Groot who, during the reign of James IV (1488–1513), arrived as a refugee from Holland and started a ferry to Orkney. His famous house with eight walls, eight doors and eight windows, with an eight sided table within – so designed so that no-one in his extended family could claim ascendancy – is now a green mound beside the building site of the hotel.

This tragedy of perception is compounded by the civic authorities constantly proving, through planning, social and cultural strategy – or lack of it – that they too do not consider the physical lyricism and natural beauty of John O Groats to be a marketable asset – there must always be an 'other', something for the tourist to 'do'. It seems what geology and evolution has given us is not enough. This failure to understand what Caithness truly and honestly has to offer the visitor by all the public agencies and their reluctance to promote these unique archaeological and topographical assets, in the natural glory of their existence, is why Caithness has, up to this point, remained an unknown land. Because of this the tragedy has reached its ultimate conclusion in that now, sadly, the local population fail to see the beauty and value of what is before them, so that Caithness is unknown even to the natives of the 'Point of Cats'. Nowhere else in the Highlands and Islands of Scotland, to my knowledge, is this self-depreciation and cultural estrangement so prolific and deep set as in Caithness.

3.

Stroma is the only island Caithness can lay claim to. This off-shore part of the parish of Canisbay lies two miles to the north of the Coast of Widows. It is about two and half miles long from north to south and a mile wide from east to west. Shaped somewhat like a great stone eye or like the back of a giant green turtle it sits in the middle of the Pentland Firth and as the meaning of its Norse name would indicate – Straumey, the island in the stream – twice daily it is a terrestrial witness to the temper of the tides ebbing and flowing both east and west. It is an island which often seems miraculously, like Tir Nan Og, to have risen out of the sea and although its western cliffs can rise as much as 170 feet these can offer scant protection from the vast western ocean. In 1862 a great storm – which caused so much havoc and death in the north of Scotland – swept in a huge tide of water which climbed these cliffs and washed over the island in a terrifying wave uprooting crops out of the ground and vegetables out of the planticrues and forced many people out of their homes. Such power is always potentially there in the sea. It is also in the eyes of those who live and work either side of the Pentland Firth.

Off Langaton Point, at the north end of the island, the sea does not so much lie as lurk. The Swelkie, the whirlpool referred to previously, when time and tide are right, is a swirling mess of water. This aquatic anarchy – which is governed by the moon – often has a calm centre in much the same fashion as the eye of a hurricane but with a frothing, wave-crashing turbulence all around its circumference. This fierce, swirling and restless, deceptive centre is often no more than a hundred yards in diameter and it is no small wonder that in the days of oar and sail the mariners of old treated this oceanic whirlpool with caution and respect, even with symbolic reverence. When a yawl or some other fishing boat or small schooner found herself too close to The Swelkie the crew would sacrifice an oar or a barrel or some bit

49

of decking, flinging it into the eye of the whirlpool to placate the sea gods. The Swelkie, after all, does take its name from the Norse '*svalga*' – the swallower.

With Swona and South Ronaldsay to the north east and Hoy to the north west and with the anchorage of Scapa Flow beyond, The Swelkie in full flow is a memorable sight. The lighthouse, built in 1896 by Charles and David Stevenson, stands as a proud sentinel, unmanned now but still painted a bright white – it takes its place in the vital array of the nine other lights (if we include Strathy to the west and Wick to the south) which guide mariners through this unrelenting and unforgiving stretch of water. On a winter's night the arching beams of the Pentland Firth lighthouses and those of the seven Orkney lights beyond make for an impressive display. Lonely, to the far north-west, Sule Skerry light shines alone.

Stroma, as April turns to May, is two things at least. Firstly from Langaton Point to Scartan in the south, the island is a teeming city of breeding birds. Shochads or Lapwings, Curlews or Whaups, Oystercatchers, Terns, Kittiwakes, Fulmars, gulls of every description, Guillemots, Razorbills, Arctic Skuas or Bonxies, various ducks, swans – the list goes on and on. Nowhere else along the north coast will you see and hear a display quite like this. Life bursts out of the place. Which brings me on to the second thing: Stroma, in human terms, is derelict and is slowly becoming desolate. In the 19th century the population peaked at 550. At the outbreak of World War One there were 300 people living on Stroma; in 1951 there were 108; by 1961 there was a family of four and three lighthouse keepers. Now no-one lives on the island. Oats and barley were exported from Stroma; there was a school, a kirk, a post office, a shop and a mains farm. Now there are only two small cottages and the manse inhabitable, with the school still wind and water tight – other than that the buildings on the island lie in ruins. Each house has its door open to the elements and with their empty windows and roofless condition look for all the world like skulls, or severed heads left to rot in some long forgotten votive ceremony. But depopulation and neglect is an unnecessary black ceremony and enhances nothing. The road which runs north from the Haven to the lighthouse is a skeletal spine with the ruined crofts and outbuildings set each side of it like crooked vertebrae or ragged ribs. Fulmars nest on the gables. Sheep protect their lambs from the constant wind in the lee of memories.

Nature, in a positive contrast, is all about renewal. At midday, when the tide is running from east to west, with a slight easterly wind, the sea runs north of Stroma literally like a river. It makes for a bizarre sensation for the viewer because you have to constantly remind yourself that this is the sea and not a river and that this is no optical illusion and that South Ronaldsay is not heading east – but the sea is physically pouring through the channel between the north end of Stroma and the south end of Swona. As I watch it from the flat platform of flagstone rocks beneath the lighthouse it seems to me that the sea is meeting itself in combat – water flowing over water; waves breaking over waves. At one point everything seems to boil. The tyse Cormorants, as the fishermen call them, and some ducks fly over it in acquainted indifference. At one point a Grey Seal sails past, obviously enjoying the ride, popping his head out of the water – from his own massive jacuzzi – to take pity on me who is unable to enjoy such a privilege.

The violent, fast moving current from the east runs around the north of Stroma and meets the slower, deeper current coming in from the west – the North Sea meeting the Atlantic. The result is an oceanic collision of dramatic and poetic dimensions. When the two currents converge they do so as if they are performing a dance around each other in a huge Catherine-wheel with the easterly current moving back upon itself and the westerly swings north and then back west and then dragged south as if by its own momentum or by an invisible force. It is the most graceful – but dangerous – and busy ballet I have ever seen. This sensation is heightened by the knowledge that if you participated in it you would be consumed. The Swelkie also gives off a constant roaring noise as if it is a beast in pain, as if this river in the sea is the boiling of the ocean's blood. As I contemplate this I look up and see the ferry from St Margaret's Hope going full ahead sideways down the firth.

Just to the north of the Gloup, on the west side of the island, an Iron Age fort, sentried by Fulmars and Bonxies, stares out towards the vast Atlantic. The Gloup itself is a massive hole caused by a cave roof collapse and gives the impression of staring into the centre of the earth. It is connected to the sea by a subterranean passage which heads to the west like some Neolithic tomb entrance. When the tide is in Grey Seals swim in and do what they like to do best which is to play gleefully in the comings and goings of the tide as it gurgles, sucks and splashes in and out of the narrow flagstone opening. The dramatic depression which is the Gloup, in such an epic and yet gentle sea and island-scape, sets the mind thinking of an entrance to an underworld and you would not be too surprised to see Orpheus stepping gingerly in, or hurrying out with doomed Eurydice. The natural amplification afforded by the long stone corridor of the western sea-cave fills the amphitheatre of the Gloup with all sorts of distorted moaning and groaning noises from wave-surges. Who is to say that the builders of the Iron Age fort and the Neolithic burial mound down by the lighthouse did not stand here, as I do now, making supplication to the god at the centre of the earth or to the god of the sea?

There is another causeway to the sea which runs north from the Gloup but this has been blocked off by a comparatively recent rock fall. This is known as the 'Malt Barn' and proved to be the perfect place for the Stroma folk to stash their contraband and to disguise the whereabouts of an illicit still or two. Here they put their ability to grow excess barley to good use. No excise men would ever find them or what the islanders considered to be the unfortunate but natural bounty of the sea. Many the cargo of a wrecked vessel was 'stored' in the Gloup. Who knows how many cases of spirits, perfume or tobacco are still down there? One excise officer, legend has it, was chatting to an ould Stroma wife who wore a belt from which hung various 'poakads', or pockets, and as she listened to him her skirts concealed a sixty pound wad of tobacco. This government official was an excitable type and as he marched up and down beside her, claiming to have 'stamped out smuggling on Stroma' he was treading on neat turf patches fitted over cavities full of smuggled gear.

One of the more poetic wreckings on Stroma – and as has been noted there were many in the Pentland Firth, which Robert Louis Stevenson called 'the grave of mariners' – was the steamer *Copeland* which went aground at Langaton Point in thick fog in the summer of 1888 en route from Iceland to Leith. On board was the writer H. Rider Haggard, the author of *King Solomon's Mines*, and his cargo of 500 Icelandic ponies. These magnificent and ancient breed of beasts were saved by allowing them to swim to shore. The image of these real 'sea-horses' appearing out from the fog and the surf must have been a mesmerising one for any who witnessed it. In 1890 H. Rider Haggard published his viking romance novel *Eric Brighteyes* which was the product of his trip to Iceland. Although it does betray the influence of William Morris, Haggard's version of the pithy prose style of the Icelandic Sagas makes *Eric Brighteyes*, ironically, read more like a modern novel. The image of these 500 Icelandic ponies emerging out of the sea is one which I cannot shake off easily.

—

It is usually very difficult to get close to a colony of Guillemots. For a start they nest on inaccessible cliff ledges and even from the sea it's hard to get a sense of what this late spring and early summer visitor gets up to. But on Stroma you can. On the mid-west side, in a geo that leads into a sea-cave, it is possible – if you are careful – to get within thirty or forty feet of the birds without disturbing them. One thing that strikes you about the Guillemot is that no matter the uniformity of the plumage – all posh waiter and dinner jacket – is the raucous bedlam they produce. Deep throated gurglings mix with high octave banshee-like squawkings and outright screams, and all this music moves like a wave along the ledges and through the colony and up into the open air cathedral of the geo. With the sea thundering in, crashing and booming along the bottom of the cliffs and the entrance to the cave, this is a divine music heard in no concert hall. All the while there is constant activity with the comings and goings of individuals and no matter how static the collective looks it is never still, never silent – always on the move, always producing sound. There is also that unforgettable, all pervasive and indescribable waft of guano which fills the nostrils. Where on earth, you may ask, are there comparable delights?

Just south of Red Head on Stroma's western side a huge colony of Grey Seals lies beached on both sides of a flat geo. Hundreds of them, as I lie low and down wind, doze in the late spring sunshine. They call and moo to each other in their Atlantic baritone. Like so many singing stones they enjoy their languor, as safe and lucky as any animals under heaven. Their only other natural predator – other than man – the Orca or Killer Whale, will not be off these shores for several weeks yet. So they are content just to be. Unlike the Guillemots the seals do not move unless they have to and because, for the moment, they do not have to they become as one with the geology, so that if you did not look too closely they appear as just so many grey boulders on a beach. Their conversation, when they can be bothered to make any, is of reassurance, as if they are just checking to see what is the dream and what is the ocean and if it matters if there is a difference. I suspect that usually it doesn't. You can almost see the acoustic signals rippling across the colony like the wind over the sea.

The sea can keep her signals hidden, even from Grey Seals and the pleasant dream of an afternoon can become an unimaginable nightmare. The predators had come early. What amazed me about the attack was the speed. I saw a dorsal fin, just in the corner of my eye and my heart missed a beat. Orcas are seen every summer in the Pentland Firth – perhaps twice, three times – and then they are gone. This dorsal fin, however, stiffened and moved at an increasing velocity towards the rocks beneath the cliff I stood on. Instinctively I flopped onto my belly. The Orca then suddenly turned and its wake-wave washed a seal clean off its rock. The single dorsal was joined by others – three, four, moving in swiftly from east and west. Some seals realised what was happening and made for the safety of a dry outcrop but there were so many seals and so heavy were they and so self-obsessed that by the time the first Killer Whale hit it was only then the majority of them became aware of their mortal enemies.

Then a panic of flippers, of seals arching in piebald purpose, diving this way and that, the sea a violent salt pan of bodies with whales some as long as fourteen feet circling and darting in a planned manoeuvre. There were five dorsals, then ten, then fifteen, some over four feet high, some much less as the generation span of the Killer Whale pod undertook their designated evolutionary tasks. Then for a moment the sea was still. The seals had either belly-scampered onto the safety of rocks or had bolted behind a skerry or to some other sanctuary. The whales relaxed as if to catch breath which was released in spouting jets I could almost smell. Then, just when I thought all this ferocity had come to nothing, a large red bubble of blood burst onto the surface of the water, followed by another and yet another and this seemed to re-energise the whales and I could see that each member of the pod was taking it in turn to submerge and surface and all the while the water turned increasingly red. A flock of hungry sea birds of every variety now arrived to scavenge adding to the noise and spectacle.

How many seals were dispatched I could not tell but by the size of the mature Orcas and the numbers in the pod it must have been five, maybe six unfortunates. Even a one year old Grey Seal can be as much as five feet long. These are not small animals. But they will feed a pod of Killer Whales. I never saw any pieces of carcass, other than what could fit into a Herring Gull's beak, break the surface. Only the rosé blood-stain on the sea told of the swift carnage I had witnessed, its speed and precision. The energy and violence of the attack on the seals by the Orcas had transferred by association into the seabirds who screamed and dived in a banshee orgy of blood and scraps of flesh and skin, attacking each other with as much aggression as they fought over the tiny shattered remnants of what only minutes before had been a contented seal.

After about twenty minutes the Orcas regrouped some hundred yards further out in the firth. Some leaped out of the water in sheer delight, no doubt ecstatic from the successful kill, several tons of adrenalin fuelled whale, their bellies full of seal meat, the effusions of air through their blowholes hanging onto the form of a fountain for a second then drifting into invisibility. The word majestic does not do the moment justice. Then after ten minutes or so of celebration and no doubt with a check to see if all were present and correct, the pod headed east, half submerged, their dorsal fins disappearing from sight.

Below me the sea washed itself clean against the flagstone ledges of Stroma. The birds exhausted their supply of carrion and themselves and the air folded back to the sound of the sea. The Grey Seals remained on the safety of the rocks until one brave individual slid into the waves. Gradually, in ones and twos, the other seals followed and as I got to my feet to look into the distance for the disappearing Orcas it was as if nothing had ever happened. The sea was host to a collection of liquorice coated heads once again, the wind carrying the snorting sound of dozens of noses. The Grey Seals surrounded their deaths with the reassurance of their own lives. If they grieved they did so together and overcame their loss by the necessity of their timeless habits. Death was conquered by just being. As much as I admired the Kller Whales for the beauty of their fury I admired the Grey Seals for their resilience.

—

Sitting on Mell Head, on Stroma's south western extreme, looking out west and at the great swell rolling in I am unable, somehow, to comprehend the vastness of the Atlantic. How can anyone? It occupies around 41,100,000 square miles and covers roughly twenty percent of the earth's surface. The name derives from the Greek god Atlas and the Greeks often referred to the Atlantic Ocean as the 'Sea of Atlas'. Indeed the word 'ocean', for the Greeks, meant the waters which lay beyond the Straits of Gibraltar. For them, this 'ocean', was a gigantic river encircling the world. In truth the Atlantic is the youngest of all the world's oceans, being created during the Jurassic period. Maybe because of that or despite it, the idea that way out there, beyond the sinking sun, there is another shore, far from the confines of Stroma and the Coast of Widows, seems unbelievable. Terns fly bad temperedly around my head as if to chastise me for the failure of my imagination. But out west is where the early map makers drew sea serpents and dragons; out there past Ultima Thule, was the edge of the world. The constant toing and froing of sea-traffic through the Pentland Firth does not compensate for the sheer vastness of the Atlantic Ocean. Like the ubiquitous seals who cavort effortlessly in the water below me the men from Stroma must also have developed an understanding of the empty distances of the Western Ocean and had a healthy respect for it and at the same time were never more alive or full of grace when they were upon it. I remember an old builder, Tommy Geddes from Canisbay, telling me that he once employed a Stroma man as a labourer and that, decent fellow that he was, he was clumsy and awkward on the building site. However, as soon as he set foot on a boat – especially a yawl and specifically if it was on the Pentland Firth – his entire demeanour and personality changed – he was in his natural element. All clumsiness fell from him and he became as careful and as graceful as a ballet dancer.

As I recall this I see a Bonxie's nest – huge and flat, like a compressed grass sombrero, with two hen sized eggs in it all dappled green and black and such a perfect camouflage that you would never see the eggs or nest until you were almost on them. I detect a dark brown presence lurking not far away and in light of the Bonxies' fierce reputation I move off the headland, reflecting that the land, as it was for the Stroma labourer, is not its happy home.

Stroma has never been lucky in the respect of who owned the island. The Sinclairs assumed title when they became Earls of Caithness in 1468 and since 1574 when George Sinclair of Mey, youngest son of George, Earl of Caithness, 'served heir of entail to his brother William in the lands in Stroma', the island has been divided up between various branches of the Sinclair dynasty. To this effect a wall and its remains can be seen dividing the island from east to west. This sense of being, physically, 'the island in the stream' has always placed a duality over Stroma's identity. It is 'Scottish' by means of being in the parish of Canisbay but in many ways the island was more Orcadian and the Stroma dialect of Scots had as many Norse words in it did Scottish. This division was resolved, so legend has it, between the Earls of Orkney and Caithness as to who would rule the disputed island by charming the native snake population. Half were taken to Caithness, where they thrived. The other half were shipped to Orkney, where they perished. So it was judged that Stroma belonged to Caithness.

Now it could be deduced that it would have been better for Stroma to have become Orcadian, as the political snakes which abound on the mainland of Scotland have never done much to maintain life and culture on the island, as the contemporary derelict state of the island bears witness. A more practical attitude to matters both political and strategic has always come from the islanders themselves. As instanced in 1155 when the 'last of the Vikings' Svein Asliefarson, who based himself some of the time in Caithness and some of the time in Orkney, was being pursued by Earl Harald of Orkney. Castle Mestag, the remains of which can be seen on a stack in the south west of the island, was reputedly one of his hideouts. Because of this, or the weather, Svein pulled up his ships on Stroma as some of his crew were natives. Earl Harald saw this and landed his forces upon the island. The weather got worse and soon a gale was blowing which meant neither the Earl or Svein could get off Stroma. Amundi, a local chieftain, saw the dangers and brought the two adversaries together and reminded them of the 'peace treaty' they had agreed for that winter. This was now Easter so supposedly Amundi desired peace for the Christian festival – a comparatively recent novelty for the Pictish-Norse natives of Stroma. To this they both agreed and to clinch the deal Amundi – and this is strange – got the Earl and Svein the Viking to share a bed.

Other than the Sinclairs, who were content to receive rents but to absent themselves from actually living on Stroma, one curious family of 'owners' were the Kennedys. In 1659 John Kennedy of Cairnmuck in Aberdeenshire was granted a wadset of land on Stroma. Now there are conflicting versions of who the Kennedys actually were, where they came from and how they came to the island. According to James Calder in his *History of Caithness*, they were a respectable family from Fife who married into the Traills of Blebo in that county and were related also to the Earls of Casillis and Robert Stewart, Earl of Orkney, and this is how they came to Orkney. But I think the Stroma version is much more likely and anyway it is much more colourful.

John Kennedy, the story goes, killed an old friend to stop him from digging a ditch across a public road. Life indeed must have been cheap in 17th century Aberdeenshire. So Kennedy fled to Stroma.

Material life on Stroma then was very basic so the arrival of a family with lavish goods and chattels raised an eyebrow and many a story. One was that John Kennedy was a pirate and all these riches were the result of his ill-gotten gains. This is logical if you think of the frequency of wreckages on or near Stroma and that piracy was rife in and around the Pentland Firth at that time. One aspect to this narrative was that Kennedy's wife was a Greek, the daughter of a merchant, and that this lady had decided that Stroma was a safe place for her treasure which consisted of two chests of gold each of which took twelve men to carry it. So it was that they established themselves on the island where the 'Greek wifie' grew a herb garden as she was skilled in medicine. Traditionally the Kennedy's house was on the north of the island – no trace of it remains, although Calder in 1861 said that it was still inhabited. There are references to a 'Mrs Kennedy' in 1724 who kept a herb garden but she was no piratical Greek but the more mundane Janet Kennedy, the daughter of William Forbes of Craigievar in Aberdeenshire.

The Kennedys other claims to posterity concerns their mausoleum at Scartan on the South East of Stroma. This is where the customs of Stroma become very curious. In 1792 Bishop Forbes wrote of what he saw at Scartan:

> This island is famous for having dead Bodies of Men, Women, and children above Ground, entire, and to be seen for 70 to 80 years, free of all corruption, without embalming or any art qtsoever, but owing, it is thought, to the plenty of Nitre that is there. The Bodies become very brownish through length of Time; but so as that the Visage is discernable by any Friend or acquaintance that ever had seen the person alive.

Here, beneath a doo'cot, the Kennedy clan laid their dead in coffins on stools rather than bury them underground. According to the Reverend Alexander Pope, the famous 18th century Minister of Reay:

The vaults being on the sea-edge, and the rapid tides of the Pentland running by it, there is such a saltish air continually as has converted the bodies into mummies – insomuch that Murdo Kennedy, son of Carmunks, is said to beat the drum on his father's belly!

Margaret Aitken, who left Stroma in 1961, has said that "A septuagenarian of my time on Stroma could recall boys playing football with Kennedy's skull, and chasing girls with his leg bones."

This deliciously un-Christian sport has a match in 1721 in the less than sporty pursuit, but highly typical behaviour for a Sinclair, of William Sinclair, the Laird of Freswick, who 'acquired' Stroma from the Kennedys. According to Calder, 'Accounts differ as to how they lost their property; but the general belief is that it was forcibly seized upon – a mode of acquiring land very common in the north at a period when might and not right was the leading rule of conduct'.

William Sinclair made siccar, as they say in Scots, this 'conduct' by going to the mausoleum at Scartan with an 'official document' and placing a pen in the dead hand of the last of the Kennedys he traced his signature onto the paper. Two men were made to witness this unusual transaction. One, reportedly, committed suicide sometime after the event and the other only confessed to his part in the gruesome business upon his death bed.

If this is both sordid and comic so is the fact that Stroma has been considered as the location for a prison – a Pentland Firth Alcatraz – and in the 1950s as a prize in an American TV quiz show. This last surreal twist was contemplated by a Mr Hoyland, who bought the island in 1946 for £4,000 and was an umbrella manufacturer from Yorkshire. Comedy concerns itself with an individual's humanity, with a society it has more to do with death, in as much as death defines comedy in relation to the individual. Tragedy touches Stroma in the islands relationship to the vastness, the beauty and the bleakness of the space it inhabits both physically and historically.

John Maynard Keynes once wrote that to maintain an effective demand in an economy it would be better to pay men for 'digging holes in the ground' rather than they should be unemployed. He did add that a more 'sensible community' would find something more socially useful for them to do. In the late 1950s a harbour was constructed at a cost of £30,000. The Stroma fishermen had been crying out for years for a decent harbour but the County Councillors of Caithness had always thought that at any resource spent on the island was 'a waste of money'. 'A pound spent on Stroma is a pound wasted' is the wisdom recorded in the *John O Groat Journal* from a certain Councillor Abrach Mackay. Ironically when the harbour was built the wages paid to the local men who worked on its construction gave them the financial wherewithal to leave and to build houses on the Coast of Widows. Just what Maynard Keynes would have made of result of this particular job creation would be a fascinating economic essay. It has yet to be written. Meanwhile the bones of the empty houses bleach in the salt wind. H. Rider Haggard's 500 Icelandic ponies still rise up out of the sea of myth.

4.

A family of grey seals lounge about in the gentle surf by the slipway at the Clett of Brough. Their noses sticking out of the water betray their Gaelic name: '*ron*', meaning nose. They are as equally interested in me as I am in them. Slightly further out towards the Clett a bull is expressing a somewhat lazy attraction to a female. The sun breaks out. It's as if the morning is just too fine to be wasted in so much effort. I study the scallop shells I found in a natural midden, amassed by humans, seabirds or otters, or the sea itself – I have no way of knowing – some ways back along the cliff-path towards Ham. Their perfect pink geometry amazes me. They are as smooth as pearls. They remind me of the jewel which is supposed to embedded somewhere in the cliff just below the lighthouse. Legend has it that it can be seen at night from the vantage of the Firth. Several attempts with cannon and chalk have been made to pinpoint this natural treasure for viewing in daylight and on dry land. All these attempts have failed. Many have said that the jewel has fallen into the sea due to a rock-fall and is 'lost to all eternity'. One other legend has it that the Dunnet Head lighthouse is doomed as there is supposed to be a fissure which runs right round the portion of rock it is built on and that it will, eventually, fall into the sea. In the eastern lee of Dunnet Head, with the sun picking out all sorts of cracks in the formation of the headland and the Firth crashing about in its perennial sea-surging business, I know there will be few moments in my life better than this. In the long scheme of things what do jewels, or even lighthouses, actually matter? My instincts swim with the seals.

Up on Dunnet Head, by Bourifa, is our family slice of the parish. Two peat banks roughly one mile from the lighthouse road. Here, in early April, my father, my brother and myself would come on our sturdy Fergie tractor and turr out a new bit of the bank, if it needed it, and cut peats and scale them out with graips, in lines to dry, to be ready for the setting up later in the month. Our mother would join us then for the setting up is back breaking work and another pair of quick hands was needed. If it was a still night the midges would come and with them the cleggs, or horseflies, which seemed to prefer the female of the human species. My mother reserved what little hatred she had for the cleggs. If you looked up from your labour and down over the hill to the north east you would see the other families from the village – the Mackenzies, the Hendersons, the Oags – all like us, head down at the peats and stretched out in a tapestry of heather and bog which had little changed from the Middle Ages.

In May we would take the peats home in a rickety trailer of my father's own design and with himself at the helm off we would trek across the bogland and dhu lochs, through the maze of pools and green and brown mossbanks and black wetness which lay each side of the rough approximation of a pot-holed track which led to the Brough road, my father satisfied with the fruits of his labour, his trailer full to the brim and his two boys crouched and clinging on the top like a pair of collies. Then it was home for the ancient ritual of the sculpting of the peat stack, which in my father's hands was a thing of great beauty and which would see us through the winter. Often I would see men come to talk to him when he was busy at it and of course the conversation was important but they were keeping a craftsman's eye on how the stack was progressing. My father would do the same to others in his turn for how well you built your peat stack said a lot about you as a man and a person. This was a matter of pride as well as necessity. There was a lot of talking in front of peat stacks by the men of the parish of Dunnet as May turned to June. I still find myself peering critically at peat stacks where ever I find them and it is a rare thing now, either in Scotland or Ireland, but the old aesthetics stay firm. That we would physically consume this art always gave me pleasure – and still does as I think on it now – because it strikes a chord deep down inside as to the justification and function of art: that it must always have a purpose, that it must be useful. There is a saying that the women from the west have, and it is, 'You will never know a man until you burn a peat stack with him'.

On the west side of Dunnet Head there is the 'Cave of Gold'. This is a sea-cave just past the Chapel Geo. On many maps it is given in its Gaelic version '*Uaimh 'n Òir*'. In my mind this cave, which cannot be accessed by land, is central to understanding memory, myth, creativity and to how a people subjected to invasion, spiritual and cultural assault preserve their identity, their humanity and how they relate to their environment and the natural world. For this cave represents cultural and narrative convergence. Firstly there is the story of how a young bouyag was walking along the shoreline somewhere between Murkle and Castlehill on the western side of

Dunnet Bay when he came across a mermaid relaxing in a rock pool. Legend does not inform us as to who started the conversation but whatever passed between the two of them it seemed to please them both – for he was a handsome lad and she was very beautiful – and they met regularly at the same spot. Now this romantic rendezvous went on for some considerable time during which the mermaid lavished luxurious gifts of diamonds and pearls and gold upon her lover. So our bouyag's status in the parish changed and although no-one had the slightest idea as to where his new found wealth came from he proved to be popular with all, especially the local girls to whom he gave presents of some of the mermaid's jewels. He enjoyed the attention so much he began to forget his date with the mermaid. This did not please the mermaid and she warned him of the consequences of his rashness and his new found love of wealth, for now he would ask her for presents rather than wait to receive them. One day when her patience had been exhausted the mermaid took her mortal love for a sail in a very beautiful boat to a cave on Dwarick Head where, she told him, all the wealth of all the ships that were ever lost on in the Pentland Firth or on Dunnet Sands was kept. His addiction to wealth was so great that he could not resist so that when they got to the cave he eagerly went inside. No sooner had he begun to be amazed by the sheer quantity of gold and jewels he saw piled up before him than the mermaid began to sing and then a piper appeared and began to accompany her and the greedy *bouyag* slowly fell asleep. The mermaid then fastened him to the cave wall with chains of gold. There he was bound for all eternity. It is said that if you go up to Chapel Geo when the sea is booming in from the north-west you can still hear the piper playing.

This yarn has echoes in another story of the 'Piper of Windy Ha'. Here the figure from the otherworld is a fairy but still concerns the stock in trade young bouyag. This time is was a herd boy, a certain Peter Waters, who was idly dreaming his day away in the summer sunshine by the fairy well of Syza when a beautiful lady dressed in green with long red hair and blue eyes shook him awake.

"I have come to make a man of you, Peter," she said.

Peter jumped to his feet.

"Beautiful as you are I have no desire to be married!" he exclaimed.

"I am not offering you marriage", she said "but something of a different kind."

She then produced a beautifully bound bible and a handsome set of black wooden pipes with the chanter and drones mounted on silver.

"Make your choice," she urged him "for the book will make you the greatest preacher in the land and the pipes will make you the greatest piper."

After great thought Peter chose the pipes although he confessed to the fairy woman that he could not play a note.

"Pick up the pipes, Peter, and we will see how well you can play."

So he did and to his amazement he could play as he had never imagined he could and music of such beauty that the deer in the forest stopped to listen, the birds stopped their singing and his cattle began to dance. He finished playing and thanked her. Of course, there was a condition.

"You have to meet me here on this day seven years from now at the hour of the rising moon", and she made him swear that he would and he so did. She then vanished.

Peter went home with his fantastic pipes to Windy Ha and no-one would believe his story until he started playing and then, like the cattle, the people could not help but start dancing. So it was that Peter Waters became very popular and as a result very rich as he was in great demand and paid accordingly.

But time passed and soon the seven years came and went and the day arrived when Peter had to return to the Well of Syza on Olrig Hill where he had previously met the beautiful green lady. So he tucked the pipes under his arm and set off to meet the fairy and Peter Waters was never heard of again.

The third strand to this legend of '*Uaimh 'n Òir*' (the Cave of Gold) concerns the legend of the MacCrimmons, the famous pipers of the Clan Donald, as described in Sorley MacLean's famous poem '*Uaimh 'n Òir*'. Although the origins of MacLean's poem are from various folk sources, of which the two cited above are brief examples, the poet uses the myth to explore deeper and more revelatory attitudes to and aspects of art in particular and creativity in general, especially in relation to a cultural or social loss. In MacLean's case it was, as he perceived it, the 'dying' of the Gaelic language.

In the poem there are two pipers. The first enters the 'Cave of Gold' lamenting that he has not got three hands – two for the pipes and one for the sword – in order to fight the 'green bitch' of death. He has turned his back on the beauties of the landscape and the world and is determined to meet his fate. When the second piper enters the cave he has four arms – two for his pipes and two for his sword and shield – he prophesises the inevitable decline of the Gaelic way of life and has chosen to leave it behind but is determined to go down fighting. In the third section of his poem MacLean fuses the two pipers together and concludes that the only thing which can defeat '*gall' uaine bhais*' (the green bitch of death) is the pipe music of the MacCrimmons but only if it is played for its own sake, if it is '*'n shoals gland dha fhéin*' (a pure light to itself). Here, of course, is the echo of Orpheus entering the underworld – as have the two pipers – unhindered by fear, bereft of culture and the beauty of the natural world and in lamentation of that fact; yet they, unlike Orpheus who tries to escape, go down, playing their defiant pibrochd.

What the myth of the 'Cave of Gold' – in its variations found in the mermaid of Dwarick and the Piper of Windy Ha and the poem by Sorley MacLean – offers us is a metaphor as to how art and by extension a culture and civilisation endures. The Pictish culture might have been overcome by Norse in Caithness and Gaelic in Sutherland and both subsequently by Anglo-American materialism; the pastoral life may have gone, destroyed by clearance, enclosure and ownership; the old belief system may have been broken and been replaced by orthodox Christianity or by its more severe Evangelical off-shoots; the very land itself may be trashed and tarnished; all this may be true but what the 'Cave of Gold' makes apparent is that the people will always find a way to be true to themselves and if that cultural and spiritual inheritance cannot be expressed openly then it will go underground and be manifest in folk culture, in what is called superstition and, most magnificently and perennially, in art. This is the positivity and the good health story contained in what Jung called our 'archaic heritage'.

—

To walk through the canopy of trees of The Planting in Castletown and to look north across the perfect parabolic curve of Dunnet beach to the village of Dunnet some three miles on the other side is to come from one reality into another and to enjoy one of the most lyrical views in Caithness. With its fringe of rolling yellow dunes, capped and contained by the needle-green of the marram grass and with the Atlantic surf constantly pounding the open sand-expanses of the beach, Dunnet presents itself more like an island rather than the western extent of the Coast of Widows. To the west, where the croft parks and scattering and clutter of houses subsume into the white incongruous pseudo-authority of the 'House of The Northern Gate', Dwarick Head rises slowly from the harbour of The Niss at its feet into a green steep meadow and then into brown heather and rock.

Here is where I went to play as a child: the village, the beach, the headland – these were my childhood trinity and no matter how much the village, the beach and even Dwarick Head change, to my mind they will always remain essentially the same. They are my three great signifiers and any memory, any purpose to life lived or to the future, would be meaningless without them. This has nothing to do with rationality but is my own internal and necessary superstition; this is my 'Cave of Gold'.

Viewed from the top of Dwarick Head the old crofting township of Dunnet is spread out like a cross. This is highlighted by the landmark shock-white crucifixion of Dunnet Kirk, one of the three 'Norwegian kirks' on this north coast and within winking distance of its direct neighbour in Canisbay in the western lee of Duncansby Head. The third Norwegian kirk lies west of Thurso at Reay. A kirk has stood on this exact spot in Dunnet from before the Reformation – recent archaeological information can trace construction dated to the 5th century AD. Its religious significance certainly stretches way back before Christianity when believers in an altogether different faith would come to the shrine and to the neighbouring St John's loch to walk clockwise around the water's edge early in the morning in order to be healed from whatever ailment bedevilled them. They had to complete the ceremony by washing their hands and face in the loch and by throwing a piece of money, preferably silver, into the water. If anyone was so greedy or foolish enough to take a coin out of the loch they automatically acquired the disease of the cured person and as plague and leprosy were common this was not to be advised.

The 'summer quarter' was considered the most favourable time. This belief that the loch had healing powers was held with great conviction by many in the north and people would come from Sutherland and Orkney to 'take the waters', although the practice seems to have died out as the 19th century progressed. It is interesting here to note that the neighbouring loch to St John's, Loch Heilan, has been interpreted as meaning the 'healing loch'. The bungalows and detached ranchero houses (the clutter) which now grow along the west side of Dunnet from the croft parks, instead of potatoes and barley, give graphic physical reference to the new, post-Christian, belief system of property and wealth. Time will tell which superstition or cult prevails.

Approached from the south, from the beach, Dunnet appears as a huddle of houses with the white flag of the kirk steeple signalling some kind of ancient security back to the eye. On its green finger of land, with the sea before it and above it the huge vault of the northern sky which it both seems to support and to be crushed by, Dunnet modestly but proudly asserts itself to be at the centre of the bayscape. To the north west Dunnet Head measures its miles of fossilised desert – which is the old red sandstone from which it is made – against the mighty Atlantic. With its three hundred feet cliffs and its sheer uncompromising bulk when you look at it you are left with no doubt that this is Scotland's most northerly point, that this is where the nation starts and stops. "I am Alpha and Omega, the beginning and the ending", saith the headland.

Dunnet – as the variations on the 'Cave of Gold' indicate – is a place surrounded by myth and legend and my own is just one more for the ceilidh house. Before the hotel was built in the village Mary Anne's cottage in the Westside was for generations a ceilidh house where the community would visit stories upon each other and where the cultural light was kept burning in the art of the storyteller. Now this particular croft house is a Heritage Centre and as is the nature of such places the art is gone and the culture is frozen in time. Mary Anne Calder and her man Chimmy, both of whom I remember very vividly as my mother nursed them both in their latter years, would be perplexed by this. Heritage, it has to be remembered, is not culture because culture is creativity and heritage is preservation and, sadly too often, distortion. Perhaps this is inevitable as the meaning of the name 'Dunnet' itself is a mystery. Some have it, such as Calder in his *History of Caithness*, that the name originates from St Donatus, a catholic saint. Beyond Dwarick Head and on the other side of the Peedie Sannie there is an outcrop of rock called the 'Head of Man' where there was once, so legend has it, a chapel – the nearby geo is called 'Chapel Geo' – where a hermit lived. The chapel, which was a sanctuary and place of penance, was dedicated to 'St Donatus'. Whether this 'St Donatus' is the same 'person' as Bishop Donat, who was a Norwegian bishop of Dublin in the 11th century, is unclear. Others claim that the name comes from an Iron Age hill fort which once stood on Dunnet Head. Duncansby Head has similar claims as to the origins of its name. The outline of such a fort can be seen quite clearly on St John's Point which lies to the east of Dunnet.

In matters pertaining to meaning in Caithness place-names I always think it is helpful to say them out loud in the Caithness dialect. In this regard 'Dunnet' is rendered as 'Dinnad'. This brings it close to Dunadd, or *Dùn Add* (the fort by the river Add) in Gaelic, the Iron Age hill fort and capital of the ancient Celtic kingdom of Dalriada, near Kilmartin in Argyll. There are two Iron Age burial mounds which snuggle behind the dunes of Dunnet beach just as there are the remains of a Viking longhouse sleeping beneath the sandy soil in a field as the main road turns from the beach up to the village. With a fresh water loch, a free flowing burn, plentiful pasture for animals on the links beyond the beach, which provided both a fishery and shelter for boats, Dunnet must have always been a prized site for settlement. Now, at the other end of different cultural journey and since the village has become the favoured residence for a commute to Thurso or Dounreay, it is still that.

My first memory of the world was of a longhouse by a beach, but this was a different kind of longhouse, as it was four blocks of council housing set next to each other in a row and containing eight two bedroom houses. As the central duality contained in the myth of the 'Cave of Gold' indicates humanity has two choices: material or cultural wealth. The township of Dunnet into which I was born in the 1950s and grew up in throughout the 1960s was not a very prosperous place. There was no extreme of poverty but neither was there an extreme of wealth. I had no idea about 'class' and all of that until I went to Thurso High School where all the country bairns encountered the 'Atomicers' who, whether they were more or less well off than ourselves or not, carried the English class system in their social outlook. Therefore the Thurso High School years were often difficult for many of the gentler spirits from the crofts and farms of the north coast.

One thing I learned very early on at secondary school was that what was often glibly called 'human nature' in fact did not exist, other than that it was a construction or a result of society. The society of peak-nuclear Atomic City Thurso in the 1960s was a very different construction from the hayfields and tattie parks of Dunnet. The result was that my expectations were different, in as much as I expected to participate and be included for who I was rather than shunned and excluded because I was shy or had no money.

The Viking-Council house system I grew up in was egalitarian by necessity as well as design. When my mother was out on her rounds and my father was off in the fields my brother and I would be looked after by several other families – fed and watered and put to bed and nothing thought about it. It was as if the eight houses had connecting doors. All the children in Seaview Cottages had the same experience and in that way we learned to appreciate other people, were extremely well socialised and enjoyed a freedom unknown to our urban contemporaries. As I realised when I went to Thurso High our primary school was tiny – I can't remember there being more than twenty-four of us at any given time and the one teacher, Mrs Docherty, had to teach all seven years at once – but it was the world to us and it was secure. This real social security was cemented by the village hall where there was always concerts and ceilidhs, especially at Christmas; by the Kirk where there was Sunday school and even by the shop, where everyone went.

There were, of course, downsides – I resented Sunday school intensely because it encroached on my 'freedom'; and because I could read and write before I went to school – Mrs Docherty seemed to find this difficult – I did not enjoy the experience of state education one bit and spent a lot of time 'off school' being 'ill'. I caught every available ailment and disease going: measles, flu, bronchitis, asthma, mumps – the list is long and when I had run out of one I just caught another and so the cycle went on. My real education was undertaken in bed reading books. Robert Louis Stevenson was a favourite but so was Hans Christian Anderson, the brothers Grimm, Dickens, Scott and anything else, including Enid Blyton, I could get my hands on. Fortunately when we moved from Seaview to Dwarick Cottage the house was full of books and my Uncle George More, my mother's brother, always encouraged our reading so there was, literally, a never ending supply of material, including a complete set of Arthur Mee's Children's Encyclopaedias. In fact my first memory of recognising words and coming to terms with printed language was with a child-friendly version of the Iliad and the Odyssey and in a wonderful version of the tales of King Arthur and the Knights of the Round Table. This was well before the official version of reality and learning which came with Dunnet Primary school. This was what my mother read to me each night.

It is difficult to rationalise the extreme dichotomy of the linguistic fissure which was mandatory for all children to experience at primary school in the North Highlands in the mid-20th century. On one hand you had the cartoon world of Dick and Dora and Fluff the cat as drawn up in the junior primary reader and then there was the apocalyptic Jacobin poetry of the King James Bible, especially the Old Testament. Needless to say for one who relished the reality of Hector and Achilles, of Lancelot and Gawain, poor old Dick and Dora had no purchase. Genesis and Exodus, on the other hand, because of the music of the language, sounded familiar. Even so the language of the school was standard English and the language of the playground was broad Caithness Scots. So it was that for a time the world of my education and childhood existed in parallel realities. As time went on these parallels became evermore distant from each other until, inevitably, they became two separate worlds. The world of school became intolerable as I did not want to inhabit that version of reality. For me the language of freedom was found in the dialect trinity of the natural world – the beach, the headland, the village – and in the imaginative universe of books. This was my own version of the 'Cave of Gold'. Here I hoarded the treasure of words and chained myself willingly to the cave-walls of story.

No-one becomes a writer by desire alone: it is the result of a series of accidents more than anything else. I happened to be born into a society where, and at a time when, people were the valued currency. My lasting memory of childhood is a list of names – not the family familiars of MacKenzie, Mackay, Gunn, Sutherland, Manson, Swanson, Sinclair, More, Campbell or Robertson and the others but rather the more intimate by-names of the characters who inhabited the community drama of Dunnet, the village and surrounding crofts. Names drawn more from the world of drama than from the school register, such as Black Roddy, Cuba, Cheordie Crack, ay Pipers, Chimmy Pandora, Donnie Coyote, Chimmy and Mary-Anne oh ay Niss, ay Heid an a Half, Goardan's Cheemie, Heilan Doanal, Beeg Doanal, ay Nurse, Sanny an Cathy ay Post, Cheordie Loogs, Bougswa Wull, Sanny ay Worm, Alice ay Organ, Peedie Cheordie, Peedie Hectrag, Beeg Doanal, Casino, ay Pope, Poopie, Ploot, Bogdanof, Chack Twash, Nan ay Shop, Diesel Doanal, Bandy Peter, Charlie Neep, Charlie Buck, Soup Soy, Pintle, Chonnie Rox, Doupie Dan and so on. These were the human landmarks and mythic signatures by which every bairn navigated the physical by-ways and psychological highways of a community linked by the agricultural calendar and the tide as much as blood.

—

No matter how much the land held us it was the sea which defined us. When I was a boy there were three deep sea captains, all called MacKenzie, who called Dunnet home. This definition often resulted in weird and naive tribal behaviour. Once when one of the MacKenzie skippers was taking his ship, a huge passenger liner, through the Pentland Firth en route to America – or it could have been anywhere – almost all of the village piled into whatever cars, vans or tractors that could be had and transported ourselves to Dunnet Head. There, in a slapdash line, as the majestic ship passed below, the folk dipped their headlights in honour and celebration of one of their own who had, in our eyes, reached the pinnacle of human achievement: he was a sea captain! Captain Mackenzie blew the foghorn of his mighty ship in answer to the signals of his clan and everyone was proud. We all watched as the lights of his ship slowly disappeared into the darkening western ocean.

This idea that the true nature of the people comes out of the ground and that the official record of their lives is a chimera is a strong one. The notion that art, or indeed expression or performance, is a thing which only a few privileged individuals can enjoy is an alien one to me. In Dunnet at Christmas or New Year, or a wedding, or after the peats, at a harvest-home or whatever was the occasion, performance was the nature of the event. Everyone was expected to do something and again I learned early on that if you could not play an instrument or sing your best friend was poetry. A poem was always treated as a good as a song and if not quite reaching the heights of the fiddle or the pipes it meant that you had something to contribute and to participate was the whole point of the gathering.

As a result I have never shared in the existential angst many modern artists carry in regard to their art. In my experience creativity was never on the periphery of society – it was central to it and on the ceilidh floor in the public domain. Neither was the artist expected to live on the margins of the group – we may have been physically at the margins, distant geographically from the centre in 'British' terms but we were central to ourselves which was only natural – indeed such a notion of marginality was unthinkable because the piper delivered the post and the singer was in the shop. So it follows that the natural spirituality of the people cannot be contained within orthodox Christianity and that the practice of ancient traditions and customs is neither at odds with the Kirk nor incompatible to it or its rituals and symbols. Myths are maintained not only in the sound of the wind as it blows through the boor-tree but because they are necessary for the people, who are surrounded by timelessness, to measure time – not in the linear sense, but in the psychological sense. This deep desire will out face any form of modern media. Myths, as they pertain to human psychology, are not about harnessing us to history but enabling us to develop and change as a society. The writer, the artist, cannot objectively stand outside this process as they are part of the process, they must describe the changes they see and in so doing become part of the subject. The burial mound on the coast beside Ham is 5,000 years old. If it is true, as I believe it to be so, that the art of the people who built it comes out of the ground then it is also true that the people come out of the ground with it.

So it was with my tiny life. I embraced the structures which were presented to me. The headland, the bay, the village: this was the trinity of my play. Inside of that there was another trinity: the house, the hotel next door, the kirk. One was domestic, the other social and the third official: in each of these is another trinity and so on. This then the matrix of everyday reality and how my 'human nature' was constructed.

At the centre of the village of Dunnet sits the kirk. I could have written the 'dead centre', but that would be inaccurate. Christianity, like all religions, is a codification of experience on the one hand and an inability or reluctance to understand history on the other. Physically the village has grown around the kirk-site and over the centuries it has changed as the belief system practised on the site changed from nature worship to the creation of the gods of the Celts and then the Norse, to the coming of Christianity – Celtic at first, then Roman and now Protestant. However, the ongoing relationship between the human and the supernatural reforms and distils the physical constancy of the Kirk, of what it means to the people. The fading gravestones which surround the present building hold fast to this relationship like satellites to a mother-ship. Here lie young women who died in childbirth. Beside them their sisters who lived to be old women of ninety. There are men drowned in many distant oceans, their names chiselled into the sandstone of memory beside their brothers who drowned in the Pentland Firth or in Dunnet Bay. But mostly these people are not dead. Their essence is carved and pencilled onto the pine pews of their own kirk. In this way, as it were, they have symbolically come out of the ground.

It is best to visit Dunnet Kirk on your own, in late spring or early summer when the light is clean and gaining in confidence. When you do you quickly realise that the place is empty of people but full of people at the same time. Kirks are not restricted to believers nor are they reserved solely for them. In fact it is better to enter the place as a heathen because then you can see its beauty without any prejudices. A kirk, if it is anything at all, is a place for the coming together of the personal and social and for the quietness which helps to highlight and enrich both.

Dunnet Kirk is loud in its quietness and despite my atheistic nature I believe it to be one of the most beautiful buildings in Scotland. It is not fussy. Shaped like a cross in the 'Norwegian' fashion, as are its two other contemporaries in Reay and Canisbay. The exterior is

Puritan white and the steeple rises modestly complete with bell. At one time a light shone in the belfry window to signal to shipping out in the bay. Inside all is Scandic cool with robin egg blue and white-wash walls with the darkening varnished pews fanned out in a three way spread like rowing benches on some ancient galley. In the middle, before the first pew, stands a lectern on which rests a bible and when I run my fingers over it I trace the first lines of the Song of Solomon, 'Let him kiss me with the kisses of his mouth: for thy love is better than wine'. At the apex stands the pulpit and before it is the font from which my brother and I were baptised. The vaulted ceilings seem to hold the memory of the voices who sang here. From these aisles my mother and father and various other members of my family received a final earthly psalm before they crossed the river to the hill of sleeping.

On the pews are the signatures and doodles of those who have made the crossing in ages past. As the lengthy hours of the time-bending sermons crawled on, tired and bored, young and old, idly made their mark into the soft wood; doodles and copperplate names; caricatures of neighbours and lines of unknown significance. But most beautiful and moving of all are the various drawings of elegant sailing ships – some fourteen or so of them in various rigs – on which, no doubt, the carvers had sailed or, as children, had eagerly watched navigate through the firth or at anchor in the bay waiting on weather. Little did these innocent inscribers imagine that their doodles would now be considered as art by a future visitor who searches for significance in everything but who, nonetheless, is one of their own. Art is a social act although it comes through the blood-fuse of the individual. On the pews of Dunnet Kirk is the modest art of a modest people and for that it possesses an integrity and a gentle intensity because it is a celebration of existence. It captures a moment and in that moment one can see the definitions of the individual and their society.

The sheer longevity of Dunnet Kirk, from pre-Christian, through the Reformation and Disruption to the present, has attracted many preachers of note. Two of the most remarkable – and completely different – were the Reverends Timothy Pont and Thomas Jolly.

Pont was born in 1565 in Fife and was a graduate of St Leonard's College, St Andrews. He was minister at Dunnet from around 1609 up until his death in 1614. He was an accomplished mathematician and surveyor and it is for his achievements as a map maker that history claims him. James VI was impressed by the advantage that these charts offered a naval power and decreed that Pont's maps, the first to give definite place-names and specific contours, be published but because of the political chaos of the time that never happened. But the Reverend Pont's maps were published, after his death, by Johan Blaeu in his *Atlas Novus* in Amsterdam in 1654. It would be interesting to speculate how much the seafaring skills of his Dunnet congregation influenced his cartography and how much this contributed to the success of the Dutch as a sea-going power?

As a Fifer it may come as no surprise to learn that the Reverend Pont in 1609 was a shareholder in one of King James VI's other apocalyptic schemes, namely the settlement and plantation of Ulster, to the tune of 2,000 acres and 400 shillings. To help bring order and security to mariners was one thing and could be argued as 'good Christian work'. Participation in the slaughter and removal, however tangential, of fellow Christians – albeit Catholics – from the province of Ulster in Ireland was work of a different kind. The plaque commemorating his life and achievements which hangs in Dunnet Kirk makes no mention of the Ulster Plantations.

The Reverend Thomas Jolly, it seems, was in nature as he was in name. He was born in Kincardine in the Mearns in 1854. His time as minister as Dunnet was a good one for him and he is recorded as being a genuinely popular minister. When one considers the fractious time the middle of the 19th century was for the Church of Scotland it is instructive to note that when the Disruption of the Church of Scotland into the Established and the Free Kirk finally came in 1843 the majority of the Dunnet parish stayed loyal to their minister while almost all the other parishes of Caithness went over *en masse* to the Free Kirk. Thomas Jolly obviously benefited from that loyalty.

He administered to his congregation medically as well as spiritually as he always had a cabinet full of medicines and such-like for whoever came to him in need. He similarly dealt with his congregation in an honest manner from the pulpit. Calder in his *History of Caithness* has this to say of the Reverend Thomas Jolly:

> He never indulged in vague declamation, or in any of those extravagances of gesture and expression that are so taking with the uneducated vulgar. He chiefly addressed himself to the understanding of his hearers; and while he gave due weight to the fundamental doctrines of religion, he always insisted on the practical effects which those doctrines were intended to produce. The matter of his discourses was always instructive, clear, and well arranged, and his style of composition singularly neat and chaste.

One incident which is informative of these 'practical effects' was the cutting of the minister's peats and for the Reverend Jolly this was annually done by two willing local men, Tam Allan and Jock Calder. On one occasion after the peats had been carted home and the peat stack built the two men were called into the manse for their 'denner'. After the meal, as they were partaking of their dram, the ever social Reverend asked Tam Allan, who was the senior of the two, what great changes he had seen in Dunnet in his lifetime.

"Weel, meenister," replied Tam, "Chock an mahsel here hev seen three great wunners in oor lifetime."

"Oh, and what are these three great wonders", enquired Reverend Jolly.

"Weel, they've pitten a kirk on e Hill o Barrag, a lichthoose on Dinnad Heid and noo here's Chock an mahsel eitan fish an tatties wae siller knives and forks in e Manse in Dinnad."

The Reverend Jolly laughed out loud and immediately went out of the room to inform his wife of the 'three great wunners'. Here was a man, you may suspect, who knew the map of the human heart better than his predecessor who knew the coasts of Scotland but who perhaps turned a blind eye to the blood-price of emptying Ulster of her natives. One gets the impression that the Reverend Jolly saw things exactly as they were.

So Dunnet marks the western extreme of the Coast of Widows and the Atlantic end of the Pentland Firth. From here to Duncansby is the rocky top lip of Scotland. Its marvels, as I have tried to show, are many and unexpected. The future direction of modern Caithness will impact on this craggy coast and leave its mark just as much as the past has left its stony paw print. If the predictions, whether based on engineering or aspiration, about tidal stream energy, about the renewable energy potential of the Pentland Firth in general, come to pass then the Coast of Widows will enter into a new phase. If the native people will benefit from this bounty remains to be seen. Experience has shown them that they get nothing from anything other than what they work for and create themselves. There is no nostalgia or charity in multi-national industry and for them local is just a location. What is certain is that the tide will ebb and flow as it has done since the beginning and if humans are to survive on this coast they will have to plough the fields and fish the sea and in so doing their lives will blossom and pass in their radiance and time and become memory and then myth. As I walk down from Dunnet Kirk and through the hotel car park I see the pink and creamy blossom of the two apple trees my mother planted hanging over the dry-stane dyke of her hard won garden and my memory goes back to the salt taste of these northern apples, of the sweet ocean texture of the strawberries she lovingly nurtured and which exploded in the mouth like a wave of soft fruit on the beach of the tongue. So then do the apples and strawberries become part of my own myth. But if life is to have meaning and resonance then it has to have signifiers whether they are the drawings of sailing ships or salt soaked apples and strawberries, it matters not. They just are.

As I approach the beach I look over the bay toward Olrig Hill which sits behind Castletown and to the east of its sister hill of Clairdon. These are Caithness hills so are minimal in their measure but sometimes from hills you can see more than the view spread out below you, sometimes you can see into the other side of meaning. So it was in 1014 for a certain Dorrud of Murkle – which could be translated, mischievously, from the Norse '*Myrk-hal*' as 'holy smoke' – who on the morning of Good Friday went outside and saw twelve women riders approach a woman's house on the top of Olrig and disappear inside. He walked up to the house and peered in through the narrow window. What he could see was the entire group of the women with a loom set up before them. In place of weights they used men's heads and their intestines for the weft and warp. For heddle-rods they used blood-wet spears, a sword was used as a beater and for the shuttle they used an arrow. As they worked they sang and chanted a long song about blood raining from the sky and of how the web of man was now being woven by the Valkyrie. What they were weaving was the fate of those who took part in the Battle of Clontarf which was fought between the forces of Brian Boru, the High King of Ireland, and the forces of Sigtrygg Silk Beard, the Viking King of Dublin. History has often simplified this important conflict as being between the Irish Celts and the Norse Vikings but there were Irish and Norse on both sides. In reality the battle was bloody and confusing and although the forces of Brian Boru could claim victory on the day, King Brian himself was killed and the real winner was the King Sigtrygg Silk Beard, who ruled Dublin for almost a decade afterwards.

Also a casualty in the Battle of Clontarf in 1014 was Sigurd the Stout, the Earl of Orkney, who was killed along with most of his followers in the cause of King Sigtrygg Silk Beard. With him went down the infamous Raven Banner of the sagas. Sigurd had an impressive Viking pedigree as his grandfather was none other than Earl Thorfinn Skull-Splitter and his mother was the sorceress Ragnhild who by the time she wove her son his magic banner had already disposed of two husbands. Prior to Clontarf Sigurd the Stout was involved in another fight this time with a Pictish Mormear called Finnleik, or Findlay. Finnleik's forces outnumbered Sigurd's seven to one so he went to consult his mother. Ragnhild's reply, as quoted in the *Orkneyinga Saga*, is a classic of Icelandic literature:

"If I had thought you would live forever" she said, "I'd have reared you in my wool-basket. But lifetimes are shaped by what will be, not by where you are. Now take this banner. I've made it for you with all the skill I have, and my belief is this: that it will bring victory to the man it's carried before, but death to the one who carries it."

The finely made banner was delicately embroidered with the figure of a raven which, when it was unfurled, seemed to be flying. Against Finnleik at the Battle of Skitten Earl Sigurd won the day but two standard-bearers were killed as soon as they raised the Raven Banner. At Clontarf Sigurd's luck ran out as the standard-bearer was killed immediately. The Earl asked Thorstein Hallsson to carry the standard but Amundi the White said "Don't take the banner, Thorstein, all who bear it get killed." So Thorstein refused. Then Sigurd asked Hrafn the Red. "Carry your own devil yourself", said Hrafn. Then bravely Sigurd said "A beggar should carry his own bundle" and the Earl ripped the Raven Banner from the flag pole and stuffed it beneath his chain mail. In no time he was killed by a spear.

When the Valkyrie had finished weaving they took the finished cloth from the loom and tore it to pieces between them with each keeping a piece in their hands. Seeing this Dorrud scrambled down Olrig Hill as quickly as he could and went back home to Murkle. As he looked up he saw six of the Valkyrie mount up and ride through the sky to the north and the other six likewise rode to the south. Good Friday in the Christian lexicon is the day of sacrifice, the day of Christ's crucifixion. At Clontarf thousands of men were sacrificed in the power struggle of ambitious men. This is a constant of history.

As I cross Dunnet beach and look back at the village the 'white flag' of Dunnet Kirk surrenders itself over to me. It is no raven; it bears the colour of the dove. Colum Cille, or St Columba, means 'dove of the church' in Old Irish. But according to the sagas it was not St Columba or St Donatus or any other Celtic saint who brought Christianity to the 'Province of the Cat' and it was not the love of Christ either but a Viking warlord and the fear of death by which the Gall-Gaels of Kataness were baptised. The story goes that around the end of the 10th century – before Clontarf – King Olaf Tryggvason of Norway was on his way back home having been away for four years plundering and pillaging around the coast of Britain. The reason for this lengthy spell at sea – Vikings usually went raiding after the crops had been planted and were back for the harvest – was that King Olaf's wife Geira had died and he was so overcome with grief that he took to the high seas to heal. King Olaf had been baptised in the Scilly Isles after consulting a seer who prophesised a great future for him as a ruler and that he would have many people baptised. One of the first people King Olaf Tryggvason and his fleet met was Earl Sigurd the Stout of Orkney who was a-ship off South Walls at the East end of Hoy in the Pentland Firth. Earl Sigurd was about to set off on a Viking raid himself. King Olaf sent word to Earl Sigurd's ships that he required Sigurd to come over to his flagship as he wanted to speak to him. When the Earl succumbed to the King's wishes Olaf told him that he wanted Sigurd and all his subjects to be baptised. Then the

Norwegian King added:"If you refuse, I'll have you killed on the spot, and I swear that I'll ravage every island with fire and steel."

Despite or because he had a sorceress for a mother Sigurd could see what a bind he was in. He accepted baptism and became the most unlikely Christian in the history of the faith. The Earldom of Orkney, which included Shetland, Caithness and East Sutherland, followed suit in time. Just to ensure there was no backsliding on Sigurd's part King Olaf took the Earl's son Hundi with him as hostage to Trondheim. So it was that the blessing of 'the dove of Christ' descended upon the Coast of Widows.

—

Landscape, like art, is often not about what you see but about what you feel. Travelling from Duncansby to Dunnet is a fluid, sensory journey through the tides of time of the Pentland Firth. To journey from the white sands of Sannick to the book-end grey flagstone slabs of Castlehill harbour is to colour experience from the human palate of the people who have lived and still do on this exposed linkage of cliffs and from those who interred their family in the burial mounds of Ham.

The road to another coast beckons; 'a pure light to itself'. The sea-bird's chicks will have hatched by the time I get there.

Chapter Three

THE GREY COAST

1.

The 'Grey Coast', as made popular by Neil Gunn in his 1926 novel of the same name, runs for some sixty miles from Helmsdale at the mouth of the Strath of Kildonan – the medieval border between Caithness and Sutherland – to Noss Head in the northeast of Caithness like a huge stone wall. The gentle landscape of the East Sutherland is abandoned by nature as you go north and the Ord of Caithness rises up in dramatic quartzite and granite fashion with the skyline kissing the land at some 700 feet. This impressive physical barrier runs west to east from Morven and the Scarbens to the 400ft high granite cliffs of Berriedale Ness. Before the advent of the modern A9 the old road precariously hugged the cliff-tops and must have been a formidable undertaking for any un-familiar traveller into the Caithnessian component of the 'Province of the Cat'.

The best way to get a sense of this sedimentary edifice, a relic of when the floor of the Ocean of the Orcades rose up after the ice had retreated, is by sea. From the Moray Firth you see a cavernous, honeycombed, geo fractured, craggy altar, massive and beautiful by varying degrees. The sea smashes its salt head against its feet in a perennial ceremony. From the sea you can fully understand what Caithness is: a rock plateau upon which people struggle to live.

This view is what fascinated Neil Gunn. All his novels – in fact, everything he wrote is about this struggle, these cliffs, this sea. On this eastern seaboard the fate of countless lives has been sealed. On the Grey Coast history has washed like waves and towards the plight of the humans who are born and perish upon the sedimentary plateau the sea displays complete indifference. The individuality of particular human lives is a marked contrast to the foreverness of the sea. The sea, as far as it is in the bounds of description, is perennial. On the croft parks and jagged acres of the Grey Coast humanity has struggled for the best part of 10,000 years to create a society, a collective, a cultural identity. The evidence is in profusion from the grey cairns of Camster to that marvel of human continuity which is Yarrows. Brochs, burial mounds and standing stones in circle, ellipses and arranged in mysterious rows: the Grey Coast has them all.

From the sea all this life, this activity, looks impossible, irrelevant almost. But from the sea they came to the northlands of Caithness. Admittedly the first ones might have walked in across the land bridge of the southern North Sea but of them there remain only Mesolithic shadows. By coracle or wooden craft of some kind the settlers we can justifiably call our ancestors came here. From the sea it is obvious why. The land rises out of the Moray Firth like a stone wave. There is nowhere else to go. To find some geo, some bay or landing place and to climb up to the top of the cliff and to look out over the flowing miles to the Pentland Firth in the north would have been a marvel to behold. It still is. They put their stones up in recognition of the impossible, to map their aspiration, to mark their success. Their vitrified hill forts remain like burnt stone hats. Brochs like giant bobbins in some intricate weave mark the fabric of the land. Their burial chambers welcome the living, still, as they were meant to welcome the dead. These people were strong, tenacious, wise and gifted. They give the Grey Coast a human acoustic I do not think you get anywhere else in the beautiful north. Here is the true nature of Caithness. Here it is impossible to be alone.

This personality is ingrained in the fiction of Neil Gunn like strata through rock. Such is his success that it is impossible to view this landscape other than through his eyes. From his first novel in 1926, *The Grey Coast*, to his farewell to fiction in 1954, *The Other Landscape*, the land, the cliffs, the sea, the people; they are the subject and object of his creative life. These cliffs are the stage upon which, in one form or another, are enacted all his dramas. The people come and go – from Jeems, Ivor, Maggie and Tullach of *The Grey Coast* to Urquhart, Menzies, Annabel and Catherine of *The Other Landscape* – they sing, dance, live and die upon this sedimentary platform. Some, in the course of the narrative may leave – walk city streets, see different horizons – but they all, in one way or another return. In their variations and differences is their continuity. What Gunn did was notice and record. But he also loved. It would be impossible to write the novels he did if the author behind them was not capable of and did not display that primary, often misappropriated, human emotive elastic-passion we know as love. In his 1991 book length study of the work of Neil Gunn, *The Fabulous Matter of Fact*, the critic Richard Price, after two hundred pages of tightly packed argument, has this to say of the four main characters in *The Other Landscape*:

> By remembering and respecting Annabel and Menzies, and also by being themselves, Catherine and Urquhart show that it is love… that must rise from and transform humankind's suffering. Ultimately, Gunn's vision is as matter-of-fact and fabulous as that.

What in that white hot creative journey of twenty-eight years, from *The Grey Coast* to *The Other Landscape*, his first and last novels, did Neil Gunn actually leave us, other than a long documentation of compassion? I would argue what he left is a door. We can open it how we please but when and if we do and go through it then we enter into that other landscape, that other Grey Coast – we come upon ourselves. This idea is central to any understanding of Neil Gunn's art and it is also central to understanding, by inclusion, ourselves. It is what history is all about. It is how we recognise the present. It is the stuff of which the future is made up of.

In his sort of biography, *The Atom of Delight*, published in 1956, he writes of the boy who 'comes upon himself'. This, of course, is a Zen Buddhist moment and much has been made of this aspect of Gunn's poetics, mainly by those who cannot be bothered to get emotionally tuned to his cultural origins, which are much more interesting than any other thing he became interested in, that he drew upon in later life, in order to explain himself to himself. The boy who 'comes upon himself', whether he is in *The Atom of Delight*, or *Highland River*, or like Finn in *The Silver Darlings*, is like the folk of the future coming upon the past and seeing themselves in it. This recognition is the human continuity in history. It is the primal signifier in our dance through time. Other than flagstone, sandstone and granite, this is what the Grey Coast is made of. It is people.

What is, as anyone can see who travels the road north, a series of irregular fields, hills, bogs, villages and crofts is also – and this hidden – a bloody corridor along which have marched and rode the armies and bands of barons, earls and chiefs who pursued their own particular ambitions, generally to the cost of and despite the desires of the people. The sea slaps indifferently at the foot of the cliffs no matter what happens on the ground above. All Neil Gunn's life, his art, was an exercise in asking 'how' and 'why' all this human palaver, for good and bad, came about.

As I have mentioned, despite their stones, the first settlers upon this coast are like shadows. This adds to the poetry of their remains. The truth is we do not understand them at all. Just what do the stones at the 'Hill o Many Stanes' align themselves to or mean? What actually were the grey cairns of Camster for, what was their significance? Why did the people of the Iron Age build so many brochs – around a hundred and fifty – in Caithness? Just what did happen to the Picts?

Did the Vikings kill them all as one Shetland historian somewhat ludicrously asserted recently? In fact, have the Vikings made much of a difference to the history of Caithness and does the popular attachment to them indicate a cultural insecurity which grazes on the thin grass of the anti-Gaelic prejudice which has existed in one form or another in the local aristocracy since the coming of the Normans?

These questions, and more, are the salt scent in the sea-breeze of time. For as much as Caithness, like its sedimentary rock foundation, is built upon a fossil record of plant and animal the actual historical record of human activity is scarce. Calder's *History of Caithness* of 1861 does its best to chart human progress in Caithness from the 10th century but his two primary sources were Torfeaus (who was an Icelander who wrote a history of Orkney in Latin in Denmark in 1690) and Sir Robert Gordon's *Genealogical History of the Earldom of Sutherland*. Sir Robert lived between 1580–1650, which was a particularly bloody period in Caithness's history, even by North Highland standards. According to the Rev Angus Mackay, the scholarly 19th century historian of *The History Of the Province of the Cat*, it was Sir Robert Gordon himself who was responsible for the wholesale destruction of Caithness's civic record, sometime around 1611, when, during Sir Robert's invasion of Caithness, documents dating from the saga period were consigned to the flames. So, prior to the 17th century, there literally is a 'dark age' of Caithnessian history.

So there is nothing particularly 'fabulous' there and not a lot of 'fact', either, in the 'history' as provided by those like Sir Robert Gordon whose desire for power guided his pen. What must guide humanity, of course, is what guided Neil Gunn's pen and that, as Richard Price has indicated, is the pursuit of love, wherever it can be found. Indeed it is a story of love – admittedly of love 'gone wrong' – which I think will help us to see how this tension between Celt and Norman manifested itself in actual events and how these 'events' continually, though time, broke like waves over the coast of people's lives.

Helen Gunn of Braemore – the 'Beauty of Braemore' – is a story, if it was not so brutal, could easily come from a book of fairy tales. But the history of Caithness, despite particular attempts to make it such, is far from a fairy tale. Neither is the story of Helen Gunn strictly history. For the two hundred years prior to the mid-15th century, when these tragic events were supposed to have happened, we know little to nothing of the history of the Clann Gunn.

The story runs that Dugald Keith, chief of the Keiths of Ackergill, had an unhealthy obsession with the daughter of Lachlan Gunn of Braemore. Despite offers of land and property from the Keith the proud father would not give up his pride and joy, Helen – who was about to be married to her childhood sweetheart, Alexander Gunn. Dugald Keith was unused to not getting what he wanted and on the day of the wedding he swooped down on Braemore from the north with a hundred of his clansmen, slaughtered all the men attending the festivities, some fifty in number – including Lachlan and Alexander – and carried off the traumatised Helen to Dunbeath Castle, the keep of his ally in blood, Sutherland of Dunbeath.

The story does not get any better. For two months the 'Beauty of Braemore' was kept locked up in Ackergill tower only to eventually hurl herself from a window to her death on the flagstone cliffs below. Legend has it there is a flagstone with a woman's imprint upon it at Ackergill. Legend also has it that her shade wanders the castle and the cliffs in the form of a 'Green Lady'. What history shows us is that by this time – the 15th century – the nature of land ownership, society and native power structures was changing.

During his reign (1124–1153) King David I of Scotland introduced feudalism, which is the hereditary system of landownership and patronage and the legacy of the Norman hegemony in England, into Scotland. In the Highlands this displaced the Celtic tradition of '*dùthaich*', which translates into English as 'land, native country or territory over which hereditary rights are exercised'. This meant, or corresponded to, generally, the homeland of a clan. Almost all clan disputes after the fall of the Lordship of The Isles in 1493 were as result of the supplantation of the concept of '*dùthaich*' by the granting of feudal charters, by or through the Crown, to chiefs which did not correspond to the actual boundaries of their traditional clan lands. This, inevitably, led to conflict and one after another the Stewart Kings of Scotland sat back and watched the bloody feuds unfold.

This is not to say that they were dispassionate or passive observers. In the far north of Scotland they were absolutely not. I have referred in Chapter One to Alasdair mac Mhaighstir Alasdair's phrase '*Mìorun mór nan Gall*', which translates, roughly, as 'the great ill will and hostility of the Lowlanders'. This 'hostility' found its first organised manifestation in the formation of bishoprics throughout the Highlands and by the time Andrew became the first Bishop of Caithness in 1146 the process was well established. The transformation of thanes and chieftains into the secular hierarchy of Earls, Lords and Barons and the hereditary privileges they granted to their feudal inferiors such as marischals, sheriffs, baillies, stewards and constables found a spiritual complement in the hierarchy of the increasingly influential Church of Rome. The bishops and their priests slowly but surely eradicated the influence of the Celtic Culdees who had administered in Gaelic the more gentle Christianity first established in Scotland by Columba.

Latin may have sounded like gibberish to the natives of the 'Province of the Cat' in the 12th century but to the succession of French knights who has supported David I – the de St Clairs, de Cheynes, de Oliphants, de Freskins, de Gordons, de Fraziers etc – it was the language of power. Landed power – which feudalism was designed to create and maintain – stops and starts with sovereignty. Sovereignty is vested in the Crown which is represented by the monarch. Securing the Crown means possessing absolute power.

In his seminal work *The History of the Working Class in Scotland* Tom Johnston, who was Secretary of State for Scotland during and after World War Two, sums up the situation thus:

> As far back as the twelfth century, the King, in Council, had decreed that actual possession for four generations was no valid title; holders must secure feudal charters and the struggle and the turmoil between the twelfth and the eighteenth centuries was at bottom a struggle between the patriarchal tribe and the feudal baron, between the non-charted, semi-communist Gaels and the ruthless, remorseless, grasping descendants of the pirates who had followed William the Conqueror to the plunder of England.

One by one, over time, the Norman knights became the Crown's representatives in the north. The ancient Celtic concept of *'dùthaich'*, of the traditional boundaries of the clan, was trampled under the hooves of the Norman war-horse.

Except it remained, along with other 'quaint' notions of freedom, entitlement and equality, in the blood of the people. One such 'people' was the Clan Gunn. Prior to the rise of the Normans in the north the Gunns were the dominant clan. Their chief, 'The Crowner', or *'Am Braisdeach Mor'*, 'The Great Brooch-Wearer', according to even the sceptical Sir Robert Gordon, was 'a great commander in Caityness … and one of the greatest men in that countrey'. This was exactly the problem for the de Freskins who had morphed through marriage into the Duffus Sutherlands and were the power-brokers in the south and for the de St Clairs who, as the Sinclairs, were establishing their grip upon the Earldom of Caithness.

The Keiths, on the other hand were a curious crowd who, although nominally Celtic, had come to Scotland from Germany and found favour in the court of King Malcolm, David I's father, who granted them lands in Inverugie in Aberdeenshire and then in 1354 they inherited Ackergill in Caithness from the Cheynes. R.P. Gunn has the date of Helen Gunn's terrible abduction as 1426 although there is no way of knowing for certain. What is certain is that this event – provocatively planned, no doubt, by the Norman ascendancy to undermine the Celtic commonality – led to a long period of feuding between the Gunns and the Keiths. This fruitless and fatal cycle of killing embroiled the Mackays of Strathnaver as well as the Macleods of Assynt and came to a bloody conclusion – of sorts – when what was left of the Gunns ambushed the Keiths as they passed through the heights of Strath Ullie, or Kildonan, in the closing years of the 15th century and under a shower of arrows wiped out the Ackergill Keiths, the grandsons of the notorious Dugald.

So it was that the Scottish Kings kept their power fresh in the north. This was exemplified in 1424 when James I returned from imprisonment in England and was crowned King of Scotland. Obviously feeling threatened by potential mutinies emanating from the Highlands and to ensure his ludicrous and ultimately destructive 'divine right of Kings' he called for a gathering of all the Highland Chiefs in Inverness in 1427. He subsequently arrested forty of them, executed a few and threw the rest in jail. Having the clans at war with each other kept them from making war on him.

Even all of this was not enough for the Stuart dynasty. Every aspect of the Celtic world they hated and felt threatened by. James VI had as one of his many obsessions the 'civilising' of the Gael. Like his antecedent, James I, he employed a cunning rouse to inflict his will. He invited many of the Highland chiefs aboard his royal ship anchored off Mull on the pretext of participating in a religious service and while his guests were at their supplications the ship slipped anchor and sailed south where the chiefs were all imprisoned. A 'good trick' repeated. Ten months later, in 1609, he released them on the condition that they sign the infamous 'Statutes of Iona'. This nine of them duly did. These 'Statutes' were the first articulated dismantling not only of the concept of '*dùthaich*' in relation to land tenure but the very idea of Gaelic culture itself. Bards, the tradition bearers, were to 'be apprehended, put in the stocks and expelled from the Islands'. This was followed up in 1610 by an act of the Privy Council in Edinburgh which while it proclaimed the desire to establish schools in every district of the Highlands the 'act' had a much more apocalyptic overtone, so that:

> ... the youth be exercised and trained up in civilitie, godlines, knawledge, and learning, that the vulgar Inglische tung be universallie plantit, and the Irische language, which is one of the chief and principall causes of the continewance of barbaric and incivilitie amangis the inhabitantis of the Ilis and Heylandis, may be abolisheit and removeit.

The proud but humbled Highland chiefs who signed the 'Statutes of Iona' had to send their sons to schools in the Lowlands of Scotland to be educated in English and if they did not do so none would be recognised as inheritors of their fathers' lands or be accepted as a tenant of the Crown. So now, in Scotland, we have the direct connection between language and culture and the right to hold or own land.

It is in the light of all this that we must view the incident of the 'Beauty of Braemore', for behind every fable there is a reality. The social and economic fallout from this transitional process of feudalism into imperialism informed the work of Neil Gunn. His fiction offers a direct and informing counterpoint to the subordination, subjugation and assimilation of what was considered an inferior and therefore naturally subservient culture by the superior, advanced and developed 'civilitie' of the Stuart monarchs and their subsequent incarnations.

During his lifetime, as a writer, he was not alone in attempting this but what I would argue made Gunn stand out amongst his contemporaries was that he was a hard headed realist. On one hand he shied away from the impossibilist position of his friend Christopher Murray Grieve (the poet 'Hugh MacDiarmid'). Gunn knew that a

Scottish 'soviet', as MacDiarmid called for, would never engage the crofters and fishermen of the Grey Coast in the 1920s and 30s, no matter the cost of the repeated betrayals of the government in London. On the other hand he also rejected the defeatism of the 'Celtic Twilight' movement as personified by Fiona Macleod (real name William Sharpe), Neil Munro and others. Gunn had no patience for the ineffectual resignation that this romantic cul-de-sac – a residue of the 19th century – offered his fellow Scots. The twin peaks of 'beauty' and 'tragedy' may rise out of the hinterland of Celtic myth and enter into the novels of Neil Gunn in one form or another but he understood them to be the signifiers of fiction not of history. The sheer pressure of Gunn's artistic ambition, his cultural drive, drove him far beyond the dichotomy of 'beauty' and 'tragedy', literally, into another landscape, which, of course, is the seed-title of his last novel of 1954, *The Other Landscape*.

If Gunn was at all drawn to a Celtic light it was to be found in Ireland and the torch bearer-in-chief was the poet William Butler Yeats. In the novel *The Grey Coast*, when the schoolteacher Moffat reads Ivor, the young fisherman, a poem it is 'The Lake Isle of Inishfree' with its definite aspirational declaration of 'I will go'. There was no room in the cultural and political daylight in which Gunn worked for any 'twilight', Celtic or otherwise, and if Yeats, at times, did pander an Irish version of it, it was shorn of the absences and fatalisms of Fiona Macleod and his misty ilk – rather it shone illumination onto the fusion and change Gunn saw and admired in Ireland as an emergent nation.

For Gunn's vision for *The Grey Coast* was a European vision for Scotland, of how his imagined place and the actual society of Caithness and the Highlands could break free of the past, of Anglo-Norman feudalism – for what is feudalism for the Celt but the organisation of imperialism? This struggle against imperialism was also the struggle which occupied the life and work of W. B. Yeats.

The Palestinian cultural critic, Edward Said, in his essay 'Yeats and Decolonisation', which is one of the best studies of a poet's life and work and his struggle for his people's freedom that I know, discusses such conundrums as how we can assure the marriage of knowledge to power, or of understanding with violence. These questions he examines in relation to Yeats and Ireland but they could easily be applied to Gunn and to Scotland:

> 'In the Irish colonial setting,' Said writes, 'Yeats can only pose and re-pose the question provocatively, using his poetry… as a technique of trouble. Yeats goes somewhat further than asking questions … (his) poetry joins his people to their history … reminding his audience that history and the nation were not separable, any more than a dancer was separate from the dance.'

But there are dangers inherent in this and Gunn felt it. He knew the 'imagined landscape' of his fiction could easily become, to use the Irish historian Benedict Anderson's phrase, the 'Imagined community' of a new, emerging Scottish nationalism. Yeats re-imagined Ireland's mythical past in order to undo the 800 years of English occupation, to rediscover 'lost' spiritual values, to prepare the Irish nation for the new industrialised Europe and to protect it from such material and multi-cultural incoherence. The task facing a young writer in the far north of Scotland in the years after World War One was somewhat different. As interested as he was in the spiritual well-being of his own people it was the materialist Neil Gunn who wrote to a friend, when he came back after an absence of sixteen years to Caithness to work for the Customs and Excise in 1922, that 'Lybster is the poorest place I can imagine!'

The effect of World War One on the Grey Coast was both immediate and profound. The war memorials which are dotted along the cliff-top road like frozen poems in stone bear testament to the needless loss of manpower in the killing fields of Flanders which was astonishing, but not untypical, for such a rural community. The land enclosures of the 19th century concentrated the population onto the less fertile coastal strips and there the people had to live as best they could on the four and half acres which was designated in 1886 as fit to feed a family for a year and we now call a croft. That mostly it could not even feed their animals was apparent in the sheer number of herring fisheries, south of Wick and north of Helmsdale, which were set up in every burn-mouth, geo and cliff-fracture which could harbour a boat. The three hundred or so stone-cut steps at Whalligeo and the hidden harbour at Clyth lead one up and down from cliff-top to herring station but also from success to failure and illustrate the desperate struggle it was to stay alive.

The post-World War One British government set sanctions against trade with the newly established Bolshevik revolution in Russia. Before 1914 Russia and the Baltics amounted to 80% of Wick's export in cured herring. At a stroke of the Minister of Munitions' pen, a certain Mr Winston Churchill, this was lost. The herring industry in Wick and along the Grey Coast never recovered. From then on it was steady decline. The statistical Accounts show that between 1931 and 1951 almost 20% of the population of Caithness either migrated or emigrated. From the Grey Coast it was emigration which was the common solution. To Canada, Australia and New Zealand women left as widows from the slaughter in the trenches; children left fatherless with their childhood ended far too soon; the landless; the boatless; these were the people the county could not afford to have leave and in the main did not want to leave but they had to leave nonetheless. If Neil Gunn 'came upon himself' in Lybster in 1922 he came upon himself emigrating.

The Grey Coast is his novel of this time. It is also his most Caithness and his most angry novel. Many critics refer to the 'bitterness' to be found in it and other novels such as *The Lost Glen* and *Butcher's Broom*. This is to misunderstand the specificity, the particularity of Neil

Gunn's art. The setting of *The Grey Coast* is, 'A grey strip of crofting coast, flanked seaward by great cliffs, cliffs "flawed" as if in a half-sardonic humour of their Creator to permit … (a) fishing creek …'.

Also the language spoken by Jeems, Tulloch, Maggie and Ivor has by far the largest vocabulary of Caithness Scots words of any of Gunn's novels and the entire syntax of the English language in the narrative is constructed in a way which implies that it is not the first linguistic recourse of either the speakers or the writer.

The 'anger' in the novel comes from Gunn's perception that this dismantling of a vibrant society, which itself was created from adversity and clearance, was as needless as it was destructive. When Caithness haemorrhaged her people the economic generator bled dry also. With the able bodied went the possibility of a future. This sense of things falling apart is a strong atmosphere in *The Grey Coast*.

But it is far from being all about darkness and disunity. In as much as the relationship between Ivor and Maggie in the novel represents the sympathy and harmony which can be achieved between landscape and humanity their love-affair is the illumination of the light and colour which is the great natural benison of the eastern seaboard of Caithness and which stage-lights the passion two ordinary people can have for each other. In Maggie and Ivor Gunn shows us human possibility. In fact the last two words in the novel are 'searing clarity'.

To view Neil Gunn's achievement as I view it, to see the history of the Grey Coast as I see it, is to see a novelist, an artist who attempts to distance the experiences of his people from those of their colonial and imperial masters, those who would deny them a history. The characters in *The Grey Coast* are all, with the exception of Moffat the schoolteacher, native. In *The Other Landscape*, the novel which bookends his creative career, only Catherine is local. It is as if the two novels predate and predict the settlement of Caithness by various economic migrants such as those who arrived through Dounreay in the 1950s and 60s or the property boom of the 1980s and 90s.

Gunn knew that any political or economic 'distance' can only be achieved through the recovery of the land. It is not 'bitterness' which permeates his poetics but the sense of loss. The 'anger' is only focussed on the act of appropriation itself; it does not have attached to it any nostalgia or sentimentality. This distancing is an act of creative resistance. The recovery of the land begins in the imagination of the artist. In a world where history has been either deliberately destroyed or re-packaged, where even thought or enquiry are treated as suspicious, then, as Edward Said has noted, 'a poet who can stimulate a sense of the eternal and of death into consciousness is the true rebel'. Said was thinking of Ireland and Yeats. I am thinking of Caithness and Gunn.

But an 'imagined community', whether it be a county or a nation, however free it thinks itself, still has the negative DNA of accepted stereotypes, false myths, pointless feuds and artificial traditions which colonialism and imperialism leave behind as trace elements. An 'imagined community' can even dare imagine itself independent but if its liberation does not involve, in the words of the radical Algerian philosopher Frantz Fanon, 'a transformation of social consciousness beyond national consciousness' then its future may well become a stultifying version of its past: a gruesome repetition. In other words, we can get ourselves to the river but we cannot actually cross over: the wave of history is somehow stuck at the foot of the cliff.

That is the danger. But cliffs are dangerous places. In *The Other Landscape*, although we see the story through the eyes of Urquhart the narrator, the central character in the novel is the reclusive composer Menzies, precariously perched in his cottage on top of the Grey Coast. His last masterpiece, which Urquhart finds as a manuscript unfinished on a table, is called 'Cliff Symphony'. Menzies has by this time met his death falling from the cliff, the very same cliff he had descended several months earlier to rescue some wrecked fishermen. That same storm-lashed night claimed the life of his beloved wife Annabel who died giving birth to their still-born child. This double tragedy sends

Menzies, literally, into a downward spiral. He shuns society, grows dependent on the rum he has discovered in a cask washed up in a hidden cave at the cliff-foot. It is his desire to claim the last of this fortuitous bounty which leads to his accidental, if inevitable, fall.

The Other Landscape, despite what these incidents indicate, is no nihilistic indulgence. It was Gunn's last major creative achievement – if we set aside *The Atom of Delight*, which was his attempt at autobiography – so it is full of metaphysics, of optimism and promise. The novel ends with Urquhart and Catherine, who have married and had a son, revisiting the graves of Annabel and Menzies. This sense of recurrence, of events happening before they are understood or of being predicted; of a second chance at life, of moving into what Edward Said has called 'the second movement of decolonialisation', all of this and more pulses through the novel in the folk songs Gunn gives Annabel and Catherine to sing. These songs of cultural continuity counter the increasing incoherence of Menzies self-obsessed ramblings, his strange, half realised elemental music. This 'incoherence', the gulf between language and meaning, finds its mirror now when politicians talk about the economy and the financial collapse of 2008. It is as if the Lybster of 1922, when Neil Gunn the excise man came back to meet himself the writer, where poverty for the many was the price of political incompetence by the few, is being recast now in a strange repeating drama, a recurrence where nothing is learned.

The similarities between the economic depression of post 2008 with that of the 1920s and 30s may be deceptive in their material manifestation but the hardships of the 'hungry thirties' of the 20th century are at least history: the deprivations which have begun and are to come can only be imagined.

All his political life Neil Gunn, although an anarchist in spirit and instinct, was in reality an advocate of Scottish independence. He would have applauded the passing by the Scottish Parliament of The Abolition of Feudal Tenure (Scotland) Act which became law on 28th November 2004. Overnight all feudal superiorities were abolished and there was no compensation to landlords and no feudal estate was allowed to be created from that day on. No longer, in Scotland at least, can a monarch or a Duke issue warrants and charters declaring that the land they desire is 'terra nullius' – land which belongs to no-one. The concept of '*dùthaich*' may be consigned to the past but so, at last, is feudalism – or at least, through the 2004 Act, it has no future in Scotland. '*Dùthaich*', on the other hand, can be reintroduced.

When I stand at Dunbeath and look north along the Grey Coast it is hard to imagine that the land belongs to anyone. The foreverness of the indifferent sea is a constant music and the 'recurrence' of economic collapse seems a distant abstract notion. Yet history does wash upon the Grey Coast in waves and the cliffs do represent the age-old struggle, the only meaningful reality; for in the end the people are the land. They give it meaning. This simple idea is at the heart of *The Grey Coast* and *The Other Landscape*, of all Neil Gunn's work. Helen Gunn, the beauty of Braemore, can now, perhaps finally, rest in peace and our history awaken from its vandalised sleep.

2.

When I was ten years old my mother planted two apple trees by the north wall in the garden of Dwarick Cottage. It was 1966. We had just moved into the house a couple of years earlier from our council house further up in the village, but up to this point those two years had been a period of transition, of upheaval, of clearing ground and planting, of building renovation and decoration, of making a house a home.

So when my parents closed the door on our comfortable post World War Two council 'longhouse' the first significant part of my life, the innocence of my boyhood, closed with it. In that little semi-detached house, part of the 'Viking row' of four blocks of two, I had learned to speak, to read and write and communicate with my fellows. In 3 Seaview Cottages I was formed. It was, perhaps more so, for my elder brother. So when my mother planted those two apple trees – one a 'cooker', the other an 'eater' – it was as if she was planting us, or for us, the tree of knowledge.

For the twenty years or so that I called that house and garden home I watched them grow – when my logical mind said that they wouldn't – and bear fruit just as Mrs Gunn's two boys grew and bore fruit and whether I was the 'eater' or my brother was the 'cooker' is still a subject of discussion between us. Unlike us, however, the trees never grew that tall. The topiary of the Atlantic wind saw to that but they reached the top of the drystone wall which surrounded the garden and the fruit was always small and hard. Yet when you bit into them the apples released onto the tongue a rushed sensation of salt and sugar, the essential sweet and sour apple-ness of the north of Scotland. It was as if both the earth and the sea were melding into a harmony of taste yet competing for the palates recognition.

These apple trees represented for me the next stage of my boyhood which was the period of recognition of and consolidation in the world, of a secondary rather than a primary schooling. So it was inevitable we would both leave the walled Eden of Dwarick Cottage if we wanted to consolidate what we had learned to recognise. With the tragic death of my mother in 1986, shortly followed by my father's four years later and the subsequent selling of the house, that second period of my life came to an end. Although it was inevitable it didn't feel that way at the time. In fact I felt a kind of stripping away of things: as if the scythe of death had gone through my family as easily as my fathers used to go through the hay.

The trees are still there, mercifully spared by the new owners who cut down other trees which had every right to live in the real world as they do in my memory. The two apple trees still bear fruit and I still, when I go to the hotel which is just over the wall, pick a couple of apples and taste again the sweet salt taste of family life, of indigenous pleasure and pain. Yet I do it, by necessity, from the other side of the wall. The wrong side, if you like, because now the native ground is owned by others who live their own lives and inhabit their own relationships with the house, the garden, the trees.

I could be forgiven, in the pale light of time, for offering this up as a rough metaphor for the Scottish, the Highland, the Caithness writer: that they must repossess their own native fruit, their own self-grown heritage, from out with the walls of their own place, to reclaim their memory – which is their right – by default, even illicitly. In his play *Translations* the Irish playwright Brian Friel, has one of his characters keen how 'a civilization can become imprisoned in a linguistic contour that no longer matches the landscape of fact'.

It was with the memory of this 'landscape of fact' and the taste-memory of my mother's northern apples which I always carry and am reminded of when I walk the hidden, mysterious and empty strath of Langwell. Running north west from the Berriedale Braes Langwell cuts a narrow defile south of the Scarabens from the east coast to the foot of Morven. To the south the Ord of Caithness blocks the northern half of the 'Province of the Cat' from its southern sister with a granite determination. This landscape of glacially scraped hills and burn cut straths – Kildonan to the south, with Braemore to the north and Langwell in the centre – is the heartland of the Clan Gunn although there is more to be seen, in archaeological evidence, of their Pictish antecedents and the Iron and Bronze Age settlers before them. Of the Gunns there is little trace left, there houses having been burned in the days of the 18th centuries turn into the 19th and the remaining stones used to build sheepfanks or estate walls. So yes, here again, in the heartland of my father's people, walls play a significant role in the folk memory which the landscape, in all its de-peopled baldness, offers up in quiet starkness and treeless amplification.

The 'linguistic contour' is in the names of the hills all around you as you walk up the strath through Aultibea to Wag. The hills resonant with the everydayness of yesteryear: *Cnoc an Eireannaich*, *Sron Gharbh*, *Meall a Caorach*, *Braigh an h-Eaglaise* and so on. In English they are 'the hill of the Irish', 'rough nose', 'the mound or bank of the sheep' and 'brae or hostage of the church'. This was the language spoken by my grandparents. As far as Langwell and south east Caithness is concerned it exists now only and in an often compromised form on the Ordnance Survey map which the making of in Ireland, ironically, was the subject of Friel's play. The tongue of the Gael is silent in the strath. The 'linguistic contour' is the 'to scale' residual of the militarisation of the Highlands and Islands of Scotland. The Ordnance Survey mapping by the British government who used cartography as both surveillance and containment is like a grid-echo of displacement.

With the clearing of the people went the ceilidh house culture of the bard and before that the *filidh* which co-joined the living with the Ossianic tales of the *Fionn Mac Cumhaill* and the *Tuatha De Danann*, all of which imbued in the people a 'timeless' sense of time. This Celtic chronology evaporates in 'the landscape of fact' as you walk up Langwell, through the plantation trees which surround Langwell House and further up to the estate lodge and the gardens where the caged hounds greet the visitor with their kennet savagery of frustrated hunting. The barking acoustic of this class war is made physically manifest in the many signs bearing the sacred credo of the landowning fraternity: 'private property, no access'. Despite this being against the law of nature and of Scotland the walker is advised to press on as past all this aristo-fiddle and pseudo arcadia is the quiet grandeur of the strath itself, reaching out to Morven which now seen from the south east, as opposed to its usual northerly viewing from the Cassiemire road, appears as it really is: which is not a big green hill but a small snow folded mountain.

In 1792 Sir John Sinclair of Ulbster, the 'great agricultural Sir John' of the Statistical Account of Scotland fame and the introducer of the infamous Cheviot sheep to the Highlands, the first five hundred were 'introduced' at Langwell, cleared these eastern straths of Caithness, eighty families from Langwell and Braemore alone. This gives lie to two of the prevailing myths attached to consciousness as official history: one is that Sir John Sinclair of Ulbster was a 'great improver' and secondly that there were 'no clearances' in Caithness. Braemore, Ousdale, Langwell and other straths lie empty and the land now lies fallow and wasting. Herds of red deer roam in their controlled majesty along the road, upon the hillsides, down by the river. As one walks on one feels the shades of the dispossessed and evicted walking in resigned single file past you to exile, to the coast, to Badbea.

The monument at Badbea was erected in 1911, the year the last resident left the township, by the son of the first resident to have emigrated to New Zealand in 1838. It stands like an omphalos on the edge of the world. The ground slopes precariously from the A9 down to the steep cliffs which plunge into the Moray Firth some 200 feet below. Here the 'shades' of Langwell had to make their lives as best they could, tethering both their livestock and children to the unyielding ground and against the fierce north-westerly gales which could and did blow them into oblivion.

The best way to appreciate Badbea and to see it in all its exposure is to head along the cliffs from Berriedale to the north and to follow the old north road which hugs the top lip of the cliffs of the Grey Coast like some thin stone moustache. This is the road traipsed back and forth by Finn in Neil Gunn's novel *The Silver Darlings*. Indeed it was to the herring fishing that the men of Badbea looked to sustain the eighty or so folk who called Badbea their home. Even this dangerous and fickle living was denied to them when David Home, the son of James Home who bought the Ousdale estate from Sir John Sinclair in 1814, closed the herring fishery and turned in the mid-19th century to the moneyed leisure pursuit of salmon fishing. The days of the sporting estate had begun. The tragedy for Scotland is that they are still here: wasteful and wasting.

One of the most moving names on the Badbea monument is that of Donald Sutherland, son of John 'Badbea' Sutherland – the spiritual leader of the people – who was killed at Waterloo. Fighting for what, one wonders? In my mind the Highlanders in Wellington's army should have dispatched their officers, grabbed their Brown Bess muskets and joined the French. A victorious Napoleon at least would have addressed the issue of land law, something successive Scottish governments have been reluctant to do.

'Passive suffering', W.B. Yeats once wrote, 'is not a subject for poetry'. Here the subject the 'tough minded' Yeats had in mind was Wilfred Owen, whom he considered 'tender minded'. What Yeats valued in his art was 'whatever shares the eternal reciprocity of tears'. Without an understanding of their history and without cultural knowledge a people, like the descendants of those at Badbea, like most modern Caithnessians, cannot fight back against the forces which have dispossessed them. Subsequently the classical literature of the Gael is denied to them as is the historical narrative of just why exactly the sons and daughters of 'the shades' of Langwell, their own antecedents, are in New Zealand.

Tenacious apple trees in a Dunnet garden may symbolise the 'tree of knowledge' or indeed *Yggdrasil*, the Norse world tree, and the apples from them could represent the hazelnuts of wisdom but I doubt if either my brother or I would pass for the salmon of knowledge who in Celtic myth ate them. Maybe I am like one of those hopeless ones in the Polish poet Zbignew Herbert's poem 'The Knocker': 'who grow/ gardens in their heads/ paths lead from their hair/ to sunny and white cities'?

As a writer one's job is to report what you see. For many walking through Langwell, through the empty heartland of the 'Province of the

Cat', is purely an aesthetic experience. They see the beauty of Morven and the Scarabens, of the dhu lochs and the frost glinting antlers of the winter stag. The beauty I see is in the people and the people are gone. To return them to Langwell and to the emptied north we need a radical new politics. Owning huge tracts of the Highlands stops anything else happening, so owning land has to be stopped. Who will walk towards that hill? Is that too 'tough minded'? The 'shades of Badbea expect their poets to have paths which 'lead from their hair/ to sunny and white cities'. It is what they would call imagining a future.

3.

Dunbeath sits like a hinge on the side of the stone door of the Grey Coast. If not exactly halfway, then it is centrally located on the eastern seaboard of the parish of Latheron, strategically placed between Helmsdale to the south and Wick to the north. Its castle sits south of the river, imposing and off-white like some great square milky bird. Its previous claimants of various Celto-Norman Sinclairs of several patchworks and strains and the evolved Sutherlands and de Freskyns of one sort or another before them used its magnificent position to batter and subdue the native population to their dubious will and for their gain. Until the late 20th century the castle and accompanying estate had the unique honour of being owned by the inventor of the sticky backed label. Such are the mighty edifices of feudalism so now put to use by those to whom personal wealth matches their various purposes and dreams. According to those who knew him, the late Mr Avery, for it was he who invented the sticky backed label, was a perfectly pleasant American gentleman. Such a positive opinion would not be one which would have stuck easily, back or front, to any of the 16th or 17th century Sinclair thanes.

My childhood memories of Dunbeath are ones of sun and fun as it was the destination of choice for either the Dunnet School or Sunday

School picnics. In the green before the village hall the children could run and play in the exotic surrounds of the mouth of Dunbeath strath while the mothers and teachers and various minders made tea or organised the obligatory games such as the egg and spoon and the sack race. I say 'exotic' because the enclosed nature of the strath with its wooded sides, the river beside the hall and the harbour at the river mouth did represent a fabulous other to us north coast children whose entire life experiences were literally of wide and open spaces. There were the occasional trees in one or two gardens in the north but we, by and large, inhabited a treeless land of fields and broad, sweeping horizons.

The magical quality of Dunbeath was not lost on its native son, the novelist Neil Gunn. When, many years later, I came to read his novels, I recognised the places in them immediately, emotionally, totally. This was not literature: this was confirmation. In and through these tales, these incantations, moved and lived people that I knew at once. These were not the fabulous creatures from some imagined golden era of race memory or the heroic figures of a politically created dream world: these were crofters, fishermen, wives, mothers, children. The language they spoke although written down in English, the lingua franca none the less was Gaelic. I say 'written down' as opposed to 'written' because the beating acoustic of Gunn's dialogue is that it has the quality of the moment, of being reported speech, of being 'in the play and agitation of the mind' as the English essayist William Hazlitt would have it. Through the characters in such novels as *The Silver Darlings* and *The Serpent* I fell willingly through a window into the land of myself, a bit like the human Yin and Yang of Young Art and Old Hector in the two very different books in which they feature. The land I fell into was not the past: it was the country of continuity which had been junctioned, stunted and bled by war.

It is salient here I think to consider for a moment just why Neil Gunn's work has succeeded and endured. It is not because the novels are 'mystical' or 'historical' or 'epic', although elements of all of those conditional adjectives and adverbs can be found in each and every one of the books, but rather that he connects with readers in a unique way and it is to do with a sense of place, both real and imagined. There is also a sense of cultural and linguistic repossession at work and an openness and inclusivity about Gunn's prose style which as John McGahern said of Alastair MacLeod – another prose stylist who writes in a similar way about essentially the same people but on a different continent – that 'his careful work never appears to stray outside what quickens it'. It is this quality of quickening which gives Gunn's prose its durability and its universality. The stress of the society he describes is easily understood, and the revelation welcomed, by anyone who has looked dispassionately at themselves and the society they live in, who have heeded Socrates and 'examined' their life.

The appeal of the language Gunn uses is in its brevity, lightness and humanity and the Gaelic of Neil Gunn's novels was the Gaelic of my grandparents. It was on one hand remembered and on the other forgotten. My Gran would happily sing to the rear end of a milking cow some song her own mother taught her from the sheilings of Durness but she would not speak a word of Gaelic to her four children. But here in Langwell, Braemore and Dunbeath is the Gaelic heart of Caithness. This is the parish of Latheron which once boasted the biggest population of any parish in the county and prior to the First World War they would have all been, predominantly, Gaelic speakers.

Latheron as well as being, up to the turn of the 19th century, the most densely populated parish is also in land mass the biggest. In human demographics it is now the emptiest. These two conditions are not unrelated. The size of the parish corresponded to the available arable ground and the subsequent amount of rent extractable by both kirk and estate. Other than some strips by the coast and north eastern facing braes along the straths this was, up to the late 18th century, in short supply. Which is why Latheron is so big and some of the northern parishes such as Olrig and Thurso are smaller by comparison. The Statistical Account shows that by 1861 the population of Caithness had peaked at 41,111. Prior to 1775 there was no such thing as crop rotation and the two main yields being corn and bere with some kail grown on the poorer ground. By 1812 over 7,000 acres of land in Caithness had been drained and enclosed into regular fields. With the clearance of people from the land increasing as these enclosures expanded and with the establishment of the herring industry in Wick and down the east coast from 1786 onwards the population of the parish of Latheron swelled and it was in Latheron, because the cottar could – in theory – be financially independent, that crofting as we know it today was effectively born.

Between 1811 and 1861 some 10,000 acres of land was given over to crofting with the majority of these holdings being south of Wick and north of The Ord. Up to that time a 'croft' referred to an unoccupied piece of bogland or rough ground. A 'toft', on the other hand, was an unoccupied but worked piece of land. At the turn of the 18th century 'croft' had come to mean a piece of reclaimed cultivated land with a house and maybe a byre of some sort or small barn on it. As a result by 1861 Latheron parish boasted a sizeable proportion of the huge population of 41,111. It has been said that at one time more people lived in Latheron parish in the 19th century than in the whole of Caithness prior to World War Two. It was not unknown for over a thousand people to attend Communion at the old Latheron kirk in the mid 19th century and it is documented that the service in the kirk throughout that century were conducted in Gaelic.

These are the subjects of Neil Gunn fiction. Whether it was wrestling with the limitations of the run rig and rig and renal system of agriculture or risking their lives on the open sea at the herring fishing the crofter/fisherman of the Grey Coast had an unusual advantage in that he did not totally depend upon agriculture. This was attractive enough to swell the population to levels never imagined before. But this was no Shangri-La. Crofts were invented to keep people on the land but not to make the crofter self-sufficient. As is seen in such novels as *Butcher's Broom* one of the purposes of retaining a population on the land was the recruitment of soldiers for the British Army. The War Memorials on the Eastern seaboard of Caithness, although they claim to remember the men who fell in the 'Great War' and World War Two, harbour the poignant and questioning echoes of the Napoleonic Wars and the unrelenting meat grinding expansion of the British Empire. This organised tragedy is why, doggedly, Gunn made sure that his 'careful work never appears to stray outside what quickens it'.

Another function of crofting was that it was an attempt by the State and the estates to curb emigration. The 'dance called America' was stepped out not so gaily on the pier-sides at Scrabster and Stromness, and on the shores of Loch Eriboll and Loch Broom. In Caithness from the late 18th century and throughout the 19th emigration was more like a slow waltz or a steady drip rather than the 'mania' it became in the Western Isles. In the opening decade of the 20th century, however, the step speed increased when over a thousand people left Caithness. A sizeable majority of these were from the parish of Latheron which because of the size of its population and the vulnerability of the crofting-fishing economy to external forces was always a district which would suffer depopulation when either the price of fish fell or the fallout from war hit home. The Grey Coast lost many, mainly women and their children, after the slaughter of the trenches left them widowed, fatherless and poverty stricken.

Other than the novels of Neil Gunn, which are works of literary art, there is no real history of this coast, as there is no real history – or sustained detailed narrative – of Caithness in general. There are, as I have highlighted above, Calder and Mackay and also the various and valuable pamphlets and short studies on aspects of specific subjects and places but no Caithness equivalent of William Thompson's *History of Orkney*. When one reads the various texts on herring fishing or on the history of Wick the enquiring reader laments the weaknesses of the amateur historian and craves the strengths of the professional as enthusiasm for the enterprise often overtakes the structure of the narrative. Often I feel myself crying out, like Stephen Daedalus in James Joyce's novel *Ulysses* that 'History… is a nightmare from which I am trying to awaken'. In many ways this entire book is testament to that.

So what am I trying to 'awaken' from? There is no doubt that the history of Caithness – I suppose like all 'histories' – is epic. The job of the poet is to draw on history in order to free the imagination from the past and to make the leap into a creative future. Gunn attempted this in *The Green Isle of the Great Deep* which is one of the most chilling versions of a future dystopia I have read because the landscape it is enacted out on is so familiar. It is, I would argue, the landscape of Latheron, but a dream-Latheron, a not-quite-Latheron.

Before they have their accident and make their descent into *The Green Isle of the Great Deep* there is a passage which Gunn hints at the predicament of the creative writer and the modern historian:

Old Hector looked now as if he might talk now to Art of many things and times of long ago. In the moment that could wait, all of life could be told. A strange and silent smile, such as Art had never seen before, glimmered on his face, and in that moment Art entered into his heritage and he loved Old Hector and the presences of all those who had been here before, alive or dead.

Here we see the eighty families walking down the Langwell strath in 1792 to Badbea, to the invention of crofting, to the fishing, to the other side of the world. This is the highly charged landscape of the votive offering and the ancient gods, the daylight gods and the gods of darkness, carved on rocks or in the imagination. 'Art entered into his heritage' as if he were both awakening and somehow dreaming at the same time. Like the political organisation of the crofters which would come into being in the 1880s Art was both entering into 'his heritage' and 'coming upon himself', another leitmotif of Neil Gunn's poetics. But whatever it was something was being assembled, organised, deployed.

When Young Art and Old Hector finally fall, suddenly, into the hazel pool where they have been gathering 'the nuts of knowledge' while at the same time landing a twenty pound cock 'salmon of wisdom' and go down into 'the deep' they emerge in a landscape familiar yet strange to them. 'I don't know the place at all', said Old Hector, 'though I seem to remember it, too. The sea looks a bit bluer than the sea at home at this time of year.'

This is the beautiful, hard country of revelation, the dream-world of consciousness: 'the other side of sorrow' as Sorley Maclean put it in his poem 'The Cuillin'. But this is also the land of a new politics – of 'the coast watcher' and 'the Seat of the Rock'. This is Gunn's totalitarian nightmare, drawn from life experience, of having 'entered into his heritage', his unconscious mind where the folk stories, poems and incantations of his childhood mingles with the Jungian idea of the 'collective unconscious' and the fear of Stalinism, or of any 'ism' for that matter. In the Highland heartland of Caithness, in her *Gaidhealtachd*, in the snow-capped hills and on the granite plateau of Latheron parish this new politics, Gunn argues, has to be nurtured and made benign. For this new vision for the country of Scotland is woven from the individuation and the atavistic culture and beliefs of the people, this hardy breed of survivors, of workers, of dreamers, of croft makers and herring gutters, of tradition bearers and exiles, so it must be a politics of enlightenment and freedom or it is nothing. It is still there that hope. I feel it enter into me as I walk north along the coast from Dunbeath to Lybster. No government act, no racist legislation, no ignorant Highland councillor can deny it for it is as Old Hector says:

'So deep … that we can only come out through the bottom.'

'Where?' (Asks Art).

'In the Green Isle of the Great Deep.' And lifting his fingers in a silent hush, Old Hector turned to his task.

That 'task', for all humanity, is to make the future inhabitable, to 'awaken' from the nightmare of history as Joyce would have it. At the very end of his kind-of autobiography *The Atom of Delight* Gunn addresses the question of how to go 'deeper into the consideration' of the 'second self', which is a parallel consideration to Joyce's, and he concludes: 'But that seems so large if not impossible a task that it would be more than has been earned at this point if the boy has given intimations of it.'

The coastline walked by Young Art and Old Hector is also a parallel experience. What 'has been earned' is the right to discuss the possibility of a future for the people of the Grey Coast as they find it now. It strikes me that the 'boy' has given out plenty 'intimations of it' and although 'it' is difficult to detect due to educational shortcomings and because of the absence of an authoritative history even more difficult to articulate those 'intimations', although not quite in the Wordsworthian sense of 'Thoughts that do often lie too deep for tears'; but 'it' is there in the gleanings of the old culture and folk memory which rises up into modernity when plunged into the dark pools of oppression. 'It' is something that ensures that the people's voice is not drowned. That 'it' moves 'rising up on the other side of sorrow' or, as Sorley Maclean has it in one of his other masterpieces, *Hallaig*, '*chunnacas na marbh beò* / the dead have been seen alive'.

4.

One winter a large black cat was reported roaming along the north coast of Caithness and Sutherland. Photographs of disconsolate and sardonic crofters posing beside the gristle and gnawed bones which were all that remained of various sheep were common in the local press from November to February. It was a panther, a lion, a huge dog, a golden eagle, a demon; that some beast, or something, had been slaughtering ewes and consuming the greater proportion of the carcass was evident for all to see. Something had to be done. That was the consensus. But nothing was done. That was the reality. For in truth, what could be done? Search parties roamed the night from Reay to Bettyhill at various times for several months and found absolutely nothing.

This is how history is recorded. The result of actions are there to be seen but as soon as humanity goes in search of the causes in order to understand the effect then humanity becomes like a search party roaming a rocky northern coastline in the dark in pursuit of something they do not believe in and are not equipped to recognise even if they find it. Their very action insures they will not find anything and the more they convince themselves the opposite is the case the more certain is the futility of both the exercise and the outcome.

If a wise person came along and said that the killings of the ewes was due to an escapee from a zoo; a feral population of large black cats which have roamed the north of Scotland for years; random acts of savagery by large dogs which have escaped from their owners: no-one would believe them. All anyone knew for certain was the result. Ten men around a dead sheep have ten subjective reasons for the animal's death. Unless the theory for that death coincides with their own they will not believe it and why should they, for no-one can prove they are wrong.

It is interesting that from Wick to Lybster there was once a railway. It was opened on July 1st 1903 and closed on 1st April 1944. Despite the Duke of Portland's plans to the contrary it never made any money. Like the mad enterprise of the railway north of Tain it was, however, built for that purpose. In Lybster's case it was herring. For the Duke of Sutherland it was the business of the sporting estate. The railway still goes to Thurso because of war and the subsequent nuclear experiment. Once the last container of decommissioned – or not – nuclear waste heads south who is to say how long that will continue? Like similar capitalists the Dukes of Portland and Sutherland depended upon coal mines in the north of England for a lot of their income, they were not the philanthropic saints of popular legend. They were the opposite. So the Lybster railway closed even in a time of war and from a lack of sufficient tons of herring.

But history is about more than war and herring, even for the fought over bogland which is the 'Province of the Cat'. History is not really concerned about the doings of Dukes. It is more about the great baggage of the everyday, of the incidentals and tiny details of the stain human blood leaves on the mosaic of time. Not much of it makes any sense, even in retrospect. Most of the episodes happened even when the protagonists desired the opposite of the recorded outcome. The train, once out of the station, must go to its destination. In Boris Pasternak's epic novel of bits and pieces, *Dr Zhivago*, the hero Yuri Zhivago, dies of a heart attack on a streetcar, or a tram, in Moscow, in 1929, the very year Stalin achieved supreme power in the Soviet Union. This is what Pasternak termed 'the locomotive of history'. The novel does take place before, during and after the Russian Revolution. But *Dr Zhivago* is not 'about' the Russian Revolution. It tells a story about human history and of survival. More love is shown in the hoarding of potatoes and firewood than in treating the wounded or burying the dead of the Red militia. This is how we recognise history as being related to the majority of humanity: by details, tiny fragments of experience. This is because history is made by the majority and not by Dukes or the vainglories of Kings and Emperors.

When the train stops at Kinbrace or Forsinard and the traveller looks out of the window, for no apparent reason or for the best of intentions, what they see is the result of one ill-thought out set of actions. Resistance to the sheriff's officers and the agents of the factors operating on behalf of the Duke of Sutherland or Sir John Sinclair of Ulbster was low at the turn of the 18th century because of what had happened before the centurys (singular) groove had been cut through the straths. When your culture is dissolved under you on the instruction of the state and when the ministers are telling you it is the will of God, shooting Patrick Sellar will not stop the train, or start it either. This is not to justify not shooting Patrick Sellar, rather it is an attempt to put yet another piece of the human mosaic on the threshing floor of history. For history to operate everyone has to understand that the locomotive is unstoppable. Yet justice comes with the passing of time. Stalin is as unloved as Patrick Sellar. The Dukes of Portland and Sutherland, past, subsequent and present, are seen for what they are: landowning capitalists. The 'locomotive of history', inevitably, passes them by. The majority, after all, have laid the track, made the machine and they drive and crew the engine. The majority is the detail of history. Which is why, because it is overly concerned about this Sinclair Earl or that Sutherland Duke, the history of the north of Scotland, as it is popularly understood, is in fact a fiction.

5.

Walking in Latheron, the vast rolling parish, is like walking back in time. It is the biggest parish in Caithness. It, in the 19th century, was the most populous by far of all the districts in the 'Province of the Cat'. The name itself is surrounded by mystery but the most obvious, and I suppose the most accurate, is that it derives from '*leiter ron*' which in Gaelic means 'sloping land of the seals'. As Latheron slopes from the west down to the east this, as ever in Gaelic, seems the practical origin but there are theories that it derives from '*ladhran*' meaning prong or claws or from the Norse '*hlatha*' which can either mean a barn or a pile of stones. As Gaelic was the spoken language of Latheron from after the Picts to the 19th century a sloping land of seals it must be. It is also a sloping place of meaning too.

What fascinates me about Latheron is the human dimension. From the end of the 18th century and throughout the 19th to the First World War the parish was jam packed full of people and most of them displaced. Other than Dunbeath in the south and Lybster to the north there are no centres of population. The harbours at Latheron and Latheronwheel did constitute what in the *Gaidhealtachd* is termed a '*baile*' or township. Mostly it is what passes or passed for crofting; the sporting estates rolling to the west like a plague. But here, in Latheron, there was another significant minority category of peasant which the Napier Commission and the subsequent Crofters Holding Act of 1886 did not address. They were the cottars. The landless ones who came and went with the wind but who had always been there and they were the ones which the agricultural 'improvements' of benevolent yet self-serving landlords trampled into the bog of history; or the ethnocide which is commonly called the 'Highland Clearances', dispersed to the far away, unknown lands of the British Empire. In Latheron, almost like the stones themselves, the cottars remained: stubbornly, perennially – there.

With them was a deep and natural culture. Celtic in nature and ancient in origin it straddled that strangeness which is the difference between *baile* and the arable ground and the wild and open places. Here in Latheron, as in almost no other place I know of on the mainland of the north of Scotland, people lived their lives inhabiting several dimensions daily, thinking nothing of practising their devout and sincere Christianity while at the same time understanding the nature of shape-changing and the wiles and wherefore of the '*sidhiche*' or '*sidheanach*' – pronounced 'she' – as in 'the fairies', which is nowhere near an adequate translation of what the '*sidhiche*' are or mean.

Like everything else attached to the reality and history of the common people of Caithness there is a distortion involved when it is explained to the modern, more Anglo-centric members of society. To say that the '*sidhiche*' were as far removed from little green people with wings as Wick is from the moon is to state the obvious or to make a meaningless comparison but in the relative universe of people's understanding, when the references are so limited, one might as well say that the sea is made out of Guinness. Desirable as that may be it is obviously not the case. As in all folk culture its 'strangeness' comes from not being the practical medium of expression or way of living for those who look into it. In many ways folklorists create strangeness by recording human behaviour in an academic fashion, separated from the way of life which gave rise to the customs and belief systems in the first place. All folk culture is the product of a dynamic, not static, social anthropological structure, ever changing, always adapting, never at peace with itself.

When you ask the question: 'What is supernatural?' – you have to answer, if you have any designs on science or accuracy, that it is a preternatural belief system; something which defies science, accuracy and Christianity – which is, after all, only the current official belief system. There is a great Gaelic word '*anaghnathaicte*' which translates rather mundanely as 'unusual' but which describes and alludes to those things which could be termed as omens or portents. That is to say that in a pastoral society where the vagaries of the weather has more import than the temper of the Earl the realities of the day to day become the belief system and whether the people hail from Celtic or Norse stock they share a genius for invention; for creating an interpretative code, a lexicon of fable from which enlightenment can be gained. The reality of every day adds to the next and over thousands of years that knowledge benefits the majority and between winter and summer, from seed time to harvest, at the calving and the milking, that knowledge manifests itself in story and song, in sayings and incantations: the general magic of life.

With the land enclosures in the second half of the 18th century a displaced population crowded down to the coastal fringes of the north of Scotland. Latheron, perched on the Grey Coast, with its rough, unoccupied ground – its 'croft and toft' – was a favoured holding tank, both a refuge and a prison for these unfortunates. As a consequence Latheron with its arable acres and its upper hill ground became the perfect place for the intermingling of known and unknown, of faith and the supernatural, and into the parish from the end of the 18th century and the first decades of the 19th poured a people whose complicated psychology and ancient nature beliefs were fire-sharpened in the violence of their recent history, their physical removal and displacement from their native straths and the wholesale attack upon their society, culture and language.

Here was a civilization which had been betrayed by both their traditional chiefs and their clergy and who, over time and through necessity, turned forcefully against both instigating a political resistance based on the Irish Land League and a Free Kirk which found footage in the Evangelical Revival, a movement of the common people that spread through the Highlands from around 1800. That the political process in relation to land ownership has yet to be concluded and the spiritual energy which seethed with an angry radical polity and which burst through in the Great Disruption of 1843 eventually turned in on itself and became what John MacInnes, in his essay 'Religion In Gaelic Society', has termed 'a reclusive religion': both these aspects await a hearing in history's court.

The on-going splits within the Free Presbyterian Church indicate that insularity is still, habitually, preferred to perception and progress. It is difficult to see, however one wishes for its opposite, how this could have turned out any other way. The Clearances produced the physicality of economic poverty coupled with bewilderment and what MacInnes calls 'an intellectual and spiritual hunger'. There was no alternative place for the people to go as 1799 turned into 1800; there was no other liberal philosophy save that of 'the market' and there was no other political system on offer to lift them out of the obedience and acceptance which had so manifestly been their undoing. Organised political fight-back was still a generation away.

So it was that the spiritual hunger of the people fed out in the open, turning its back not only on the kirk walls but on the physical pleasantries of the lived world and through the emergence of a succession of powerful and persuasive lay-preachers and leaders there evolved a domination of their own society by a strict moral code which at least fastened them to their creed while emigration, exile, starvation and an early death did their utmost to loosen them from the land and life itself. Is it any wonder that the great communal psalm singing which rose up throughout the 19th century from the huddled multitudes of Latheron and other parishes could reduce those unfamiliar with its anguished poetic origins to a stunned silence? This was an outpouring of redemption that had artistic and cultural roots so ancient and deep as to be almost archaeological. The white hind of the supernatural was grazing in the township of the people and to this the reply was '*Se comhtharra cogaidh a tha seo*', or 'This is an omen of war'.

The 'war' would be conducted on earth as opposed to heaven. Many of the sites where these open air services and gatherings took place were already places steeped in traditional folk beliefs or places of significance where people had gathered for centuries. Latheron is littered with brochs, stone circles and burial mounds: all these have associations with tribal gatherings, the ancestral dead and the pagan other world of 'faeries' or '*Na Sidhichean*'. Now nowhere in any of the folk stories of Latheron do we learn of 'little green people', rather the '*Sidhiche*' were of human proportion and appearance, although there is the odd reference to them as being 'shrunken' or 'wizened'. The colours of their clothes would depend on what local dyes were available. This, of course, corresponds to the tartans of the Mackays, Gunns and Sinclairs – all of which are green and brown based. They are generally never described as being vivid in any way when they are seen above ground. There are many legends of the fantastic nature of fairydom when a mortal ventures down into the mound.

But the '*Sidhiche*' are beings not of the domestic realm, the township or the field, but the wild open places – the high strath pastures, the Scarabens and the vast sea of bog beyond. There they rise up the colour of the earth and the heather. Indeed the Gaelic for the fairies has the element '*sidh*' which means a 'mound or hill'. Up in the headwaters of the Dunbeath Strath there are hills such as '*Sithean Corr-meille*', or 'the (fairy) hill of a thousand points' and '*Sithean na Gearra*', or 'the (fairy) hill of the hare' – the hare has its own place in the ancient gallery of spirit animals and shape-changing. If anyone walks over these hills they cannot but be impressed by the large herds of red deer which seem to appear from no-where and then disappear as easily. It is no coincidence that the red deer, the '*fiadh*', are known in legend as the cattle of the '*Sidhiche*'. Their abodes are known as '*Taighean-fo-thalamh*' or 'the underground houses', which corresponds again to ancient souterrains and ruined brochs. From these can be heard music, especially pipe music and it is a strong thread of folklore which has the famous pipers of Clan Donald, the MacCrimmons, learning their famous pibrochd from the '*Sidhiche*'. As with Fyfe and other pipers, as we shall see, the relationship between composition and inspiration and the 'other world' is a complicated and profound one. Music has, in many cultures throughout the world, a long association with the 'divine' and this 'divine' more often than not has a more earth-bound flavour than that of the cherubim or seraphim.

The '*Sidhiche*' are also known as 'the people of peace', from '*daoine sithe*'. In Neil Gunn's novel *The Silver Darlings* young Finn has as his sanctuary the 'house of peace' which is situated deep in the upper reaches of the Dunbeath Strath amid the ruins of brochs and souterrains. It is this idea of 'deep country' which is attractive in regard to the '*Sidhiche*'. As I have claimed earlier, and for want of a better explanation, history has washed over the 'Province of the Cat' like waves, each one pushing the earlier established human sediment before it or absorbing all trace of it completely. Who built the brochs? Who did the Picts displace when they arrived in the north and in turn that happened to the Picts when the Norse and the Gaels arrived? In his book *Clans and Chiefs* Dr Ian Grimble offers an indication in way of an answer, or at least a suggestion as to the origin of the Clan Gunn:

> What seems … likely is that the Gunns were a Pictish tribe, especially in view of the inveterate hostility that continued for so many centuries between them and the Mackays (and the Keiths) who were of Gaelic origin and had almost certainly invaded their neighbourhood in large numbers. Anyway, Picts must be looked for somewhere. They had been a more numerous people than the Gaels, a formidable power in the eyes of the Romans, and modern methods of genocide did not exist in those days. The Gunns territory (along the Caithness-Sutherland border) is exactly where one would expect to find the survivors of so many centuries of misfortune. That incomparable Highland novelist Neil Gunn felt in his bones that his people were Picts: it influenced his work deeply, and it seems very probable that he was right.

If we think of the '*Sidhiche*' as fulfilling in folk memory that echo of an historical displacement of a settled people by invaders then the reality of the fairy element begins to take on some psychological sense, if not historic. The 'Picts hooses' of Caithness, where the 'wee folk bide', were in fact the remains of pre-Pictish brochs. The 'border country' of the Clan Gunn corresponds to the land beyond the '*baile*' or township, to the 'wilderness' of '*Na Sidhichean*'. If history cannot provide us with answers or information then folk culture, even the supernatural, will.

If, from the beginnings of human settlement in the Far North, most people were bi-lingual (whether it was in some form in the linguistic line from pre-Pictish, Pictish, Gaelic, Norse, Scots through to English) then it is no stretch of the imagination to assume that most people could traditionally accommodate 'two realities'; the real and explained world, and the preternatural and unexplained world. So by extension it would not be unusual to expect to find among a God-fearing Christian society, such as the peasant class of Caithness in the 19th century, those who had no real trouble with the conflicting belief system of Christ's resurrection at Easter and the shape-changing abilities of a Latheron 'feeach' or 'witch' who can adopt the form of a hare. 'Feeach' comes from '*fitheach*', the Gaelic word for raven.

John Carey, in his study *A Single Ray of the Sun: Religious Speculation in Early Ireland*, cites the belief that the '*Sidhiche*' are a kind of fallen angel. When Lucifer rebelled against God and was consigned to perdition along with those angels who sided with 'him'; the angels who were loyal to God remained in heaven. But, as you might expect in the Celtic world-view, there was a third type of angel: those who remained neutral. They were judged neither good enough for Heaven or bad enough for Hell so were banished to the earth to reside amongst the hidden places, in the hills and distant mountains, until the end of time. I am not putting a case forward for considering the Picts, or indeed the Clan Gunn, as 'fallen neutral angels' but this idea is clearly an early exercise by the emerging Christian church in cosmological fusion, of trying to bring 'in house' a strongly held strand of the pre-Christian belief system.

One of the most unlikely examples of this accommodation in the 20th century – although his working life straddled back into the 19th – of 'folklore' by practising Christianity is by the Reverend George Sutherland of the Bruan Kirk whose book *Folklore Gleanings and*

Character Sketches From The Far North was published in 1937. George Sutherland was born into a Gaelic speaking family at Houstry, near Dunbeath, in 1854 and his fascinating record of stories concerning fairies, witches, the supernatural, hauntings and general tales of the ancient beliefs and peasant customs of the ordinary people of Latheron is all the more remarkable when one considers that he himself was a Free Church minister, a theological particularity not usually noted for its tolerance of 'other-ness', paganism or for having a sympathetic ear for the '*Sidhiche*', neutral angels or not.

What is apparent throughout Sutherland's 'gleanings' is a great sympathy for the people – which, of course, he was one – and a refreshingly non-judgemental attitude to their long held superstitions. Perhaps the most endearing quality is that of good humour. Sutherland's stories are always flavoured with the necessary comic democracy to give them if not quite a sense of the ridiculous then certainly a sense that these yarns are fundamentally a part of a very human experience and tradition and of a life all the more richer for it as a result. Whether it is about who put 'the freet' in the milk or how the corn got trampled; or about changelings; transportation through the air and through time; or stories about a Water-horse or a Water-bull, or about certain individuals who had this or that 'gift' of the second sight or of miraculous healing – each one is told matter-of-factly and with an empirical detachment which evidences in the author a great respect for both the people and their belief systems.

He is never shy to tell a story against himself. For example:

> I met Robbie the Bee yesterday and we drifted into a talk about church going. I asked him why he did not go to church on Sunday like his neighbours. Fancy the reply the droll creature gives me '*Na mise rachadh do 'n eaglais a dheisdeach is fear na sheasadh ann an cubaid caoineadh am fear tha cumail a chaid aran ris?*' Or in English 'Is it I would go to church to listen to a man standing in a pulpit and reviling the fellow that is keeping him in bread?'

Is there a hint that George Sutherland's sympathies were more than a little with Robbie the Bee than the Sabbath habit of the Kirk?

Throughout his work we find a bevy of real, remembered and imagined folk characters, 'some with second sight' or some other quality. Such as the piper Fyfe from Reay, who was reported to have had his extraordinary powers granted to him by the '*Sidhiche*' and no matter how far he travelled or in what weather he always turned up in a neat and tidy condition and was always willing and able to play. Or there was Sandy Gunn from Houstry who when he was walking one day on Cnoc nan Crask found himself flying up into the air and looking down onto the district below with the people working in the fields. The wind that caught him up deposited him back exactly where it had found him. Or the Rapid Weaver, '*Am breabadair luath*', who could weave a long length of cloth (a day's labour) in the time it took to boil a pot of potatoes. Then there was the story of a man sitting by the seashore reading a bible when along came a woman dressed in green. She asked him if there was any salvation for the like of her, such as she was. The man looked up at her and knew at once exactly what she was and told her no, that it was only for those of Adam's race. On hearing this the poor woman gave out a horrendous scream and dived headlong into the sea.

Then there were the 'witches', the Caithness 'feeachs' or ravens. A black raven on the roof was commonly understood to be a warning of death. These 'feeachs' took many forms. There were the purely psychological operators like Bell Royal. According to the Reverend Sutherland she was 'tall and strongly built and had a fine moustache and a number of straggling hairs adorned her chin'. Although she did have the habit of dressing like a man she did 'retain the use of petticoats'. Her trade was with the fishermen of Latheron. 'Give royally an ee'll get royally' was her catchphrase – hence her name. The fishermen knew too much not to take heed and give generously.

These people were known to George Sutherland and no more so than perhaps one of the strangest 'feeach' of them all, namely the 'Witch of Snaetoft' who, unlike the 18th century 'feeach' the 'Witch of Ballachly' – the original 'feeach' – had no byname nor Christian name. She was well known for putting a 'freet', or spell, on the milking and indeed her most famous chant was:

> Gether in, gether in
> cream an milk an cheese
> Gether in, gether in
> an stop no til I please!

Very early one morning a certain Betty, or Bettsag, went with the cattle down to the grazing beside Loch Rangag. There she saw the 'Witch of Snaetoft' sitting beside the water making her famous incantation. Bettsag remained out of sight and, as is only human, repeated the charm over and over to herself until she had remembered it. Then when the cattle had munched their fill she lay down and spread her aprons out in the morning dew and repeated the words:

> Gether in, gether in
> cream an milk an cheese
> Gether in, gether in
> an stop no til I please!

To her amazement and horror milk started streaming from her aprons, petticoats, from her dress and from every article of clothing she had on – as the good Reverend puts it 'a veritable Noah's flood of milk'. Unable to understand what was happening to her and therefore terrified Bettsag ran back to the croft. By the time she got home she was followed by a procession of cats, dogs and pigs all eager to get their fill of the milk. What kind of sight she presented to her brother who found her raving and lactating profusely on the croft floor is difficult to imagine. However the poor stricken girl did manage to tell him what had happened and he set off for Rangag and there he found the 'Snaetoft feeach' and he boldly related what had happened to Bettsag. She 'muttered some words' and much to the disappointment of the parish cats, dogs and pigs, the flow of milk from Bettsag's clothing stopped.

Whatever credence one gives to such a story our prejudices will be distanced and fashioned by time and the rationality of the 21st century. The latter condition was no impediment to George Sutherland and he relates that when the 'Witch of Snaetoft' either died or moved away he went up, with the curiosity of a young boy, to what remained of her bothy. On the floor, amongst a heap of rubbish, he made two remarkable discoveries and both of them books. The first he came across was a battered copy of Luther's *Commentary on Galatians* which was an unusual tome to be found anywhere in those days but especially in the residence of a 'feeach'. The second and even more fantastic was a copy of *Satan's Invisible World Discovered* by George Sinclair, who had been Professor of Moral Philosophy at Edinburgh University. This book was published in 1688.

He took both books home to Houstry. He showed them to his father. Here were the two sides of the theological universe. His father seemingly agreed with him that *Satan's Invisible World Discovered* was 'fantastic' because he made the young George go out and burn Sinclair's priceless volume.

Whatever the 'Witch of Snaetoft' was she was no 'neutral angel'. Throughout Latheron parish there are tales of supernatural harvests; of fantastic journeys at sea dependent on a string with three knots; various omen animals bringing either good or bad depending on the circumstances; of a distiller who discovered an 'eolas' – or secret word – to make himself invisible; strange processions of carts through the sky going in the direction few folk rarely took to places no-one had ever lived. All add to the pattern of everyday life – hard, unremitting and often short – as experienced by the vast majority of the people. To have a greater reality, to emboss a deeper meaning on such a pattern is a creative instinct displayed by peasant societies across the world and throughout time which is what gives these particular instances of phenomena their potency: it is their sheer ancientness, their preternatural acoustic. They resonate and endure in a way that modern Christianity does not, cannot for these episodes come from a deeper human well and are unburdened by the morality or direct instruction so embedded in Christianity.

Ironically it is not 'mere' superstition but metaphors and similes built from long experience which accommodate this embeddedness: it is a poetic notation of memory for these are survival codes. Although an element of the creative imagination as manifest in individuals is important to consider when the divination of these image-sets are concerned what is of more significance is the importance of the collective imagination. These combinations of visions, dreams, experience (remembered or actual) belief, ceremonial practices emerges with humankind from deep time and the fact that we continue to evaluate and contextualise it is proof positive of its endurance. What we must conclude then is that such hybrid nomenclatures such as '*Sidhiche*', '*fitheach*' or 'feeach', Each Uisge and the like are drawn from psychic inheritance of a pastoral and agricultural experience which is an essential part of understanding who we are and of our part in the in the ongoing human journey.

It is as if there is a curtain of radiance between the world of life and work and the other world of the phantasm or '*taidhbhse*', or the person 'blessed' or 'cursed' with the 'second sight', who inhabits the realm of the seer, who enters into the world of the '*filidh*', or more mundanely the art of the bard. On the other side of this curtain can walk the '*samhla*' or the 'astral body', or the likeness or human resemblance – the Gaelic doppelganger, the '*co-choisiche*' or co-walker. This idea of two realities walking side by side in the physical world is central to understanding how folk culture and belief in the 'other world' represent the two sides of psychology and of history, even the two sides of the brain. It is also a vital indication of where art sprung from and what function it had and has in the development of human behaviour and psycho-pathology.

The relation of the pastoral society to the land changed as agricultural 'improvement' prevailed: the relationship of humankind to nature changed accordingly. Belief systems changed also. A culture which can give rise to an easy acceptance of the '*co-choisiche*' is not going to be contained or restrained by the physicality of mere time or social alteration. Every new circumstance must be understood and this is as true of the political world as it is of the supernatural. In order for any set of realities to be understood they have to be recognised and it is this dynamic of recognition, rather than belief, which is at the centre of the human interpretation of the natural world, of all reality. As both political control and spiritual maturity were snatched away from the people of the 'Province of the Cat' as the 18th century turned into the 19th, as the unnatural concept of the Christian church and the landed estate evolved into being two sides of the one power structure, so it was that instead of the peasant being the active instigator in their own spiritual development and participant in the husbandry of the their own land they became passive receivers of denuded forms of both.

This did lead to fatalism and an acceptance by the people that these historical circumstances were natural and inevitable. There was no pattern to the events which they could recognise. Instead, where there was once connectedness, there was now land enclosure, sheep farms and the physical clearance of the population, cultural ethnocide and a society which had once enjoyed some control over their future, their fate, now found their destiny in the hands of others. Value was transformed into material wealth and, ironically, no matter the pecuniary success of those who transformed the New

World across the seas, they could never buy back what had been taken away from them. The experience for the majority was that the free market in property was as rigged as the doctrines of theology. Where the '*Sidhiche*' and their 'host', the '*Sluagh*', offered a freedom to the imagination and a link to the past that the large enclosed fields of Caithness and the open yet empty acres of the deer forests along the border with Sutherland blocked off; these enclosures denied to the people such a connection with the future. In other words, the future whatever it was, was not for them.

The 'otherworld' has another function: that of a deferred political sense of justice, or '*ceartas*' as it is known in Gaelic. This is the sense that despite everything that history has thrown at them that the cause of 'the people', the Gaels, the Celts – call them what you will – will prevail. That the stolen lands will be re-possessed, that the people will return to the straths and glens they were removed from, that they will once more acquire status and enjoy the culture and society they previously had. This sense of inevitability, almost of the Second Coming, has its roots deep in the Fenian legends of Ireland and the myth of Arthur, his non-death and residence in Avalon. The Arthurian myth is resonant throughout the Celtic world and no matter how it has been redesigned by the scribes of the Anglo-Norman ascendency of the Middle Ages, namely Geoffrey of Monmouth in his *Historia Regum Britanniae*, into Camelot and the Knights of The Round Table or rehashed into some Pre-Raphaelite fantasy in Victorian times, it still retains the trace elements of the part-mythical 6th century Romano-Brythonic warlord Urther and his struggles against the Angles and Saxons.

More locally the Brahan Seer, or *Coinneach Obhar* (Sallow Kenneth), has predicted, amongst his more famous prophecies about the 'black rain' and so on, that the Gael will 'regain our rightful place in Scotland'. This has also been attributed to Thomas the Rhymer. Messianic it may be but such romantic notions of the reversal of history has remained popular in north Highland culture and this sense of '*ceartas*' fuelled much of the myth of the Jacobite entitlement of the 18th century and this sense of 'coming again' into what was wrongly usurped. It could be argued that the very idea of Scottish independence in the 21st century has this Fenian, Arthurian idea somewhere at its centre.

All this is part of the necessary, self-sustaining psycho-mythology of a culture and civilization in decline, of a society subjected to intense historical and political pressure. The Grey Coast is one place which has witnessed the results of this pressure first hand. From the post-1746 Clearances, the enclosure of land and the imposition of sheep and deer forests, the establishment of the herring industry in the 19th century through to the subsequent emigration both prior to and after World War One, the Depression of the 1920s and 30s, World War Two and the pre and post-Dounreay economy of the early 21st century: all these waves of history and modernity have crashed over the granite and sedimentary rocks of this north eastern shoreline, washing the people of 'Province of the Cat' this way and that. That they have successfully and literally hung onto the far flung edges of Scotland with their bare hands is testament to the strength of their will and the quality of their endurance. But this is not an 'otherworld'; this is the real world.

6.

Wick is the only town in Europe with extant bomb damage from World War Two. It is a place where the ideas of the Enlightenment led directly to the charnel house of organised poverty. That the scars of war are now converted into a memorial garden and the skeletons of the past walk beside the shadows of the living or peer out from the voluminous sepia photographs from the Johnston Collection in the Wick Heritage Centre does not detract from the fact that Wick was built for human exploitation and for the exploitation of nature, to the detriment of both. There are many who view the industrialisation of the herring fishing around the Moray Firth basin from 1792 through to its peak before the outbreak of World War One in 1914 as some kind of 'golden age': I am not one of them. My mother who was a Wicker born and bred had no fondness for herring and would not eat them. When I asked her why, she replied measurably but forcefully, "Look, ids lek iss – wae hed thum Monday, Tuesday, Wednesday, Thursday, Friday and Setterday and choost for a change on Sunday wae hed a kipper!"

Her mother, my Nana, gutted herring; her father, who was dead before she was born, was a cooper. They were a team and travelled from Unst to Yarmouth when the season was in full swing but mainly they worked at Bruce's yard in Wick. They worked themselves, literally, to death.

When the Bolsheviks rose to power in Russia in 1917 the British government of the day tried to influence the turn of events through invasion and arms imports to the forces of the White Guards and when that became futile imposed, along with other Western powers, economic sanctions on the emerging USSR. For Wick this meant a loss of almost 90% of her herring export which previously had either been shipped directly to West Russia or to Germany and then on by rail into the land of the revolution. As the British state emerged from the hauteur of World War One an impoverished and wounded shadow of its former imperial self, Wick faced the 1920s with the reason for its very existence, the barrelling, salting and export of herring, reduced from a flood to a trickle.

For a brief time herring gave Wick a reason to be and a pivotal place at the centre of the 'herring world' which stretched from Fraserburgh to Stornoway, from Shetland to Norfolk and for a time Wick was the biggest herring producer in Europe. So specifically she sits 58° 27′ North, just below the latitude of the southern tip of Greenland, north of a lot of Hudson Bay and Alaska, well south of

Moscow and 3° west of Greenwich. So that is physically where she is; geographically twenty-three miles south-east of Thurso on the east coast of Caithness: but where is Wick socially, psychologically, politically? All these are vital components of what is known as history.

Well, the herring are long gone as is the white fish industry which followed it. Wick sits haemorrhaging the shades of former glories, shoring up her memories in the development of what remains of Thomas Telford's architectural masterpiece of industrial and social planning which was Pulteneytown. The new yachting marina in the inner harbour only adds to the sense of directionlessness. Somehow millionaire yachters and the rugged residual of Wick are unlikely partners in progress. Wick reminds me of Volterra in Tuscany. Here is a town which was once the proud capital of the Etruscans but because the Romans swallowed the Etruscan civilization all that remains is a series of tombs. Volterra, as the name suggests, was built on a volcanic fault so that most of the main Etruscan town, due to earthquakes and erosion, is a heap of rubble at the bottom of a 'frieze' or cliff.

Wick has yet to fall off a cliff but the metaphor, I contend, is a strong one. The wave of history has broken over the capital of Caithness and which way the waters will flood remains to be seen. Wick's claim to be 'capital' of anything is tenuous and rests chiefly on the fact that it was created a Royal Burgh by James VI in 1589. Before that its connection to historical narrative and even its physical presence was little more than a row of thatched dwellings which no doubt pointed out to the sea with the same single syllabic jab of its Norse name 'Vik', pronounced 'veek'; much the same as Wick is always, in Caithness Scots, given as 'Week'.

From The John O Groat Journal 'Anecdotes', we have the observation of a Captain Kennedy and from him we learn that when the town was created a burgh by royal charter:

From one to one hundred and fifty houses then formed the village, all of them of the meanest description, built in complete defiance of architectural rule, and scattered in every direction with the most thorough contempt for order and regularity.

This was the very polar opposite of Pulteneytown, Thomas Telford's stone essay in 19th century modernity. The 'one hundred and fifty houses' were the usual 16th century low turf longhouses with humans in one end and the animals in the other with a hole in the roof for the smoke to pass through, unchanged since Pictish and Norse times. The granting of the 'Royal Burgh' had more to do with George Sinclair (III), the 'Wicked' Earl of Caithness, his ongoing war with the Earl of Sutherland and Sinclair's weird and unexplained 'can do no wrong' relationship with Jamie the Saxt, that mercurial, cruel, brilliant and ambitious monarch with a gift in equal measure for both creation and destruction.

Destruction, however, was the reciprocal stock in trade of the Sinclair Earls of Caithness and the Gordon Earls of Sutherland and in 1588 George Sinclair and the Gordon of Dunrobin combined in opposition to burn Wick to the ground.

The previous year a follower of Sutherland – George Gordon, the Bastard of Gartay – ambushed some servants of the Earl of Caithness and cut off the tails of their horses. This was seen by Sinclair as a great insult. 'The Bastard' was pursued by a band of Sinclairs and shot through with arrows as he tried to make his escape across the river at Helmsdale. The result of this murder was various stand offs and lots of marischal strutting with truces and breaches with the Earl of Sutherland eventually invading Caithness at the beginning of 1588 with a 'commission from the Privy Council' in his grisly mitt. How these commissions were obtained is anyone's guess but it would be fair to imagine they were had by a mix of dirk and diplomacy, with a greater percentage use of the former. So it was that the Gordon was determined to put the Sinclair 'to the horn'.

The Earl of Caithness did the only thing he could: he holed up behind the impregnable walls of Girnigoe Castle and waited for the bluster to blow itself out. Having led his combined force of Mackays, Macintoshs, Macleods of Assynt, Macleans of Raasay and various others to the dance floor Gordon had to give them their head and after twelve days finding Girnigoe too hard a nut to crack they fell upon the parish of Latheron, killing innocents and stealing their cattle. Then they came to Wick which they pillaged and burned to the ground, except the kirk. John Maclean of Raasay burst into the building and found the lead container which housed the ashes of 'the heart of the late Earl'. It was duly opened and with no jewels being found was thrown to the floor. So did the mortal remains of a previous Sinclair Earl, arguably more 'wicked' than his grandson, find their final resting place.

This series of barbarisms were known as '*Creach larn*' and '*La na creachmore*', or 'the harrying of Latheron' and 'the great spoil'. In an act of compensation James VI granted Wick the status of a Royal Burgh and although Wick had held the lesser privilege of 'burgh of barony' since around 1390 she was now licensed to trade. Royal Burghs were still quite rare in the 16th century and even rarer when the recipient was but a heap of smouldering ruins. Whether the king granted the Royal Burgh status for his own usual divisional reasons (Thurso, for example, was under the influence of the Earl of Sutherland and at this time not a Royal Burgh) it was from those ruins that Wick grew.

What it grew into was Europe's 'premier' herring port with the legend that 'you could walk across dry shod from one side of the harbour to the other' on the decks of the herring Scaffies with their brown sails folding and unfolding like sleeping moths. But the herring fishing was awakening industry in the far north of Scotland like nothing else and after the Napoleonic Wars it unfolded all sleeping wings and took to the air; indeed the charred caterpillar of Wick metamorphosed into the great big bird of commerce, the like of which Caithness nor anywhere else in the Highlands and Islands had seen before. Certainly Wick in its herring heyday must have been quite a sight. But what exactly would you have been looking at?

The history of Wick has been charted, written up, misinterpreted either idiosyncratically or in prose that is as leaden and dull as a barge full of flagstone ballast. In many ways Wick only has its past, however brief in historic time that actually is. It is as if Pasternak's 'locomotive of history' reached the end of the line in this northern town. If you were to look down the track, through the tunnel of years, would any of us see that other locomotive coming: the locomotive called 'progress'? This particular machine was powered by the engine of the Enlightenment.

The explosion of ideas and technology which spread across Europe in the 18th century probably found its most dynamic centre in Edinburgh after the Jacobite Wars. Towards the century's end this creative energy had migrated north and was abroad in the 'Province of the Cat', most advocated and celebrated in the form of Sir John Sinclair of Ulbster and his 'agricultural improvements' and more constructively in the work of John Rennie the harbour builder, James Bremner the engineer and Alexander Bain the electrical inventor. Thomas Stevenson, the lighthouse engineer and his errant genius son Robert Louis, added to the safety of our shores and to the broadening of our literature, although neither had a good word to say about Wick or the time they spent there. Thomas Telford brought his considerable gifts to Caithness and through building Pulteneytown reigned in the 'contempt for order and regularity' so notably the spirit of old Wick.

The 'order and regularity' referred to was primarily in architecture and town planning but its effects could be referenced across the entire social spectrum of the essentially pastoral society of Caithness up to the 1790s. The deep Pictish, Norse and Gaelic roots of this cultural practice were difficult for the men of the Enlightenment to undo let alone understand. For men like Sir John Sinclair 'improvement' meant 'civilization' but for the majority of his tenants it proved to be displacement, poverty and exile. Land enclosed and divided up into individual plots was difficult for a residual cottar population to accommodate, so naturally inclined were they by tradition and instinct to the ways of collectivism. This 'progress' also had a linear view of time that veered out in a strict singularity from and against the native concept of time as a cyclical affair, where the present is a continuation of the past and the future is a version of the past and the present yet to come. This peasant idea is not rational but it does explain how religion, faith and the supernatural co-existed in such easy ambiance and how co-operation in the material world is vital for the survival of the majority when that majority have little access to the resources jealously guarded by the minority.

How-ever this collectivism is not 'rational'. Paternalists, whether out of self-interest such as in the case of Sir John Sinclair or for rather more humane reasons such as in the work of Thomas Telford, considered this world-view as 'laziness' and 'indolence'. One only has to look at the descriptions of the dwellings of the natives of Kildonan and Strathnaver by those who cleared off the people and then burned down their homes to see how this aspect of modernity was couched in a form of contempt which could hardly disguise its racism.

7.

As I write this it is early summer in the second decade of the 21st century. The swallows have returned, the lambs are filling out, the new calves walk now instead of staggering and the seabirds are busy upon the cliffs both north and south of Wick. The North Sea gleams uneasily under a mid-day sun. The morning fog has burned off and to the south east in the Moray Firth I can see the Beatrice Field and its adjacent wind turbines, each structure signifying the embrace of yet more historic phenomenon, the mechanical jiggery-pokery of humanity's impossible desire for cheap and perpetual energy.

The North Sea knows no such ridiculous restrictions or delusions. It may look small on a map of the world but it is a huge stretch of ocean rolling from Noss Head to the coasts of Norway and Denmark which lie far over the eastern horizon. For Wick, throughout its history, the North Sea has been its '*co-choisiche*' or 'co-walker'. When the British Fisheries Society commissioned Thomas Telford, the renowned engineer and began building the new harbour at the mouth of the Wick River in 1803, two years before the Battle of Trafalgar, the beginning of Wick's profound social and economic transformation began to take physical shape. After Trafalgar the long lost trade with the Baltic was restored as prior to that the majority of herring exports had been west across the Atlantic to feed the slaves in the plantations of Jamaica, Barbados and the Carolinas. When the Napoleonic Wars concluded their bloody business at Waterloo in 1815 the commercial business of making money could begin in earnest.

The British Society for Extending the Fisheries and improving the seacoast of the Kingdom, or the British Fisheries Society as it became known was set up as a joint stock company in 1786. To assist its passage that same year the British Government passed an Act which introduced a bounty which could be paid directly to a boat for the herring caught. No sooner had Wellington wiped the Belgian mud off his boots than Pulteneytown began to rise up into the world under the watchful eye and design of Thomas Telford who, quite incredibly, was building the Caledonian Canal at the same time. However elegant Pulteneytown appears to the modern viewer it was not, from the outset, ever going to be compared to the symmetrical terraces of Bath so featured in Jane Austen's fiction or the perfect classical squares and avenues of James Craig's Edinburgh New Town. Although Telford planned Pulteneytown to be uniform and to an extent the geometry of its street layout is exactly that but because Telford gave no exact specifications for the houses and because he sensibly gave the local builders their head the result is that no two houses in Pulteneytown are the same. That healthy old Wick contempt for order and regularity had won through yet again.

Pulteneytown was a working class project. Access to the place of work was the paramount concern. However comfortable or hygienic Telford insisted the houses were to be and despite his best efforts in stipulation few, if any, of the new houses had lavatories, or privies, of any shape or form. At the beginning of the 19th century this was not considered as important. Only later as overcrowding increased and diseases such as cholera, typhoid and diphtheria became rife would the planners learn the cruel lesson. The major concern was to make money and as the place names of Pulteneytown bear witness the shareholders of the British Fisheries Society such as Sir William Pulteney (the Chair), Nicolson, Wellington, Vansittart, Breadalbane, Huddart, Dempster, Sinclair, Argyle and others were keen to be associated with that pursuit.

This was Upper Pulteneytown. In Lower Pulteneytown where the inner harbour was situated and where the cooperages and herring yards were between the shore and the brae the streets were named after the lower caste artisans such as Telford himself, Burn the architect and Williamson the fisheries agent and so on. Class was in the very layout of Pulteneytown: rich men above with poor men at their feet.

My mother's people, the Mores, who had been drawn to the klondike of herring in the hope of a better life were crammed into what the Glaswegians would call a 'single end' above, ironically, a jewellers shop, on Union Street in Lower Pulteneytown. Like many before them their lot was exhaustive labour and the sanctimony of the Enlightenment did not prevent the baronets of the British Fisheries Society encouraging hundreds if not thousands of other 'lazy', landless, homeless and hungry Highlanders to join them, my great-grandparents and their children, to fuel the cogs of the industrial machine.

As has been noted much has been written about the history of Wick, most exhaustively in Frank Foden's 1996 study *Wick of the North*. Iain Sutherland, too, in all his works has proven himself to be a mighty Wick patriot. But the Wick I love has little to do with these official records of material progression nor do I make any special claim as to Wick's significance other than the fact that it exists, that it is one half of my consciousness and that the ordinary people of the town have always had a healthy disdain for civic fictions and have instinctively formed a community with more of a liking for truth as opposed to history. One 'truth' is that before the coming of the herring fishing, the industrial pursuit and processing of '*Clupea Harengus*', Wick was a small township by a river where nothing much ever happened. I imagine the natives liked it that way and despite Gordon of Dunrobin burning the place to the ground in 1588 their lives would have had a beautiful percussion beat out in the natural dramas of everyday reality. Another 'truth' is that however successful the herring industry was in Wick from the 19th century's beginnings to the First World War – and Frank Foden spends two thirds of his 800 page book charting that 'success' – it was doomed to failure as all essentially destructive monocultures are.

As a new model town Pulteneytown was a barracks for the workers of capitalism and was as far away from the planned economy and socialist idealism of Robert Owen's New Lanark as it was possible to get. Although created slightly earlier the 2,500 workers who operated the cotton mills of New Lanark when they were at their peak of production were better housed, fed, educated and their children's welfare provided for than the Enlightenment refugees who crammed into Pulteneytown could ever have hoped for. The mills of New Lanark survived unto 1966. Pulteneytown as a working fishery did not. The British Fisheries Society was concerned principally with making profits for its shareholders and the grinding contradictions of the liberal free market regulated, or not, the welfare and destiny of the fishermen, fish gutters and the like was decidedly not its concern. As a result poverty was more common than plenty.

Of the cultural life of the people history has little to say. To be civilized was to be expected to abandon any resemblance of indigenous, even residual cultural traditions so that if you were a Gaelic speaker coming into Pulteneytown to live and work in 1815, if you wanted to progress, you adopted Scottish speech and custom. In turn if the Scots desired to better themselves they took on the resemblances and manners of the English ascendancy. As Karl Marx has pointed out, 'The ruling ideas of an epoch are essentially the ideas of the ruling class of that epoch'. So it was in 19th century Wick.

But how easy it is it to abandon your culture? For is culture not everything which has made you, come before you, all the natural deposits of consciousness whether they are habits, skills and acquired abilities which have developed out of the whole of pre-existing belief systems and material culture? To improve upon this is the natural progression of culture and nature. What the like of Sir John Sinclair of Ulbster meant by 'improvement' was the wholesale destruction of that cultural legacy, that inheritance, in order to start again, to begin the process of civilization through industry, land enclosure and the replacement of humans by animals who provide a more profitable return at the market through wool or meat or fees for being shot such as deer and grouse. To interrupt in such a fashion the time-framed conscious development of humanity is to create alienation, hesitation, confusion and insecurity. For centuries humanity may have struggled with nature in order to secure our existence but the business of the British Fisheries Society and the capital investors in Pulteneytown was now the management of humanity and to achieve that the strict boundaries of class had to be maintained.

So, unknowingly, the new industrial working class of Pulteneytown inhabited this on-going contradiction: they were indeed constructing a new culture, but it was not theirs. All their efforts created wealth and power for others. It was in the organization of the production of herring exports and in the initial fishing where the contradiction became manifest. As the technology increased so too did the exploitation of both the workers and the herring to the extent that the material machine began to strangle the life out of the former while initiating the near-extinction of the latter. In this process civic history records the growth of production – how many boats, how many barrels, how many tons of fish – and all of this seen as progress, as social development and a contribution to the general good. In linear history the dictum runs that nature has dominated humanity now humanity dominates nature. The 21st century ruins of Pulteneytown and the empty harbour at Wick suggest that the cyclical nature of time prevails in the end and that markets – and the not so mystical forces which drive them – come and go.

So how did the people of Pulteneytown survive? Well, in many ways they did indeed create a new culture. It must be remembered that for Caithness, for the 'Province of the Cat', this was all brand new and if the enclosure of land, the removal of the indigenous people, the creation of sporting estates and the setting up of a herring industry were specific instances in the grand plan of 18th century Enlightenment social development then these instances in the 19th century were transitional with no such fixed outcomes. The evolution of capitalism and the urbanisation of lived human experience – Pulteneytown being a micro-example – meant that products such as wool and herring assume the social form of commodities, things that are bought and sold and consumed. In Pulteneytown we see the first example in the north of Scotland of people becoming commodities.

From Stoer, Lochinver, Assynt and the western seaboard in general, the cleared of the inner straths, those too poor to afford to emigrate, walked the hundred or so miles to Wick in their thousands – or sailed from Lewis which was common – to participate in this transition, to add their not inconsiderable cultural weight and experience to the creation of this new culture of urban industrialisation. It is estimated that between 1849 and 1859 as many as 80,000 Highlanders had come to Wick to work at the summer herring season which usually concluded towards the end of September. From pastoralism to industrialism is a long walk. Many never returned. They either settled, drowned at sea – the loss of life due to inexperience was high for the Highland incomers – or were claimed by the three headed hydra of Cholera, Typhoid and Diphtheria. The fact was that they walked and sailed to Wick to escape destitution. The Crofters Holding Act was not passed until 1886 and from 1811, when the Pulteneytown harbour opened, until then was the time of eviction, clearance and emigration. It was also the time of turmoil in Europe, of war, of revolution, of land agitation in Ireland and in the Highlands, of crop failure, potato blight and famine. These were the black, hard years for the Highlands and Islands of Scotland. The herring fishing out of Wick at least offered a little cash.

The quest for cash makes commodities out of us all. The product of herring was cash rich for the British Fisheries Society and the 'entrepreneurs' on the board. Cash flowed through the hands of merchants, curers and ship owners alike, with the trickle down eventually reaching the fishermen, who on average, by 1850, might earn £10 for a season. The herring girls got a fraction of that. But still they came, scarcity driven and hungry for life, however hard.

By 1859 there were seven harbours in Wick Bay. There was an astonishing ninety curing yards. There was on average 1,000 boats in these harbours; 600 locally owned and crewed; 250 or so from the West Highlands and Lewis in particular and the rest from the many fishing villages dotted around the Moray Firth. Wick, as it emerged into the 1860s, had a resident population of around 6,000. In the fishing season this increased to 15,000 with, on average, as many as 3,000 young fisher lassies who gutted the 25 million herring which had been known to have been landed in Wick during a single day.

To slake the thirst of these hard working individuals Wick has forty-three 'licensed premises' – which could mean anything from a hotel to a pub to a shebeen with two barrels, three planks and a bucket. During the season all these people, when they did not sleep aboard their boats beneath the sails, had to be lodged and in Pulteneytown they were accommodated, wherever there was space, literally like the herring in the barrels they packed: commodities, both fish and human.

Human interaction such as this and at such close quarters creates pressure. On Saturday 27th August,1859 at approximately seven o'clock in the evening in Market Square in Wick this pressure finally found a release. It was not pretty. It was violent and it was over in a matter of days. The results, however, were rather more long lasting and indicate that this 'new culture' created by industrialisation was not without its friction no matter how exhausted most of the 'commodities' felt most of the time. The 'War of The Orange' or '*Sabhaid Mhor Inbhir-Uig*, the Great Wick Fight' proved that energy can be found from somewhere when the principle of justice, of *ceartas*, is found to be selective. Or when people are just too run down to think straight.

It all started innocently enough. The Market Square was full of stalls and sideshows as was usual for a Saturday during the season. Hundreds of people milled about. Young lads did what they have always done when cooped up in a small town – they paraded the streets with an eye on the talent. The day's catch had been landed, gutted, barrelled. There would be no more work until the first herring were landed on the coming Tuesday. A young fellow can take his ease for a bit, see what's going on, get 'the crack' and have some fun. Likewise the girls, but more sedately for this was the 19th century. The older men could have a dram or two and catch up on how everybody else was faring. If truth be told 1859 was not a vintage year. The landings were down on the previous year and the money was not as good. Still, there was three weeks to go and who knows, a couple of good shots and it may all come right yet. In the pubs, on the streets and on the way to the prayer meetings, which were always well attended – the Whitechapel Free Kirk with an average attendance of 1,200 boasted the biggest Gaelic speaking congregation in Scotland – this would have been the main subject of conversation.

That soon changed. A young boy from 'The Lews', as Lewis was known at the time, bought an orange from a stall. On his way to show it to his pals he stumbled or tripped or something, anyway the orange fell from his grasp and an older Pulteneytown boy picked it up. When the young *Leòdhasach* asked for it back the Pulteneytooner refused. Perhaps he threw it to a pal. Whatever happened the young lad's blood was up and in time honoured Highland fashion he charged at the older boy who easily repulsed him. Seeing two of his fellow islanders nearby he called to them and they came to his aid and without too much ado returned the orange to the young lad who had bought it. What happened next no-one really knows. There is the story that one of the older Lewis men was drunk and punched the Pulteneytooner but whatever it was the result was that within minutes hundreds of people were involved, some three hundred or more, the sideshow stalls in the Market Square were demolished and previously sensible people were knocking several shades of manure out of each other. What became apparent at once was that there were two sides: local Caithness Scots speaking men and Gaelic speakers from the west. This is significant.

The police were called and two brave Bobbies entered into the riot. Now these were county constables, members of a different force from the Pulteneytown police whose domain was south of the river. Here, again, there was a dichotomy. But such was the respect for authority at that time – it would soon be lost – that the fighting stopped and the police managed to arrest one of the Lewis men who had come to his young fellow islander's assistance. They proceeded to frog-march him to the police station in Victoria Place, just off Bridge

Street but on the Wick side of the river. This 'injustice' incensed the Highlanders and they tried to rescue their man. The locals decided to protect the police and the fighting flared up again. By this time the streets were jam packed with people more interested in seeing what all the fuss was about rather that getting involved in the conflict. So it was that the two Bobbies had to take a detour and eventually detained the arrested man in the Court House which was next to the Police Station. This was immediately surrounded by angry Highland fishermen. The police sent a 'snatch squad' out from the Court House into the crowd to arrest one of the ringleaders. The crowd grabbed a hold of this individual and with the police tugging from one side and Highland hands from the other all the clothes were ripped off the man. Eventually he was buckled into the Court House. This enraged the growing crowd outside even more and they threatened to demolish the building. Things were quickly getting out of hand.

Now it has to be remembered here that in the thirty years or so that Highlanders had been coming to Wick to work at the herring there had been no trouble socially, not so much as a single arrest or any recorded incident of a breach of the peace. So where had this violence come from? A relatively unspectacular herring season could not explain it. These were almost to a man and woman God fearing people. So why were they fighting like demons on the street on a Saturday night at the end of August? As it turned out it was all to get a lot worse.

By this time it was just after eight o'clock and there were around 2,500 people crammed onto Bridge Street. The Chief Constable of the county police mustered a force of special constables and he sent a messenger to contact the Fishery protection ship *Princess Royal*, which was at anchor in Reiss Bay to ask for assistance. Perhaps this agitated the crowd because it was a signal for stones to be thrown with the result being that some windows in the Town Hall were broken and armed with makeshift wooden clubs from the mangled stalls in

Market Square some hundred Highlanders stormed the jail. Quite what they were expecting to achieve by this, other than the rescue of their two comrades, is debatable. Soon it began to get dark.

Worried that the 1,500 or so people who were due to empty out of the prayer meetings would swell the already dangerous numbers of people on the street there were various pleas made for the crowd to disperse, clear the street and go home. These were ignored. So the police did what police always do in such situations: they mustered as many men as they could and baton charged the crowd. This did succeed in dispersing the problem but only to the two ends of Bridge Street – locals on the High Street end and the Highlanders on the Lower Pulteneytown side by the then Rosebank House, across from the present Mackay's Hotel. Now it was getting Biblical: two warring tribes separated by a river.

At this point the Pulteneytown police joined the fray. It was now half past nine. Gangs of young Wick lads had formed and had begun attacking anyone who spoke Gaelic or who wore what was considered 'Highland garb'. Several of the victims were bible carrying Christians fresh from their prayer meetings. Things were deteriorating and would do so further. On hearing of these attacks the Highlanders charged, as is their custom, across Bridge Street and a vicious battle ensued, with the Wickers at the other end. Again the police intervened and a calm of sorts was restored. Blood, by this time, was on the flagstones and more blood would be spilled before the whole sorry, violent and strange affair was over. By midnight Wick was quiet.

Sunday was also quiet but with a nervous atmosphere hovering over the town like an electric cloud. This is ironic because at this very time in 1859 the planet earth was subject to the largest geomagnetic storm ever recorded and the Aurora Borealis could be seen in the south of Europe and in the Americas as far south as Cuba and telegraph communication systems around the world were knocked out. Luckily for Sheriff Russell of Wick he managed to wire to

Edinburgh, via the nearest telegraph station which was in Inverness, for a detachment of troops to be sent to Wick as soon as possible before the giant solar flare engulfed the planet. If they had only looked up at the sky they may have been humbled into pacificity. Tragically this did not happen.

It's difficult to look up when your head is down and as it was the good Sheriff, along with the rest of the authorities in Wick, had more earthly and immediate problems to contend with: principally, how to maintain law and order in the 'Capital of Herring'. As Monday morning came along that prospect looked hopeless as by nine o'clock around 4,000 excitable folk had gathered outside the Court House to await the outcome of the sentencing of the two arrested men and their mood, Aurora Borealis or not, was not good. Again futile pleas were made for them to disperse but the crowd had another opinion: they stayed put. It was decided then to release the prisoners on bail. This brought no calm and fighting broke out and heads, again, were being broken. About noon a detachment of retired soldiers in uniform marched along Bridge Street and order of sorts was restored by about two o'clock in the afternoon.

But Wick was far from normal. No boats had gone to sea and all the commercial businesses were closed. The cooperages and herring yards, carters' sheds and gutting stations: all were deserted. People stayed indoors. The many pubs, however, stayed open. It didn't seem to make any difference for all that week Wick was quiet with bands of vigilantes under the authority of the Sheriff patrolling the streets. By Thursday most of the fishing boats had put to sea. Early on Saturday morning the *Prince Consort* arrived from Leith with a force of 100 men of the West Yorkshire Militia. The authorities felt, at last, they were getting on top of things. They were wrong.

At ten o'clock on Saturday night the Sheriff was just about to announce to the assembled heads of the police, vigilantes and the military that because it was 'all quiet' they could stand down when news reached the meeting that there had been a series of stabbings in Pulteneytown.

The police were sent along Breadalbane Terrace and there they discovered that eleven men had been stabbed in the space of ten minutes, mainly about the head and neck. The perpetrators had been a gang of young Wickers who had spent the night roaming Pulteneytown and they had attacked indiscriminately, the mere sound of a Gaelic voice was enough. Although many of the injuries were serious, none were fatal. The whole sorry business had reached a truly ugly point and now it was at its most explosive. But just when it all could have become open civil war with running street fighting the whole incident quite suddenly stopped.

Led by the women of Wick the local people downed their weapons, carried the wounded into their homes and attended to their wounds. A spontaneous and collective horror combined with shame overtook the local people and it was as if, for the first time, they could see clearly the madness of what had happened, that they had allowed to happen in their own community. This sensation spread throughout the town and the week long animosity fortunately was all that bled away.

On Sunday the kirks were full to bursting. Ministers ground their gums in sermonising. On Monday morning a young lad from Ulbster was in the cells charged with serious assault and Wick Bay was full of the open brown sails of the Lewis herring Scaffies as they set course for home, the remaining weeks of the season abandoned. By Tuesday there was not a Stornoway registered boat left in the harbour and hardly a Highlander could be found in the town. 'The Great Wick Fight' was over.

But the social fallout lingered longer, most notably in the pages of the two Wick based newspapers, the John O Groat Journal and the Northern Ensign. The 'Groat' took the view that the entire affair was the fault of 'the Highlanders' and that they should have been punished severely for what 'they did'. The 'Ensign', throughout the episode, advocated toleration and that the violence had not come from 'nowhere' and also that the relations between the two communities had up to that point been amicable and that only a minority had been actively involved. The 'Groat' replied that 'toleration was weakness' and only encouraged the kind of behaviour which had resulted in the trouble. The 'Ensign' rebuffed this with the truism that such intolerance generated reaction in people whose real struggle was in trying to earn a living. This ding-dong went on for years.

It is interesting to note that the Northern Ensign ceased publishing in 1926 and that the John O Groat Journal is still going – if not 'on strong', then certainly active. The 'Ensign' was by far the more progressive of the two newspapers and its demise does not seem to have changed the editorial outlook of the 'Groat', especially its keen knee-bending to royalty and its ambivalent coverage of things Gaelic or Highland. It is sad to relate but elements of '*Miorun mór nan Gall*', 'the great ill will and hostility of the Lowlanders', Alasdair mac Mhaighstir Alasdair's phrase from the 18th century, still holds a regrettable chauvinistic resonance in civic Caithness. This 'ill will' was certainly a component in the backdrop to 'The Great Wick Fight'. Which is ironic because the vast majority of the people of Pulteneytown, and a majority within Wick itself, were either first, second or third generation Gaels who, one would suspect, should have had no hostility to Gaelic speaking fishermen. But attitudes change. The alienation manufactured in displaced individuals as result of the Enlightenment idea of 'progress' induced a shortening of cultural memory, a denial of history and a hardening of reaction. To raise yourself out of poverty you must abandon your past, goes this credo; aspire to the social, cultural and political aspirations of the ruling class and cultivate the necessary 'other' – in this case Gaelic speakers form the west – in order to qualify your own significance and to explain away the forces which are holding you back. The history of humanity is strewn with these divisive and manufactured instances.

It is also interesting to note what else was going on in the world in 1859 when the Wickers were having running street battles with people who were just like them save for language and with the 'super-Aurora' blazing un-noticed above their heads. If the 'Groat' and the 'Ensign' represented the duality of mid-Victorian society Charles Dickens' novel *A Tale of Two Cities*, published in 1859, also had as its narrative the duality of the poor and the rich which resulted in the French Revolution. Despite the High-Tory moral tone of outrage as postulated by the John O Groat Journal the ruling class in the Far North of Scotland preferred the working class fighting amongst themselves rather than threatening their interests.

Another significant book published that year was *On the Origin of Species* by Charles Darwin. One wonders if he would have revised a little his findings on human evolution if he had been on Bridge Street on Saturday 27th August 1859? What these two works represent is the emergence of a counter to the accepted liberal idea of class and ownership as 'natural'. Darwin showed that 'natural selection' was a different process altogether from that pursued by the Countess of Sutherland and Dickens illustrated what happens when the 'un-natural selection' of aristocracy refuses to acknowledge natural justice. What was forming was the idea of science as rational, where the processes of nature provide evidence for those with eyes to see it. These forces had just rocked the very foundation of the British East India Company with the result that by 1859, as a result of the First Indian War of Independence of the previous two years, or the 'Indian Mutiny' as it was popularly mis-known, it was transformed into what became the 'Raj'. Two years hence the American Civil War would tear the States apart. In 1859 one of the seeds of that conflict was planted when John Brown was executed in Virginia for his part in the Harpers Ferry raid.

Wick, like every little town, was preoccupied by its own parochial concerns but it was not and never has been isolated from the events of the world. As the town moved through time and the 'glory days' of the herring fishing came and went either side of World War One and as Wick experienced the 1920s she was a harder, hungrier place and all the certainties of the 19th century lay dead and buried on the Somme. The Enlightenment had metamorphosed into the Depression and the pressures of the post-war experience compressed and shaped the people of Wick as they did the population of the rest of Europe. 'Civilization' was doing what it always had done: it was reducing everyone to wrecks.

Strangely one of the central metaphors in Dickens' *A Tale of Two Cities* is the sea. He uses it to represent destruction. For the people of Wick the sea provided them with the means to life, even though it extracted a heavy human price. The '*co-choisiche*', the 'co-walker', was a hard, demanding provider. All along the eastern seaboard it bred a psychology into the people which was a mixture of their deep-race memory of 'fate' and the evangelical flavouring of every new wave of drum-banging Christianity which offered the deckhands and fishwives a quicker rung up the ladder to heaven. More often than not it stripped their joyous nature of all its natural happy foliage and left them as bare stumps of intolerance and catechism. It also, from time to time, co-mingled with the almost indestructible sense of justice that they would never lose, no matter what the Victorian age threw at them. In 1920 another such episode in the saga of 'civilization' was to unfold in Wick. Somewhere in it there was the sense of justice, or '*ceartas*'.

—

Before he was dragged off to die *en route* to the Siberian gulag in 1938 the Russian poet Osip Mandelstam declared, 'I am nostalgic for world culture'. As I stand at the Fishermen's Rest on top of the Pulteneytown brae and look out over the emptiness of Wick harbour and dream myself back into the sepia photographs in which our history is captured, I know exactly what he meant. My nostalgia is not for those bygone times, or for that lost industry, but rather for all the human potential which in effect was wasted here. The energy of that, or rather its familiar or likeness, its '*samhla*' as it's called in Gaelic, dances before me like a beautiful woman or like my grandmother as a young girl, all cheekbones and shawls, on her way down Union Street in the ever-lit summer morning to the gutting pool beneath Broadhaven across the river. The pub door of the Mountain Dew bar swings open over the road behind me and two young men pour themselves out and into a taxi which has come to collect them. The electric pepper noise of Saturday night follows them and as the door swings closed behind them and the taxi pulls away the ghosts and shades of all that lost human potential cease to dance and parade before me as the reality of the glimpsed pub conversation of contemporary Pulteneytooners is sucked back into silence.

'World culture' began when the first human turned the first sod and planted the first seed. The words of another Russian, this time Leon Trotsky, follow me as I walk down the Blackstairs, past the bomb damage and the Memorial Garden and out onto the cobbles of Union Street, rounded and polished by countless thousand feet and the iron rims of cartwheels.

> Let us recall first of all that culture meant originally a ploughed field, as distinct from virgin forest and virgin soil. Culture was contrasted with nature, that is, what was acquired by man's efforts was contrasted with what was given by nature. This antithesis fundamentally retains its value today.

Trotsky said this in Moscow in 1926. For those Pulteneytooners carousing in the Mountain Dew bar, for some of them at least, 1926 was when history becomes memory. I remember my grandmother, my Nana, very well when she was an old lady with her hair in a bun and an endless supply of pan drops. She walked up and down these cobbled streets when Trotsky stood up to deliver his speech that February night to a club in Moscow. What she acquired was through her labour, the nimbleness of her hands and fingers to gut forty herring in a minute. The sea, unlike the land, is always virgin and what she gave she insisted had a price. Those who benefited were few: for the many, after World War One, it was as if they had been totally contrasted with nature, almost to the point of alienation. It was as if their spirituality, their true nature, had gone back into the burial mounds in the straths and hill country of their ancestors where, like the *Sithean*, it had retreated into the earth.

I walk along Bridge Street, the location for much of the violence of 'The Great Wick Fight', and look at the deceptive façade of the closed Bridge Street Kirk which, when you enter into it, opens out into a descending fan-like auditorium which could, and often did, seat over a thousand worshippers. I look back across the bridge to the war memorial glinting in the evening summer sunlight.

The First World War rationalised for the new industrialised working class of the Far North of Scotland the formulated industrial pursuit of profit for a few at the expense of the many through the exploitation of the North Sea herring shoals. As the Mansons, Swansons, Mowats, Calders, Hendersons, Gunns, Bannermans, Mackays, Macleods, Mackenzies, Macdonalds and others marched off to the Western Front, many meeting their doom, there would have been a strange familiarity for those who saw the future in the wide, dead, oily eyes of the countless millions of herring gutted, salted and barrelled in the yards of Wick.

Killing on an industrial scale was just another instruction from on high. Throughout the 19th century they were expected to abandon their culture and sacrifice themselves to the processes of landlordism with its land enclosures and clearance, then to provide the labour in the creation of a single product capitalist concern where poor wages were their reward for procuring the vast wealth enjoyed by the shareholders of the British Fisheries Society. In the killing fields of

Flanders they were expected to give up their very lives in the name of the British Empire and the pattern on the flag.

The virtue of this deadly pursuit and the rightness of its cause were championed by their local press and hallelujah'd like a joyous hymn to death every Friday morning in the pages of the John O Groat Journal from 1914 to the Armistice. For many of the lucky few who survived the artillery, machine guns and gas, they knew from experience that this was the propagandist psaltery of a dream world. Nothing was really the same after 1918 and not just because of the lost export to Russia. The war memorials which sprouted across the 'Province of the Cat' like so many stone flowers – and for which the people themselves had to pay – bore witness to the human price paid by innocent infantry in the wrong struggle. What followed was depression – both economic and psychological – depopulation and for Wick and from 1922 to 1947 there was a prohibition on the sale of alcohol in the town, just to ensure that nothing, oppression-wise, was left to chance.

By the 1920s the industrial machine had the people of Wick firmly in its grip. History shows that for the majority caught up in this situation the only freedom they can achieve is through the machine itself. This contradiction was at the root of the problem faced by the fishing community of Pulteneytown and for every other fishing station along the Moray Firth at that time. Technology was creating new forms of culture. Steam had, by and large, replaced sail. The 1,000 fishing boats working out of Wick in 1859 by 1920 had been reduced to 100. Instead of embracing revolution as their contemporaries had done at the Russian end of the herring trail the people of Wick were subjected to war, its aftermath, poverty and one evangelical religious revival after another which led to the increase of their oppression and the stifling of their intellectual development. One episode which illustrates this social compression and highlights the political contradiction was the tragic-comedy of the 'Vote No-Licence' which was acted out in Wick between 1920 and 1922 and led to the town being 'dry' for twenty-five years.

In many ways this entire episode highlights Trotsky's contradiction. This was democracy but also the absence of democracy. The legislative hub of it was Lloyd George's Welsh whin-baggery anti-booze hobbyhorse. This became Parliamentary in 1913 when the House of Commons passed the Temperance (Scotland) Act. In those days Scotland was always in brackets. This was an adaption of the Temperance Act for England and Wales but banged into shape to meet the requirements of Scotland's different laws. It was an unusual piece of legislation in as much as although it was an Act of Parliament it required a local ballot in any burgh or parish or defined community to implement it and it required 35% of the electorate to vote for 'No Licence' in their area and all sale of alcohol in any form, in public, would cease. Also, once it was passed, it could be re-balloted in three years.

There were three main reasons why all this came to pass. One was that 'drink' was seen as a major factor in deprivation in the slums of Scotland. Why these slums were in existence was not the concern of those who advocated prohibition. That would have displayed a political consciousness which went beyond the tambourine. In Wick in 1920 this awareness was not recorded. There was poverty in Wick. Disease and want led many to an early rendezvous with the cemetery. But compared to a city like Glasgow Wick was a small thing.

The second thing was the Temperance movement itself. This, too, was a child of the Enlightenment. Except instead of looking out it looked in. As has been noted Wick was a civic body prone to religious fevers. From as early as 1840 there had been the Pulteneytown Total Abstinence Society and far from being, as one would imagine, a little thing, it built a hall for its meetings which accommodated 1,000 people. Also the Wick and Pulteneytown Free Templars were formed in 1870. There was also the Society for the Propagation of

Christian Knowledge, the SPCK, which like the KGB in Soviet Russia, did its best to stamp out all connection with reason and history. After World War One it is no surprise to see the SPCK doing its 'work' in Wick. It had been trampling the psychological heart of the Gaels into the dirt of landlordism for the past hundred years and more.

Wick was a ripe fruit. It was duly plucked. All of the above does not mean to say that the Temperance movement was a centrally controlled organisation like one of Trotsky's soviets: it was not. There were many local associations and groups, mainly connected to kirks. However it was extremely effective. The Bridge Street Church and the Sisterhood who met there made this 'second thing' an unstoppable force. Their ability to influence, especially the emerging middle class such as ministers, lawyers, bankers, doctors and businessmen was considerable. Also considerable was their ability to raise money. This money came from the working class. You do not fill a 1,000 capacity hall with doctors and lawyers. There were more fishermen in Wick in 1920 than any other trade. These fishermen all had extensive families. This is where the third reason arises: poverty.

It wasn't the poverty of no money. It was the poverty of delayed money. Fishermen, unlike every other trade, 'settled' at the end of a fishing season. It was in April for the winter season, September for the summer season and December for the Yarmouth fishing. When a fisherman 'settled' he paid off all his debts which had accrued up until then. This system had been, by 1920, in operation for one hundred years. Most of the pubs in Wick, at this time, were around the harbour area. The crew could wait there while the skipper went to 'settle' with the fish salesman. There may be as many as eight to a crew. Everyone stood a round. After eight drams everyone was inebriated. Also they were happy. It was the end of the season and everyone was getting paid. This is where the trouble started.

Somehow poverty and the chicanery that goes along with it is always the 'third thing' in any story of the working class. So it was in

Wick. Meeting in pubs to 'settle up' was all too handy. Serious money changed hands in these premises. Not all of it, sometimes not any, got back to the wife in the Pulteneytown single end. Drunken fishermen seldom make sense. But shark finned publicans never miss a trick. Being diddled out of your cash by a bar owner was common. He, after all, was keeping a tab. Also the business of fishing boat ownership was all divvied out in shares. Mostly the crew owned a share in their boat but after World War One this system itself was being 'rationalised'. By 1920 a lot of the shares were owned by publicans, doctors and lawyers. This is why the hypocrisy of the Temperance movement is hard to stomach. If a man has no cash and he is standing in your bar then the tab must be paid somehow. This is when publicans began to own fishing boats. This is also when the working class fisherwomen organised themselves and this is when the Temperance (Scotland) Act became a reality.

The artificial poverty suffered by the fishing community – hungry children, women dead from stress and malnourishment at too early an age, poor housing – all this had to be addressed. The clamour for a 'No Licence' referendum in 1920 was a symptom of this poverty but it was not a solution. The Representation of the People's Act of 1918 meant that women over the age of thirty could vote in a General Election. In 1916 the London government set up The Liquor Control Board. This was an emergency wartime organisation which controlled the drinking of the munitions workers of Britain. It wasn't wise to have intoxicated people making the artillery shells and bullets. What it meant for Wick was that there was a total ban on the selling of spirits in the north of Scotland. This was aimed at the thousands of men stationed at the two navy bases of Invergordon and Scapa Flow. It was an effective piece of legislation, the result of intense committee work – something Lloyd George was good at – in as much that whisky was almost impossible to get – unless you made it yourself – north of Inverness.

The social effect on their men folk was not lost on the women of Wick. All these reasons came together on 10th of December 1920 when there was an election in Wick which 77%, under the terms of the Temperance (Scotland) Act of 1913, voted for 'No Licence'. The 35% clause was easily met. There was much wrangling, in and out of court, by the Licence Holders (Local Veto) Defence Association – and they managed to stall the inevitable by almost two years. But on 29th May 1922 all twelve pubs, six hotels and eleven licenced grocers in Wick closed. They had 'no licence'. Did the lot of the deckhand and the fishwife improve? The answer is no, it did not. In fact the economy of Wick up until World War Two took a sharp dip. This was a fact that the Licensees were quick to point out. But no matter that the vote was renewable every three years the solid citizens of Wick voted for 'No Licence' no less than four times. It took another world war to change that.

The immediate effect was on public drunkenness. But as it was, in 1922, at the beginning of the summer fishing season, drunkenness was rare at that time anyway. Two other instances of this soft parade of civic gormlessness was that the first major meeting of the Temperance movement was held in Market Square – the very venue for the start of 'The Great Wick Fight' of 1859. The other consequence was that the publicans of Wick, post 1922, did not suffer as the 'Templars' desired. Most of them were already rich, and continued to be so, because of the shares they owned in fishing boats. All of this, I imagine, was not lost on my Nana as she tramped down Union Street to the gutting pool. This was the echo of Osip Mandelstam. This was the nostalgia for world culture.

This nostalgia had its opposite, its other parallel, its own '*co-choisiche*' or 'co-walker'. It was the organisation of the people's own oppression. If this oppression had a music it was a soundtrack supplied by the cruel melancholic somewhere else compositions of the Salvation Army whose leader in Wick in the 1920s was the miraculously and appropriately named Captain Dry. Pulteneytown itself was a 'somewhere else' sort of place. It was an idea of industry landed on the northern end of the Grey Coast and the notion of the 'Vote No Licence' was a concoction from out with the native recipe. In their poverty and exploitation the people of Pulteneytown, of the north in general, were still being 'improved' and made ready for 'civilization'.

All these prescriptions for change and the soul deadening, brass-rasping cacophony of Captain Dry and his Sally Army band and the entire flagellation of prohibition and the pseudo-salvation of the Evangelics came, over time, to be seen for the social and economic sado-masochism it was. When World War Two came along it gave, on the surface, something for the people to fight for, as opposed to against. By 1945 'progress' was seen as something the people could determine for themselves, at least notionally. So it was that on 10th December 1946, in an act of deliberate duplication of the date of the original 1920 vote, a fifth poll under the Temperance (Scotland) Act was held and 1,500 voted for continuance and 1,941 voted for a repeal.

By 1947 Wick was 'wet' again. Wet to welcome a new war. This was World War Three and as was only reasonable no-one could be expected to contemplate such a thing sober. This was the hangover Wick enjoyed from so much sobriety. But the Cold War, as it became known, signalled Wick's abandonment by the forces and processes of history which by 1999 had begun to fizzle out in the Royal Burgh. Wick began to shed its civic clothes and return to the sleep it had arisen from in the 18th century. The new millennium was to see Wick almost naked and decidedly drowsy. It became like a stone scarecrow on a flagstone headland. Captain Dry and his hellish hounds of progress and civilization had sucked all the blood out of the people. The new 'Enlightenment' had arrived with the nuclear age and as we shall see Dounreay rose up, a factory to silence, some thirty miles away, yet another wave of history to break over the coast of the 'Province of the Cat'.

Chapter Four

THE GRANARY BEYOND THE FLOW

1.

Once the sacrificial blood had flowed away after World War One Caithness tried as best it could to get back to normal after the slaughter and waste of the trenches. The waves of history may rise up and break over the 'Province of the Cat' and the tide of time ebb and flow, a pastoral people become settled and semi-industrialised, the land enclosed and the arable pattern re-arranged – but the human heart must still beat out its persistent rhythm across the sedimentary plateau of the Far North.

With his heart no doubt beating faster than usual my grandfather took his young wife and came to farm at West Greenland in 1924. This was the year of Lenin's death and the beginning of Stalin's purges in the newly recognised Soviet Union, of Hitler being thrown in jail for his part in the Munich Beer Hall Putsch and when Ramsay MacDonald became the first Labour Prime Minister of Britain. If he stopped at the bottom of the farm road as it leads up to West Greenland and looked out over the northern sea what thoughts of the future went through the mind of young Donald Gunn?

Situated on a rise behind the Links of Dunnet the handsome tree surrounded sandstone farmhouse commands fine views over Dunnet Bay, Dwarick Head and Dunnet Head and west out into the distant

Atlantic. The sunsets at harvest time – or the hairst as it was always known – as viewed from West Greenland, are amongst the most beautiful, vivid and sustained I have ever seen. The salt spray from the breakers in Dunnet Bay, as it is pushed eastward on the wind, mingles in the air with the smell of grass and September barley and to the nose and tongue is pure sensation, the ozone taste of the deep ocean gentled by the surface scents and perfumes of the farm land. The light from the sinking sun highlights the sustaining flatness of the links-land, the lengthening shadows somehow lending even greater distance to the horizon and the dappled orange clouds encase the sky with both intimacy and infinity. You really get the sense and feel of the Norse creation myths when you stare out at the autumnal Atlantic and that Sól actually will be consumed by Fenrir the World Wolf at the Ragnarok of each day's ending. Donald Gunn and his wife Georgina would see the fire of war fly in on the wings of spitfires and on the decks of battleships before fifteen years of their domicile at West Greenland was out.

The farm directly to the west of West Greenland is called Thurdistoft (or fields of Thordis) which means that these lands were settled and worked by the Norse immigrants well over a thousand years ago and by the Picts before them. They chose well for these modern acres represent the western extremes of the great axis of the prime arable ground in Caithness, the granary beyond the Flow, which stretches south-east from Greenland along the strath of the River Thurso, through Loch Scarmclate to Loch Watten where the Strath Burn turns into the Wick River; then north to Freswick and south along the Grey Coast to the Ord. From the north coast at Dunnet the barley grows in a broad avenue which runs along the Coast of Widows from Barrock to John O Groats. West of Thurso the good ground extends in a fertile strip to the east of Reay. These are the places in Caithness where the Norse left their language in the place names of the county. They show that the Norse were far more than mere Vikings or pirate raiders: the

Norse, like my grandfather, were farmers. But my grandfather was a Gunn, a Celt, and the good farm land of Caithness represents around 30% of the land mass of this eastern half of the 'Province of the Cat' which is Caithness, the point of cats. The other 70% is Celtic and is given Gaelic names: this is *Ghallaibh*, the land of strangers. This cultural duality is the celebration of the history of Caithness. It is its richness and its strength; its mystery and its appeal.

Whether Pict or Norse if you showed those early farmers around Caithness in the mid-18th century they would have easily recognised the place and the agricultural methods as being much the same as that of their own time. By 1775 this began to change. Crop rotation and the introduction of new crops, plants and animals; the use of new iron ploughs which replaced the *cas-chroim* and the Reestle plough – all these new technologies and innovations took hold as the population began to grow. Yet the single most radical measure, a literally shape changing process, was the enclosure of the common lands and the drainage and opening up of new, dormant, arable land. By 1790, in Caithness, the enclosure of this 'new' land and the replacement of the old run-rig system of growing crops by the now familiar rectangular field had begun. Principal architect in this was Sir John Sinclair of Ulbster. His cultural stock was neither Celt nor Norse for the Sinclair, or de Saint Clair, was a Norman.

Ulbster, itself a farm, with a Norse name – '*bólsataðr*', which means farm or steading and has been abbreviated to the suffix 'ster' with Ulb or Ulf a farmers name which pre-dates the Sinclairs, sits in a gentle strath just south-wst of Sarclet on the north end of the Grey Coast. To approach it down the muddy track from the road is to approach neglect and authority wrapped up in silence. The first thing one sees by the gate which bars the way down to the farm building is a sign which informs you of the invisible presence of concealed twenty four hour closed circuit television cameras. When and if you resign yourself to surveillance and negotiate the gate and make your way down to the steading what you find is an abandoned farm, dripping melancholy and dilapidation. Beyond the Victorian desolation lies the chapel of St Martin, a strange and exotic construction, unique in Caithness, which sits square to itself beside a field of ripening barley.

Set in the centre of a walled rectangle with a boor tree in the north-east corner the four-sided cupola domed chapel is the burial site of the Ulbster St Clairs, the first Norman aristocratic adventurers of that name to gain a toehold in Caithness. They first arrived in Scotland around 1070 on the back of the marriage of Malcolm Canmore, King of Scotland, to Margaret of Wessex, by way of Hungary. These St Clairs were of a very different cultural hue to the majority of the future generations of Sinclairs whose surname evolved from those early and eager followers from Saint Clair-sur-Epte in Ile de France of William the Conqueror of Normandy. The St Clairs landed at Ulbster around 1476 when William St Clair became the second Earl of Caithness. It is at this time that the surname 'Sinclair' came into being.

Like everything else the Sinclairs touched the chapel of St Martin has all the signs of faded majesty and mystery mixed with the rubble and ruin which is the historical signature of this particular family's ambition. Ten stone steps lead up to the south facing doorway of the chapel. Inside and under a wooden roof cover there is a stark white-washed stone floored fire placed interior. Two small wooden shuttered windows face north and east. It is a handsome building – beautiful even. Its spiritual integrity and architectural symmetry stand at odds with the cold political desires and material appetites of its creators. At odds too with the legend of St Martin himself, the Bishop of St Tours in 372 and who died in 397, who famously gave half of his cloak to a beggar. Nonetheless this remnant of a French Catholic past adds some lustre to the harvest scene of these distinctly Presbyterian Scottish acres.

The yellow lichen covered slate roof points up into the grey hairst sky. The cast iron weather vane flag on its crest is rusted to solidity, bearing the coat of arms of the Ulbster Sinclairs and the legend 'I S 1700'. The ubiquitous dead who lie beneath the flat flagstone gravestones keep their own council. To the west a burn flows past and out into the Moray Firth, where on the shoreline there appears to be no visible remains of a mooring place or any sign of a pier. To the north-east and spreading out towards the herring hamlet of Sarclet – and the 'seat' of my mother's own people, the Mores and the Christies – the field of barley blows in the Sunday September wind waiting for the combine. The rustling ears of the grain breathe in and out the hissing music of history. A meal mill stands wheel-less, waterless, almost roofless by the weed choked burn.

All claims to anything in history are dubious. Here at Ulbster the Sinclairs physically originated their feudal overlordship of Caithness by simply coming ashore. Here was where the old Celtic world began to erode into landownership, titles and power. How ironic then this beautiful desolation? How unlike in its needlessness is it to Caithness at her best, in late August, early September, just before the harvest begins when the bread-wood-cut colours of grain pigment the county in their patchwork quilt of sandy ochres of varying degrees of difference? Barley, both winter and spring varieties, are the modern base-load crop with still a significant insistence of corn fields that appear to hold the sun's honey-light longer than barley which, when grown *en masse* as is now the cash requirement, reflects the sunlight back into the air. This, too, has its particular beauty as it illuminates the immediate vicinity of the fields with a lovely yellow light. The barley throws the light back into the atmosphere in a delight of being: the corn drinks the sunlight down into the very earth to give the soil a welcome taste of heaven.

When finally, inevitably, the combine harvesters enter the fields the hue and colour of the patchwork quilt of parks takes on another transformation. As the winter barley is cut and then the spring, the grain harvested and the straw baled, the vibrancy of the ochre becomes less insistent, more restrained – the sharpness of the light seems to bleed into the ground taking the summer with it and again, when the bales are stacked into the modern gilts under roofs or plastic, the dilution of colour continues until autumn floods the fields with her thin yellows, pale browns and sleeping greens. The carpet is laid for the rain soaked winter, with her violent bursts of snow and cementing frosts. It is then that all colour is petrified for the season.

Before that, though, the land is a bustle of activity. Combines shave down the infantry of the barley. The tractors and trailers catch the grain or transport the round industrial bales from the back of the infernal baling machines to their storage place. The back roads from Watten to Westfield are a constant convoy of farm vehicles driven by workers who themselves are driven by weather and the clock. The hairst is a time of doing and no opportunity offered up by good weather can be wasted. Night and day it goes on until it's over. Then there is a stillness across the farm-land, for a period, before the ploughs are prepared and the whole cycle begins habitually, necessarily, relentlessly again. Yet even industrial farming must relent for a moment and it is possible, if you so desire, to see the music of the season played out in a field somewhere at night with the harvest moon shining, with Venus on her starboard bow, with the crop half cut in the field and the nodding heads of the barley anointed silver in the beatitude of the moonlight and the wounded beast of the combine speared by its own silhouette beside the shadows of the furrows of straw. An owl, perhaps, may roost upon a fence post.

Then it is possible to follow the track of time back to the Iron Age when the same processes were enacted, the same moon shone down but on a different necessity, a less relentless activity, when the technique of man had advanced to the point where it was no longer a constant struggle with nature, for by then humans had reached that historical place where they had developed the ability to ensure their existence. Agricultural technique has advanced the organization of production. Production has given rise to the tyranny of the market. The market has demanded an increase in production and human technique – our technology – has delivered quantatively. The fields must become bigger. The yield must increase. The owl flies from his observational stab, cries out into the night and beats its wings over the empty historical space where the ordinary people of the 'Province of the Cat' lived their lives. Here is where they raised their families, enjoyed their happiness and endured their sorrows and whose presence upon the land is like the moonlit shadow of the passing owl. With the clearance of settled populations prior to the land enclosure of the 18th century's end the human mark of a thousand generations was, for the most part, rubbed out like a chalk mark off a board.

From around 1792 when the first clearances in Caithness began up to 1830 the amount of land under cultivation had doubled and blossomed to approximately 100,000 acres. Sir John Sinclair of Ulbster brought in experts in 'Paring and Burning' from Cumberland and little by little, year after year, by digging, burning, potashing, draining – both bogs and lochs such as Durran, Alterwall and Seister were drained in this endeavour and their 'marl' spread upon the newly enclosed fields – the acreage of both converted and enclosed land grew. Seaweed from the shore and shell sand from the beaches were burned together with the heather and added to the soil-mix. New crops such as potatoes and turnips became common. However historians may dress this process in the fine new clothes of 'improvement' the result was that many thousands of people were removed from their native place and set upon the sea coasts like so many gulls. The creation of roads and the building of estate walls in which Sir John engaged these refugees and paid them in kind with meal or 'free rent' so that they would not immediately starve, only seemed to highlight their exclusion form their own country. This has been seen by scholars of the past as 'humane' but the direction of travel of such largesse for Sir John was towards his own benefit which was, after all, the entire point of the enterprise.

As has been noted we could take Thordis from his 11th century 'toft' and up to the point in historical time of the first land enclosures Thordis would have recognised the land as being very much like his own. By the middle of the 19th century he would feel like an alien in a strange world. Gone were the division of land by 'Tacks, Wadsets and Townlands' – a 'tack' could support some twenty small farms – which constituted an 'estate'. All of this without fences or walls, which would be unknown to Thordis and only came into being around 1775 when the regular rectangular field systems which is the mark of modern Caithness agriculture first began to take shape. Richard Pococke, an English Bishop of the Church of Ireland and a noted anthropologist, when travelling through Caithness in the summer of 1760, wrote to his sister his impressions of the landscape – a landscape which in a few years would change beyond recognition:

> When we came to the summit over Sir Patrick Dunbar's (Stemster) house, we had a most uncommon prospect of the broad vale in which his house stands, of another separated by low hills or eminences, with a great number of gentlemen's seats, and two churches in view, two large lakes, the fine mountains of the Paps, and that ridge which bounds the county, and the ground rising gently on all sides; but what is most singular spots of corn all over the county, contrasted with such a mixture either of heath or pasturage as rendered the face of this northern country very agreeable.

The land the Bishop looked out on was almost treeless, except the elder or boor-tree, which as Calder has pointed out 'thrives everywhere, and without much protection from the Northern blast'. This hardy quality of survival as demonstrated by the boor-tree was shared by the native people. Beautiful as the landscape was to a visiting bishop the social reality was that the majority of the 22,215 population, as recorded in 1755, lived lives in and out of scarcity. A severe famine in 1782, when early snow and frost decimated the harvest, highlighted this fragility and forced many to move to the central belt or to emigrate. Yet despite all this the husbandry of the land known to Thordis had maintained a steady population for centuries. Change came, in historical time, relatively suddenly and its manifestations socially and economically were dramatic. The practice of almost two thousand years disappeared in less than fifty. With it went the people it had evolved to support. After 1800 the purpose of agriculture was to make money.

The 'great number of gentlemen's seats' as noted by Bishop Pococke in 1760 came to about fifty and were mostly owned by Sinclairs of various branches of the family. Sir John Sinclair of Ulbster, born in Thurso in 1754, had the biggest estate holding of all and by the time he became a MP in 1780 this constituted about a quarter of the county. The other main estate at this time was that of the Dunbars of Hempriggs, who were a branch of the Sutherland Duffus minor nobility. Other than these lords, baronets and lairds, the lave, as the rest of the population were known, were tenants.

These tenants may have had little or no rights – and in some case little better than slaves – but they were industrious and productive. Like the county itself, by 1700, most of the exports from Caithness were raw and unprocessed. However in that year it is estimated that around 864 tonnes of grain was exported from Thurso in the north and Staxigoe in the east to Leith, Newcastle and Bergen. By 1790 this had grown to 971 tonnes and in 1793 to 1,295 tonnes. From off the hill ground came the black cattle, that true and timeless measure of value and wealth throughout the 'Province of the Cat', and by the 1790s Caithness was sending, annually, around 3,000 head of these sturdy beasts to the drovers' trysts at Falkirk and Crieff. This new found wealth brought the Sinclairs out of their draughty old castles and into sumptuous new mansion houses or 'Mains' as they were known, or inclined them to do up their keeps such as at Keiss and Barrogill.

So, despite or because of Thordis and the owl, the Enlightenment – as dreamed up by the philosophers in 18th century Edinburgh – came to Caithness wielding its double edged sword of progress and innovation, disinheritance and emigration. As usual it was left up to the church ministers, through their reports to Sinclair's *Statistical Account of Scotland* in the 1790s, to report enthusiastically on how beneficial the Age of Improvement was to the lot of the common people. Whether viewed as venal or informative the *Statistical Account* is a landmark piece of social inventory. Unfortunately it does not tell the whole story.

By 1802 2,500 acres of common land was removed from public access, its benison stolen by landlords and this was quickly followed by many thousand more acres. The walls and dykes, built by the dispossessed people themselves, sealed this stolen land into modernity. By 1840 almost all the common land had been enclosed, but by that time a lack of capital had temporarily halted 'progress'. The landlords quickly turned to whatever would increase revenue. The tenants had by necessity become labourers as they could not afford the rents for the new 'improved' land. What was once 14 shillings (60p) an acre now was let for up to £4 or £5. What this meant was that many southern farmers moved to Caithness and the once 'self-employed' tenants had to find subsistence on rough and marginal land because that was all that was left for them. If they proved industrious and improved their own arable ground or their dwelling house or built a modest byre the landlord put up their rent. Cash for the laird had to be raised somehow. As a result evictions increased, homelessness was common where once it had been unknown and squatter camps appeared here and there across the county: two at Reaster were called Beggars' Town and Paupers' Town. Add to this the influx into Caithness of the displaced of the Highland Clearances in Sutherland, such as the three hundred or so who came to Dunnet from Assynt in 1821, then the broad base of poverty in the Far North in the mid-19th century increased correspondently to the increase in pecuniary wealth of those who 'owned' the arable acreage, those at the material apex of this so-called agricultural society.

Of the Assynt people in Dunnet, the majority of whom stayed for ten years, the Reverend Thomas Jolly wrote that they 'got into arrears with their rent'. As we have seen this was not uncommon or surprising. The good Reverend could not help adding, in the somewhat nonchalant racist way which was the temper and prejudice of the time, 'that their habits not being adapted to an industrious life'. The 'industrious life' was made impossible for the majority as access to the land was denied them and their instinctive insistence upon it criminalised so it is little wonder that many of the *Assaintaibh* escaped from this lack of opportunity and soul sapping poverty on emigrant ships to Canada. For those too poor to cross the Atlantic the harshness of their situation on the newly improved land was to be 'relieved' by the brand new harshness of the herring fishing. Here was a people, literally, caught between the devil and the deep blue sea.

For these people, my own people, what use is history? Whom does it serve? Is it just a charabanc like the one my grandfather unloaded when still a young man in 1924, to move his worldly belongings into the West Greenland farmhouse? To find any answer one must walk up over the dunes of Dunnet and up through the gently sloping fields of Greenland and the three farms which both give and take their names from the district – East and West Greenland and Greenland Mains – then down past the Shepherd's Cottage, past Lower Greenland and on along to the old township by the Lochend road. Here is where my father and his brothers and sister went barefoot in the summer to school. This is to walk through the echo of a dream, to walk towards the source of history and also to the resurrection of the rising sun for in Caithness, traditionally the dead are buried with their heads to the west and their feet to the east. The road running all the way to Keiss to the north and Wick to the south is the river-road of barley that flows through the blood of the walker as much as it does the feet as they caress the Highland Council's privatised tarmac. With wide open fields bursting with grain stretching out on either side all history falls away into fragments of information devoid of knowledge and the memory of the 17th century smoke of Robert Gordon's source-obliterating fire still somehow resides in the yellowing fields. History then becomes emotion, a sensation of all the little deaths and the all the mighty slaughters. At the same time all the centuries of life fill my lungs because I can taste it on the barely flavoured air. I can hear all the beautiful Caithness voices from times gone and times yet to come in my mind. They circle my head like skeins of wild geese as the sky is blown towards Norway by the west wind hard off the Atlantic. I know I am home here, home and going away.

How strange, then, is the imagination when it comes to land? As I walk to the east I conjure up into my mind a picture of what Caithness would have looked like or become if the common people had not been cleared and if they had remained on the land and continued to work it. That the majority were swindled out of and denied access to working land that had been held in common for centuries is a matter of fact. What we see now, if we look out over these parks, is the semi-industrialised farmland which is dry-stane locked for exclusive use into the areas which were enclosed. They have covered a possibility for the many with an opportunity for the few.

Sir John Sinclair of Ulbster and Dunbar of Hempriggs had no legal title, as is understood – more or less – in the 21st century, to the land they appropriated by enclosure. That Sir John was a Glasgow University trained lawyer served him well in making up of laws to suit his purpose. From the time of the Proscription Act of the Scottish Parliament in 1617 'possession' of land had been deemed a sufficient assertion of 'ownership'. Since then legal variations on this theme has passed for land law in Scotland. It sufficed for the authorities at that time that members of the nobility, such as Sinclair and Dunbar, said that they owned this or that tract of land; and subsequently those who worked and depended on these acres could offer no proof of ownership either. Their claim has always been deemed the lesser. The lave had no legislation to assert their 'possession' and no lawyers to advocate their claim. So they went unheard and unrepresented.

Sinclair, more than anyone, knew that he couldn't be half a landowner. So he set out to become the biggest in the north of Scotland. Well, the biggest after the Countess of Sutherland who also 'acquired' her vast 1.2 million acres by rather more direct and violent means. All of this resulted in clearance, whether it's the 'Highland' version in Sutherland or the 'Lowland' apologia in Caithness. The result was the same: the majority of the indigenous population were gone.

Ironically with them went the wealth. With them, also, went the culture, which is one reason why there is no song tradition left in Caithness and very little native music. Once these good things have gone there is a poor residual resistance to the bad ideas of war, air bases or such nuclear schemes as Dounreay. Quite literally the people had nothing to fight back with. A people without a culture are like an alcoholic or a drug addict. They have to fill the void with something, anything: they have to meet a need. As I walk eastward and see the harvest coming in the more this 'need' measures itself against the yard-stick of time.

It is the relationship between the individual and the land which has changed. Time is an indicator but it is not the only one. For example when your very existence is predicated upon the benevolence of a superior then your confidence in your own objectivity deteriorates. The ability to make decisions is one of these. If what you say, do and think has no value in the eyes of the hierarchy then what that manufactures in a society is silence. Political, cultural, historical: silence is silence. It also renders that society fragile.

That is what clearance means. This is its legacy. Unfortunately what is put at risk, ultimately, is the future. So it has come to pass, for one reason or another, that farming, as it is currently constituted, has no future. It has been recorded that in the Tigris valley some 20,000 years ago there were around thirty-seven species of grass by which the people could live. Now, in the world, there are a dominant three – rice, wheat and corn. The rationalised greed of land enclosure has to be seen in this light. What landownership and crop specialisation has exposed humanity to is vulnerability. A trinity is never as secure in its base as a multitude. The human history of Caithness shows that the multitude has emigrated. As a result Caithness is a land, literally, of empty cultural spaces. That these spaces have been filled by voices from another airt and orbit is not surprising: it is inevitable. The tragedy of these newcomers is that the economic wave which brought them north will also leave them stranded amid property they cannot sell and land they cannot work: the country will be unrecognisable to them but they will be just another set of ribs in the bone-dust of history. Once a cultural space is empty it is surprising how unrelentingly it hangs onto its vacancy. Caithness, as every civilisation has found, is like that. No-one and nothing, as yet, has got out alive.

The love and potential democracy I see in a field of barley is translated, in the official historical narrative, into everything staying the same. Nothing changes as long as the land is owned by an individual or their representatives. It, quite literally, stops working. Caithness has no future if it is simply an agri-platform which allows twenty or so individuals to become even richer. What I see when I look on these fields is the recent invention of a received order, yet as has been highlighted corn and barley were produced here in great quantity before the propaganda of the 19th century modernists who insisted that everything 'before' was backward and unproductive. Caithness has always been known as a 'granary'. It will have to be again if it is to support any kind of civilization.

Civilization, as history proves, is defined by the victors in a war between the objective and the subjective. This I witnessed when

I was working at West Greenland one summer when I was a boy. My grandfather had been laid low, temporarily, by a 'turn'. Now a 'turn' in Caithness parlance can, as has been mentioned, mean anything. As we subsequently learned this was the first manifestation of the heart trouble which would eventually kill him, but this did not become clear until the doctor had been sent for – and the doctor was sent for very rarely and only when things were serious. The usual GP, Doctor Sutherland, was on holiday so up to the farmhouse drove a fresh faced young locum, all eagerness, seriousness and sincerity. He examined my grandfather comprehensively and informed my grandmother as to what had happened to her husband – my grandfather wasn't interested in such trivia. The young doctor correctly advised my grandmother that Donald, because of his heart condition, should stop working in the smiddy at every available opportunity, that he should resist smoking the vile black twist tobacco he was so fond off, to desist from the Johnny Walker whisky which was his preferred dram and to take it much easier about the farm now that he was at a 'certain age'. If truth be told no-one really knew how old he was. In his mind he was exactly the same age as he was when he first came to work the place in 1924. To me he was all time and kindness wrapped up in soot stained dungarees and my brother and I loved him dearly.

My grandmother politely thanked the doctor for his advice and apologised for troubling him. When Dr Sutherland finally came back from his holidays – at West Greenland the concept of 'holidays' was unknown – and when my grandfather was eventually dragged down to the surgery in Castletown to get further checks and tests my grandmother said plainly to the doctor, "E next time, Doctor Sitherlan, could e no sen somebody up wae a puckle sense."

The point being that the young locum's sensible advice to my grandfather was ultimately senseless – old Donald was too set in his ways to change. The irony here being that this was a man who had changed West Greenland from being an under worked and poorly maintained collection of fields and links into a healthy mixed arable farm which, to all intents and purposes, was self-sufficient. The 'good luck' of the Second World War and the newly installed RAF Castletown (Coastal Command), next door at Thordistoft, meant that he could sell the RAF his bacon and eggs from the pig house and deep litter of his own design and construction. Many other Caithness farmers benefited equally from the need to feed the massive influx of military personnel into the Far North from 1939 to 1945.

From these black seeds grows war's popularity with state capitalism for everybody benefits in this ultimate exercise in consumerism. It is pertinent here to remember that the pressure for land 'reform' which drove the enclosures of the common lands was the need to produce more quantity to supply a growing market. That market was stimulated by war. From 1727 to 1815 the newly formed state of Britain was constantly and continually at war. War was the normal condition of the state. It predicated everything. The patchwork quilt of parks and fields which stretches from Reay to Reiss is the direct result of military necessity as is the landlordism which it gave birth to and also created the useless and wasting sporting estates which currently litter and corrode West Caithness and all of Sutherland.

Landlordism without war to sustain it is a flawed system because ownership supposes not only ownership of the land but of all the knowledge and labour which has gone into the husbandry of the land and the art of cultivating it. By enclosing vast acreages landowners deny the majority an active participation in their own future. The landowner has not earned the right of ownership because owning does not acknowledge what has gone before. If acknowledgement were duly given then the benefit would be shared and progress could be guaranteed. As far as future development is concerned there is no other serious or sensible way to proceed with agriculture in Caithness or the rest of Scotland.

Land is not an invention, no matter what the defenders of Sir John Sinclair of Ulbster may claim, and cannot be patented by ownership. Ownership results in slavery because it ties people to dependency. Agriculture is the only way we, as a species, can face off the spectres of hunger and want. The argument that farmland has to increase so that yields can increase and to ensure this farming has to go hi-tech and that crops have to be genetically modified in order to be high yielding, drought resistant and pest free is a flawed argument. Only by doing all of this, the argument runs, and by funnelling huge financial resources into research and engineering will we feed the population of the future. It is a good thing, we are told, to maximise the yield per hectare and to maximise the productivity per unit of labour. This is classic neo-conservative, Americanised economic development, managed for and by big business through national governments and trade cohorts such as the European Union and its genesis is in armed conflict which is the macro-climate in which capitalism works best.

It is seen as heresy to suggest that this war-mantra of parameters as far as Caithness (and the rest of the world) is concerned is disastrous. At present Caithness may not suffer from water shortage, salinisation, soil erosion and compaction but many parts of the world not far from us do. Herbicides and pesticides create health problems for plants, insects and humans in the long term. Turning crops into 'commodities' ties farming into questionable markets and because of the volatility of these international commodity trade structures due to weather, climate and other variables prices increase and decrease alarmingly and the likelihood of poverty and debt for both producer and consumer rises accordingly.

Ancient agricultural traditions and common knowledge cannot be enclosed or patented by the concept of 'intellectual property' which on one hand encourages innovation but only the kind which leads to profit for a corporation. On the other hand investment for research into agricultural regeneration and bio-diversity, new ways of sharing and saving, is less forthcoming. This knowledge, this real 'intellectual property', is being lost.

2.

At the beginning of David Harrower's strange and beautiful play *Knives In Hens* the character of the Young Woman says to her husband Pony William, "I'm not a field. How'm I a field? What's a field?" The rest of the play is about, amongst other things, how to answer that question. The Oxford Dictionary variously describes a field as a 'piece of ground used for pasture or tillage; ground on which a battle is fought; large stretch, expanse, of sea, sky, ice, snow etc or the whole of history; area of spheres of operation, observation, intellectual activities etc.'

To understand the predicament of my native place in the early 21st century, to follow the progression of human activity from early settler to modern society and to chart that, you have to know what it is you are looking at when you look at a field.

The field, in Caithness, as has been shown, is a comparatively recent invention. Prior to the 1770s there were no big enclosed rectangular agricultural areas which specialised in growing one crop or rearing a single species. Before that the agrarian system was pastoral and suited to the needs of the native population. The pastoralism of cultural beliefs of the remaining population could not similarly be 'cleared' or 'improved' and remains a healthy counter-balance to the 'rationalism' of the 'enlightenment', even if there was no political structure in place to organise a social resistance.

From the mid-1770s the agricultural method changed to a system which maximised output and profit which enriched the new breed of landowners and fuelled the state driven enterprise of war. In effect nothing much has changed in the 250 years to the first decades of the 21st century.

It is often difficult for a modern sensibility to comprehend what this new addiction to conflict meant. To set into context just what this 'age of improvement' introduced it is instructive here to consider the life of the great Strathnaver bard, Rob Donn Mackay. He was born in the winter of 1714 and from the day of his birth to the day of his death in August 1778 the state of Britain was continually at war.

It was not until after the Battle of Waterloo in 1815 that peace, of a sort, broke out in Britain. However, with a burgeoning Empire, there was always a small war to engage in somewhere on the planet. It was as if the field of Waterloo in Belgium had metamorphosed into the big battlefield of the whole world. As empire is the consolidation of markets and materials, which is the motor aim of capitalism as generated by the British Empire, then the ultimate conclusion of Empire through capitalism is global control. Ironically it was the evolving system of capitalism which outgrew the necessity of a single nation-state dominated militaristic empire to ensure its survival and in so doing the symptom has replaced the disease and become the greater plague-threat to the future of humanity, infecting the very air we breathe and becoming a form of financial scabies.

The big battlefield of the world has reached its finite limit – unless we see space exploration as an extension of empire and markets – and capitalism, despite the cyber hallucinogen of the internet, has also reached the point where its inbuilt entropy bleeds it of its energy. On the other hand the advance in technology has meant that the concept of 'production' has lost most of its meaning. Our hi-tech gizmology now services capitalism in the way that capitalism used to service industry: industry, as a result, is the new service economy. A bright light does not need to be shone on this to see that it is unsustainable as the manufacture of wealth becomes disproportionate due to the reduction in the agencies involved. These stateless corporations increasingly see no need to contribute to the tax gathering regimes in the particular states they are located. Witness Starbucks zero

Corporation Tax contribution to the British exchequer. Google, Ebay and many others are taking a similar view and there is little the British government can do about it. Or more accurately: there is little this 'dog of a government', to quote Norman Tebbit, is willing to do about it. Next to the big field of war is the big field of capital. Both their crops are fatal.

The death of Rob Donn in 1778 effectively marked the end of the Middle Ages in the Highlands of Scotland. What had been held in common was now land possessed. It is interesting to note that in the Celtic place names of Caithness – and throughout the Highlands – there are few if any personal names to mark topographic areas or physical features. Gaelic culture tends to describe rather than possess. In the years before and after the Battle of Waterloo the landscape of Caithness was altered from the rolling patchwork of open park systems – tacks, wadsets, davochs, pennylands and run rigs etc – where bere and barley were grown and where the grazing animals were left to wander comparatively freely, to the regimented square fields so admired by visitors to the Far North today.

The price of these land enclosures was human. By 1800 thousands of people had been driven off their traditional pastures in the interior and forced to exist on the hard and precipitous coastal districts where the likelihood of having your children blown over a cliff was a constant threat. It was at Badbea, we need to remember, where the people were reported to tether both their animals and children for the same reason. Within forty years Caithness went from having a self-sufficient pastoral peasant economy which had existed for around 2,000 years to a series of staked out 'estates' where 'entrepreneurs' such as Sinclair of Ulbster and Dunbar of Hempriggs emerged in the post-Napoleonic society of North Britain as substantial 'landowners'. In almost every instance the 'title' to the land was acquired after the enclosure.

But why was this system of big fields necessary at all? The answer was, of course, to increase production of grain, meat, wool and soldiers. A people who had created a society which self-regulated itself and despite the occasional famine managed to feed itself and maintain a constant population was reduced within two generations to passivity, poverty and periphery with nothing left to sell but their labour.

Waterloo was no more the battle to end all battles than the First World War – so beloved of the Conservative Prime Minister David Cameron – was the 'war to end all wars'. The creation of the big open fields of Caithness was the organisation of agriculture to serve the material needs of empire and war: in reality they became the big fields of war.

The labour that many young Highlanders in the 19th century sold was themselves into the British Army, an army whose officer class just some decades previously had been hunting to extinction their fathers and grandfathers. Throughout the 1800s these Highland regiments were instrumental in the suppression of indigenous political cultures from the Caribbean to the Indian Ocean. This then is the dreary reality of what has gone before in the Far North of Scotland. From pastoral to property, from independence to dependence, from community co-operation to individual wage-slave: this journey has not been a beautiful experience. The spillage of blood and loss of cultural identity never is. As a result the people have been silenced politically and culturally and are unable to resist outside ideas of progress and value such as the billeting of thousands of military personnel during the two World Wars and the subsequent siting of Dounreay on our northern coast as part of the dispensation of post-war paternalism. The dependency of employment on a nuclear installation has infantilised and alienated the native population so that they neither know their past nor can imagine an alternative future.

One way to cast off the debilitating experience of history and create a new reality is through the imagination. The big fields of war can be dug up and re-thought. Currently in Caithness 95% of the food bought is not produced locally and the majority of crops grown, animals raised and fish landed are exported. The price of fuel is unregulated and artificially high. As a result everything costs more than it should. In Caithness, as in most parts of the eastern Highlands, Tesco controls the market, dominates the towns and villages and closes local shops. Consequentially take-aways, charity shops and pound stretchers of various hues blow in and out like tumbleweed. Tesco is another big field system. If it is not dug up then the food supply in the Highlands – and the whole of the rest of Scotland – becomes vulnerable. Energy production and food supply can, with a mixture of imagination and political will, be reclaimed. For example landowners and power utilities should not benefit from renewable energy – another big field – in the monopolistic way they currently do. There is no reason why an individual croft, or house, cannot have its own individual wind turbine – of scale – generating all the energy required and the excess sold off to the national grid. If food producers followed the co-operative practices common abroad then local food can find its way to local markets and prices can be contained. This is not romantic or fanciful: it is extremely practical and it is the future if we desire a resident population on the ground in Caithness and the north Highlands after the middle of the 21st century.

The big field of capitalism can also be opened up and redistributed. The crisis in the money supply and the 2008 collapse of fractional banking – RBS, BoS, Lloyds etc – shows that making money from money which relies on perpetual debt is institutionalised madness. As history has shown and as we have seen this only makes a few speculators rich and the rest of us impoverished and allows governments the opportunity to unleash their reactionary austerity programmes which demonise the victims of fractional banking – the poor, the majority. This policy will also depopulate the north of Scotland. What Caithness requires is local, positive equity banking based on community needs and realistic returns – not speculation. Our society craves a financial facility which allows it to invest in itself in order for the community to benefit. These facilities should be kept local and accountable.

Caithness is a small part of the small country of Scotland. Scotland as it is currently constituted is a minority portion of the state of Britain. Britain is a member of bigger organisations such as the UN, the EU and NATO. An independent Scotland would desire, one hopes, to be a part of the world of nations so until something better is created the UN is that field. The EU is a big field we could negotiate with to re-cultivate its purpose. NATO on the other hand is primarily a big field of war. In Caithness our sixty year relationship with the nuclear industry through Dounreay and the presence of HMS *Vulcan* and a US Navy base at Forss on our coast for almost as long has shorn from us any romantic or heroic notions as to what being on the front line of a nuclear war would mean. But as oblivion is no longer a mutually agreed military strategy and we have, as a result, no enemy it seems that the big field of war which is NATO has to be dug up and replanted.

Whether or not the people of Scotland will eventually decide that NATO is the big field of war and that we should desire no part of it will be decided in the fullness of time. But as Boris Pasternak wrote in the final line of his poem *Hamlet*: 'To live your life is not as simple as crossing a field.' Like the Young Woman in Harrower's play the Scots have yet to say 'I'm not a field.' History has shown us how the big fields of war are made. Let the history of the future show that we in Scotland at least had the imagination to remake the big fields of war into the big fields of life and the Rob Donns of that future can live their long creative lives in peace. The 'Province of the Cat' is big enough for such a dream. We certainly have time on our side, for time in the Far North is like peat: a deep running and ever growing commodity.

History has yet to prove whether the big field system we have at present will serve us well in the future. In times to come, the weather being the transitional thing it is and the climate changing to a wetter, more sustained damp period, we may view the humble run-rig system as not the antiquated and inefficient anachronism modernity says it was but rather a very practical way to drain small parcels of land for cultivation. It could be that what benefited Sir John Sinclair of Ulbster in the 19th century and fed the markets of war throughout the 20th will not ecologically benefit the land or the people of Caithness in the 21st century and beyond. For ecology to work each species must contribute to the wellbeing of all things. What the big fields of war represent is a rejection of that contributory cycle. What the people require and what the land requires is the same: an end to the intensification of technologies such as machines and chemicals which increase yield and maximise control at the expense of the physical world. The black fertile earth of Caithness has to be regenerated as has the natural and clean watercourses which spring up from beneath the ground and which flow in the burns, rivers and lochs. Agriculture has to be about biodiversity or it is, ultimately, about starvation. Would it be tragic or ironic if the 'age of improvement' led to the 'age of abandonment'?

3.

It is the first of November; *Samhain*. The day of the dead. The first day of winter in the Celtic calendar. The summer has been so poor and the autumn so brief that there are still uncut parks of green corn dotted around the county. If the combine does not conduct its solemn procedure soon then the frost will get them and the only thing that the grain will be good for is buckshee cattle feed or to be ploughed back into the earth. So the dead will join the living, which is appropriate for *Samhain* when, as myth has it, the fairy mounds – the home of the *Sidhe* – open up and the spirits of the underworld walk upon the earth with those who enjoy the light. This was when traditionally the cattle came down from the sheilings and the choice was made on which beasts would live for another year and which would be put to the knife in order to feed the people through the winter. A time of life and death.

Samhain was also traditionally a time of fire and like *Beltane* the cattle were driven between two fires to purify them, to mark the halfway point between the autumn equinox and the winter solstice, to symbolise the duality of existence. *Beltane* is the time of the living whereas *Samhain* is the time of the dead. On the last day of October and the first day of November was the time for the tribe to gather, to tell stories, to drink, for The Morríghan and The Dagda – the male and the female proto-gods of the Celts – to meet and have sex before the battle of the two worlds – for the bleeding of light into the dark, for the ultimate triumph of light over darkness, of the fulfilment of the optimism of the human heart.

On the 31st of October, on the night of transition, on Dunnet Beach, the community of Dunnet would build a bonfire which to my brother's and my eyes was as huge as a hill. All year stuff would be hoarded for this very special night. When the people gathered around and the fire was lit a slow smoky madness overtook all the children and we would run clockwise, anti-clockwise or widdershins – eventually it didn't matter – until the flames leapt up into the black Caithness night. The sparks would join the stars in the broad endless heaven and the crackling of the fire would meld with the roar of the surf and if joy was in being possessed by the spirits of the dead then joy was plentiful and the dead benign and our energy inexhaustible. Half bottles and flasks would be passed from adult to adult and the cold salt Atlantic air would be kept at bay and they would listen with concerned tolerance to the fire induced hysteria of their children for they knew that in all that noise and recklessness was the memory of the summer just passed and the promise of the year to come. They also know that we would, in time, run out of steam and would fall half-drunk from smoke and adrenalin, wound up from the sense of occasion and exhausted by the intensity of its sensation, onto the sand and there either roll around like peedie shamans conducting their own rituals with the spirits of the night or lie quite still, with heads reeling, blood pumping around our bodies as it had never done before, the sound of the surf filling our ears.

There on Dunnet Beach with the endless, timeless sea washing up her dark music, as the 1960s lost their innocence, at least one community – however imperfectly – in the melange of history understood its place in time, recognised who they were and were content with that. The winter could be faced. Soon the light would return. The *Samhain* fire had shown the way. The laughter of their own children made the people know, unconsciously – for what is the purpose of such knowledge if it is not printed high on the page of the tongue? – that their own lives were part of that fire, the illumination of that light.

History, however, is like a grinning turnip lantern – it throws light out through a grotesque and roughly cut window, only for the bright illumination to fade very soon. For as children we ran in the spirit of *Samhain*, at Halloween, the seed bere barley of the crofting run-rig of Dunnet parish, in the years before we were bussed to the big field of Thurso High School to learn of Guy Faulkes and the Gunpowder Plot, of the divine regal mania of the Stewarts and much else; where we were expected to become comprehensively 'other' which meant we had to conform to the grain-stock of the majority and to lose our nativeness, our language, to embrace the Atomic orthodoxy and become English.

But before all that there was a life to live and other than being stuck in the Dunnet primary school with Mrs Docherty grinding out her Old Testament religion and rock hard arithmetic it was lived scouring the shoreline, the dunes and the headland; but mostly it was spent, especially when the holidays were in it, at West Greenland with my grandparents, carving out our signatures on the earth beneath our feet.

Farming at West Greenland in the 1960s was, compared to farming generally in Caithness now, more like farming in the 1860s. A mixed arable farm of about 300 acres was the norm in the county then. Now, under the subsidy diktat of the European Union's Common Agricultural Policy farms like West Greenland are extinct, replaced by the monotonous mono-acres of hybrid barley strains, field after field of shivering continental cattle and Texel sheep which look more like small bears than the hardy Cheviot-cross hoggies my Uncle Jimmy and I would rescue from themselves every lambing time on the Links of Dunnet.

Self-sufficiency was not an aim: it was a way of life. The seasons ruled everything. Come the end of October there was a definite sense of the farming year, the cycle of ploughing, planting, sewing, lambing, calving, cutting and harvesting having come to a natural end. It was a time for taking stock. There were the 'harvest home' dances in the village halls. The 'thanksgiving service' in Dunnet Kirk where the Reverend Balingall would chunter on in his beautiful Argyll tones about things he didn't really understand and we would all sit politely in our family pews and sing the appropriate hymns and psalms and stare at such strange de-contextualised things as tins of peaches or cans of Campbell's tomato soup set out in a votive array before the pulpit. Occasionally there was a symbolic sheaf of corn which lay like one wing of a harvest angel, or a neep which sat like a severed head carried in from the battlefield by a respectful ancient Pictish warrior.

The centre of the West Greenland world was cattle. A herd of around fifty Hereford breeding cows was a constant, most of which, but not entirely, were reared on the farm and one bull. Whether this creature was always home grown I cannot recall but I do remember one beast, a Hereford colossus called Roddy, who my aunt Maggie had as a pet when a calf and who would follow her wherever she went, especially if she had a bucket in her hand, which was often. Roddy continued to be a pet and would meekly step in line behind her even when he stood six feet at the shoulder and weighed well over a ton and a half. She would heave my brother and I onto his back and parade us before astonished visitors as if we were young maharajahs on their ceremonial elephant.

So it was one *Samhain* morning we crossed a field. The Halloween night had been bright and even though the moon was two days past being full the sky was peppered bright with stars and the temperature had plummeted. The grass in the field was frosted white and as we made our weird procession towards the herd – a woman more like a man than many who worked the farm, a huge pedigree Hereford bull with two boys, all rag and muffin, nine and ten, sitting on his back with a mixture of fear, delight and ease – we could hear the cattle bellowing for the bull, the icy ground crunching under his massive hooves and all the while the perennial background music of the surf, the real acoustic of our lives.

The cattle were to be brought in for the winter and they knew it. The older ones were resigned and sniffed the wind while the younger heifers just stared at the space in front of them with that bovine curiosity which is a mixture of intensity and distraction. Usually there was a minor song and dance about the herd giving up their spring and summer freedom but the Caithness climate from November to March would challenge the constitution of a yak and even though the instinct of the cattle was to seek shelter they also had this deep rooted desire to roam freely and to be together. With Roddy at their head they followed on without a fuss. The conditioning to be close to the dominant male was just too engrained in them. So in they came to the freshly prepared cattle shed which made up one quarter of the steading, where they would stay over winter, protected, together at least, dry and silage fed. Their bellowing, 'boglan an greetan', sounded out over West Greenland those first few November nights like so many melancholy fog horns.

After the 'cattle-beasts' had been taken in my grandfather used to like to patrol his vacated acres, pipe in mouth, bonnet pulled down, jacket usually tied up with binder twine to keep out the chill. Invariably I would go with him on these day-long reconnaissance manoeuvres and although I knew he was thinking about the coming year – what crops would go in what field, which park the beasts would graze in first before the spring hay was brought on: all of that – I often wondered if he was actually looking beneath the fields, as if he was stripping it back like bark from a tree so that he could see the older landscape beneath, that husbanded Norse world of Thordis, the Pictland of his own ancient ancestors.

In truth I had no idea what old Donald Gunn was seeing. Perhaps he was remembering when he first came here and how it had changed – how he had changed it, how it had changed him. That the spirits of the dead walked upon the earth among the living, I suspect, he would have thought no more strange or fanciful than dunting the ash out of his pipe off a flagstone dyke for a refill of boagie-roll. Although the field-scape he looked over was artificial, man-made, recent, it was none the less his own. Like Frankenstein he looked at his monster but unlike Mary Shelley's Doctor he recognised it for what it was and he did not reject it because it was ugly, for it was far from ugly: my grandfather, again like Frankenstein, looked at what he had created and saw that it was like himself, one had made the other.

There is no journey back in agriculture, the only direction is forward. My grandfather is now one of the numberless chorus of the dead and at *Samhain* he walks again these fields and parks and acres. I think his heart would be sore at the rejection of the hard lessons he had learned while farming this ground. He would see the folly in being dependent upon a single crop, a single species of beast and on subsidy from the Common Agricultural Policy of the European Union. He would not see this expansion of production and the loss of identity as farming. He would recognise it for what it is: the industrial usage of land, an alienating, chemically induced dead end which distances the producer from both the land and the people: a process which diminishes imagination, innovation and craft.

21st century farming methods in Caithness beat out a hollow drum sound. There is no harmony. The pattern of cattle and sheep, hay and sileage, turnips and potatoes, barley and corn, pigs and hens – all on the same farm – has been ploughed into the ground of memory. Everything now is specialised, singular. But that memory and the balance it contains is mirrored in the Caithness soil itself: peaty black, sandy with a clay body to it. Given the right conditions and a bit of luck you can grow almost anything in it – any cereal other than wheat. It is a soil that both demands and allows variety. Variety, however, in agriculture is something which has disappeared.

When my mother came to West Greenland after World War Two she thought she had arrived in Eden. Newly married to Donald Gunn's youngest son she found a world in total contrast to the thin herring boned streets of Wick where poverty, wartime rationing and general want were the common experience of the hard pressed population. Her time away being trained as a nurse and a midwife at the Rotten Row hospital in Glasgow's Townhead exposed her to poverty, suffering and deprivation which far exceeded anything post-herring boom Wick could manufacture. At West Greenland there was fresh meat, milk, eggs and vegetables all year round and, probably more importantly, fresh air and wide open spaces full of beauty and light.

Here were a people similar but different from her own. They moved differently, more assuredly and without haste. The pattern of their days was not dependent on the amount and price of fish landed on the Pulteneytown quay. Their working lives were governed by the seasons of the year, by the vagaries of the weather and whether it was seed time or harvest. In habits and custom the farming community were as fastidious, kind and welcoming as her own but the relationship with earth as opposed to water made them temperamentally less anxious in the matter of religion and so unconcerned were they with the on-doings of the kirk or the significance of this or that passage in the Bible that I'm sure Helen More sometimes wondered if the Gunns were really Christians at all.

For my grandfather Heaven was a field of hay or a new born calf. His true kirk was the black, fire-bright fulcrum of the smiddy. In there he would hammer out his own strange metal psalm music to the god of a new trailer frame or a hydraulic axle. His family likewise put their love of creation into what they did, what they grew and what they raised – human or animal. God, for them, was the sun coming up and going down and the paraphernalia of all of that was kept firmly in the background – the mystery was in the everyday, in an ear of barley, in the deep wet mystic brown of a newly ploughed field. From what I could gather my mother took to West Greenland like a duck to water. She loved the abundance of it, the rhythm of it, the colour of it and above all she loved my grandmother.

Georgina Jack Mackay Gunn was a woman of the west. In her skirts crackled the old static of clearance and eviction, exile and emigration. Like my grandfather she was a Gael and the two of them, when they thought none of the rest of the tribe was listening, would converse with each other in the Sutherland Gaelic which was their native tongue. The only other creatures she would speak Gaelic to were the cattle she milked – and that with a song or a soft coaxing word – or to me when I was up to some mischief and general no good. She also sang songs when she was at the butter churn and whether they were the songs of Rob Donn Mackay, whose Bheinn Loaghall and Bheinn Hope straths were the straths of her own people, sadly I cannot tell. That love of Gaelic has stayed with me all my life. If anyone could have told my grandmother that if you spoke Gaelic you would more than likely be working for the BBC she would have laughed out loud. For her and Donald Gunn it was the case that if you wanted to get on in the 'modern world' you had to speak English. It is one of the greatest tragedies of the 'Province of the Cat' that this economic necessity has been adopted as cultural prejudice. Every time I hear a Caithness Highland councillor open their ignorant mouths and say that Gaelic was never spoken in Caithness I hear the shade of Sir Robert Gordon wish this advice to his Tutor, written in the early 17th century, that 'the Irish language cannot so soon be extinguished', but in my memory I can still hear my grandfather and grandmother talking 'Irish' in the scullery of West Greenland, I can hear that proud, beautiful woman singing an ancient Gaelic air to the working end of a cow.

Indeed her domain was the diary, the hens and the baking. My mother, who was a brilliant baker, said later that everything she knew about baking she learned from old Georgina. My grandmother's relationship to oatmeal was almost mystical. The way she handled it and spoke about it one could be forgiven for thinking that oatmeal was the elixir of life which indeed it was if you came from *Dùthaich Mhic Aoidh*, from the heart of Mackay country in the north west of the 'Province of the Cat'. Like my mother my grandmother also looked upon West Greenland as the land of plenty, as the good land, not so much 'the happy land' of the hymns but a place where hard work in a beautiful landscape provided everything you could desire. Especially cattle, which for a Mackay as well as a Gunn, was the measurement of wealth, fame, love even.

Part of the bond between my grandparents was their shared sense of exile. This was not a recent thing but it was inside them like an unstated longing. Behind their eyes was the process of history, its human cost. My grandfather's people were burned out of Strath Kildonan and my grandmother's out of Strathnaver. I did not know it then but I realise it now that their easy habit of enabling, of passing knowledge and skill on to whoever was smart or fortunate enough to receive it came from this sense of injustice. They created such a strong sense of 'home' and of being 'grounded' because in their recent history their ancestors had been refugees, dispossessed and diminished. They worked hard to create something that they would never lose, that their children would never lose. That the farm is now owned and worked by a family of Mackays would please them both.

My grandmother had what Jung termed 'archaic heritage' as an instinct. When people she had never met came to West Greenland she would speak to them in her broad Caithness dialect of Scots no matter who they were – except if they happened to come from England when she, somewhat comically, would speak to them very slowly so that they understood her. As Hamish Henderson once said of the language of the Sutherland travellers, that 'they accommodated English' in their linguistic repertoire; likewise with my grandmother with her two languages – Gaelic and Scots. She had no real reason to learn any other, especially English which hardly anyone she knew spoke.

There was also something quite relentless about her, as if she grew impatient with the shallow external realities which most people presented as themselves. She would always ask a stranger, "An far e frae?" And they would give an answer. Then after a bit, when the conversation or reply did not satisfy her she would ask again, "Aye, boot far e really frae?" It was as if she was looking deep inside you, beyond the superficial 'you' to that other more profound thing, to the reality of your origin, to who you 'really' were. In all of this I suspect she was searching for kinship, for the lost members of her clan whom she would never meet because of oceans and time and landlords and this lost fraternity somehow angered her, so if there was the slightest chance of a connection she would seek it out. She would not be denied in this, it was one way she could reclaim the past and undo the senseless cruelty of it. When she actually did make some connection her whole being filled up with a quiet light as if the small victory of a rediscovered, distant bloodline was inevitable, only natural. "Ah choost kent e wis freends oh his!" she would exclaim and for a days after life would, as a result, be better.

To make the world better – is that not the ultimate aim of progress? Is it not what the forward march of humanity is all about? The longing behind my grandmother's eyes gave away the lie to all of that and was the sign of the great betrayal of the Enlightenment and of modernity. West Greenland may have been home to her for sixty years but she and Donald Gunn inhabited it as it were the last place of exile, a refuge from the storm of events which, ultimately, as RAF Castletown manifested around them in 1939 was to prove, they could not escape.

I recall a passage from the writing of another exile, one who tragically found no refuge and who died in flight from Nazi tyranny. In 1940, on the Spanish-French border, the great German-Jewish Marxist philosopher Walter Benjamin, took his own life. In one of the last things he wrote, the *Thesis On The Philosophy Of History*, he described my grandparents' condition perfectly, although he was thinking about all of humanity:

A Klee painting named *Angelus Novus* shows an angel looking as though he is about to move away from something he is fixedly contemplating. His eyes are staring, his mouth is open, his wings are spread. This is how one pictures the angel of history. His face is turned toward the past. Where we perceive a chain of events, he sees one single catastrophe which keeps piling wreckage upon wreckage and hurls it in front of his feet. The angel would like to stay, awaken the dead, and make whole what has been smashed. But a storm is blowing from Paradise; it has got caught in his wings with such violence that the angel can no longer close them. The storm irresistibly propels him into the future to which his back is turned, while the pile of debris before him grows skyward. This storm is what we call progress.

The storm of progress catches us all in its blast. As Donald and Georgina prepared to make a new life at West Greenland in 1924 they too looked back at the 'pile of debris' which can never be remade. It was the look that was always in the corner of my grandmother's eye.

It was piling up in front of Neil Gunn that very same year as he wrote *The Grey Coast*, aghast and angry at the destruction of the thriving community he left behind as a child only to find on his return in the early 1920s the wreckage of World War One piled up outside Lybster and all along the coast from The Ord to Wick. Donald and Georgina Gunn translated their tragedy into a working and successful farm and Neil Gunn turned his anger into a brilliant novel.

For Walter Benjamin, with the Gestapo, arrest warrant in hand, hot on his heels and Franco's thugs about to send him back to Paris to certain torture and eventual death, there was to be no sanctuary, he reasoned, other than the fatal oblivion induced by an overdose of morphine in a hotel room in the coastal Catalan village of Portbou. The 'Angel of History' is remorseless, yet we as a people cannot afford to walk backwards into the future, no matter the nature of the storm blowing from paradise. We need to look forwards and shine a light out over the coming years. For that we need poets.

4.

Memory is not to be trusted. We cannot reliably explore the past with it. For memory is a theatre where images and scenes are presented and played out. For Caithness the past has been destroyed, ignored and disbelieved. Beneath the carpet of enclosed fields, heather bog and under-used estate land lies a vast archaeological record of mans' built and nurtured landscape. That it remains unexplored, unheralded and dismissed in many quarters is evidence of this northern society's strange unease with itself, its fraught relationship to landownership, power and cultural expression. At *Samhain* the dead may come out of the ground and dance amongst the living but in many ways the dead are more alive than the living, it's just that we are not encouraged to find out.

Post World War Two there was a general exhaustion within the war weary state of Britain. After 1945 the news of the extent of the terrible human catastrophe and the sheer physical wreckage acted out on mainland Europe and in Russia became apparent. The 'Angel of History' had passed over us and as if taking their cue from her backwards motion the leaders of the victorious Allies decided to go in the same direction: backwards into the future. So it was that in the north we were too ready to accept anything, believe anything – anything other than the truth.

It was as if for six long years – from 1939 to 1945 – the people had abandoned memory, burned down that theatre, forgotten who it was they actually were. Everything which was instinctive, learned and beloved was abandoned. War became the reason for being. War became everything. War roared in the skies above Hoy. War exploded in Scapa Flow. War sailed this way and that through the Pentland Firth. War stretched everyone to the point of insanity. War was good for West Greenland. Peace was not so profitable.

Every sector had to adjust after 1945 and farming in Caithness was no different. The ready and steady markets of airbases, army camps and the navy went. Suddenly having huge deep litters full of Rhode Island Reds and pig houses crammed with porking sues was no longer the goldmine it had been. So they adjusted, shrank, stayed still or went to the wall. Or, like Donald Gunn junior, they broke out, went their own way and embraced Harold Macmillan's great big post war lie of 'You've never had it so good.'

He bought a tractor, a binder and a threshing mill. Where the money to do this came from remains a bit of a mystery. Finance and the Gunn clan have never been easy or natural bedfellows. Centuries of cattle reiving along the Caithness and Sutherland border had made cash a fluid entity. My great-grandfather, George Gunn the stonemason, also mysteriously came into some money. So much so that he bought himself and his Mackay wife, Johanna, Ormlie Lodge in Thurso. He also bought for is two sons, Donald and James, the farms of West Greenland and Brawlbin respectively. In the early 1920s this was no small undertaking and even then the prices would have been substantial.

My Auntie Maggie always said that my father sold out his share of West Greenland but this was something he fervently denied. My Uncle Jimmy, forever called 'the shepherd' even though he had trained as an engineer at John Brown's shipyard on the Clyde before World War Two, always kept a diplomatic silence on the issue. He had other issues to contend with. For a start he hated being called 'the shepherd' and he also hated sheep. I would go out with him in the early spring-time along the Links at the lambing. Once we found a dead ewe with its head stuck down a rabbit hole. "Take a look aat at, Cheordie. Smothered by e world!" he exclaimed. He was firmly of the opinion that sheep had a death wish. "If e gee a cheviot three feet o binder twine an ten meenads when e come back hid'll bay deid," he would say with a mixture of resignation and astonishment, then add "Id's a fact. Thur boarn till dee, ay fooshanless craiturs." More often than not he was vindicated. I never ever heard him discuss money with anyone.

My father's target clientele during the 1960s was small farmers and crofters who could not afford the equipment themselves but still needed their crops harvested. At that time west Caithness still had many working crofts. The coming of Dounreay actually suited the crofters as they could finally achieve what fishing never could and what crofting had been set up to do: keep the men on the land while they earned their living somewhere else locally. Neither the Crofter's Commission nor the United Kingdom Atomic Energy Authority could have foreseen this unlikely harmony.

As the 1970s came along the binder and the threshing mill gave way to the Claas combine harvester and the Fergie tractor to the Ford Super Major. My father grew older and maybe it was because he had turned his own 'Angel of History' around and had a squint at the future, or maybe it was common sense that told him that the strange dichotomy of change which was taking place within Caithness agriculture, where things got bigger but at the same time got smaller, was not for him. By this time the head of cattle produced in Caithness was reduced significantly. The amount of cereals grown increased and the number of viable farms dwindled accordingly. By the 1980s big was good and the little player, the self-employed agricultural contractor and the crofter, could not compete. Encouraged and enabled by the Conservative government of Margaret Thatcher, crofters sold their land for house building and to buck this trend my father, again the financial details are mysterious, acquired a croft overlooking the Pentland Firth.

It was at this time, around 1985, that the Gunn clan fell apart. Within five years my grandmother, both my parents and my Uncle Jimmy were dead. Old Donald Gunn had died happily enough in the late 1960s. My Auntie Maggie in 2010. *Samhain* now is their time, the calendar year when death makes sense. With them went continuity and knowledge. The 'Angel of History', her wings flush with this new storm from Paradise, dragged them off. If what is left here, now that they are not around to manufacture it and guide it, is called 'progress' then we had better try to find it another name. It seems to me that everything is moving backwards into the future because agriculture in Caithness has not truly progressed at all. Rather what has happened is that the energy built up from the late 18th century and during the 19th and 20th centuries has only increased in entropy and now sits on the edge of its allotted domain embracing a darkness of its own creation. How futile would be the life experience of all of these wonderful people, of all people, if it has not allowed us to hold up a light to the dominant operational economic credo of the age and say: the free market is not free and everything which has been said or written to uphold that credo is a lie.

The lie at first is musical, it is fresh, it makes sense. Then the lie becomes architectonic: it is built into everything including the ground and our beliefs. Finally the lie becomes like a finely woven fabric which we hang on our walls and bodies and mistake for beauty and truth. Time, as ever, undoes the lie. The music loses its harmony and becomes unbearable. The ground literally moves beneath our feet and we cannot believe what we are seeing. Finally the walls fall down and with it our beautiful wall hangings and clothes, the fabric of our truth which in the end becomes so much rubble and rags. The 'Angel of History' moves ever on, backwards, away from us and we add our wreckage to the catastrophe incapable of doing anything else.

But here is a question that may vex even the 'Angel of History': what if no-one gives a damn about the past? Isn't that the risk: isn't that the risk with everything? The storm of progress may blow out from Paradise but the dead still oceans of indifference could becalm us all. The rough anarchic answer is that we are all blown forward, propelled by the inevitable drive of progress to escape the increasing piles of debris our civilization has created. It is impossible, it is futile, it is beyond reason and science, but we are driven to do it anyway.

So if forwards is the reckless, inevitable direction of 'progress' – the storm blown from Paradise – even if we cannot see it, then perhaps there is a little wisdom in looking backwards for some inspiration in matters agricultural in the vain hope that we may actually be able to learn from history. The illusory permanent big field – big shed, big budget – of the Common Agricultural Policy as administered by the European Union with its subsidies to farmers for growing this and not growing that and with its emphasis on production, conformity and yield is, to all intents and purposes, bureaucratic entropy. The big farm is agri-death in Caithness. Crofting, despite its origins and its application up to this point in time, may offer an indication of a future; a future which involves keeping people on the land and working it and in so doing offer them a productive and fulfilled life.

It is the common chorus of this long prose-poem but the issue of who owns the land and the nature of that ownership is central to harnessing the stormy winds blowing from Paradise. Quite simply – the big farms and the estates have to be broken up, redistributed in appropriately sized lots to support and service a sustainable population who will have to, if they are to have a future, relearn the principles of co-operative working and community living. This community will have to develop internal markets whereby goods and services are sold and traded locally. Tesco and every supermarket chain will become just more wreckage on the pile and this will mean that if Caithness is to have any population, sustainable or otherwise, there will have to be a matrix of localisms – food markets, energy suppliers, building materials, banking facilities etc. – so that what wealth is created is retained, as far as is possible, within the locality to work for the betterment of the society. This way progress may neither be catastrophic or blind.

This is no hippy-dippy, anarcho-syndicalist fantasy but something Donald and Georgina Gunn would recognise as being normal in the 1920s and 30s. Neither would this 'progress' necessitate a return to those times but would represent an improvement on them. Of course this is a dream but it is a dream which insists that this dynamic is the real meaning of 'improvement' in regard to agriculture and humanity, as opposed to the corruption of terms forced upon it by the likes of Sir John Sinclair of Ulbster and the self-serving interests of his class. It is also a dream tempered by technology which would demonstrate that there can be a society organised which does not depend on the exploitation of man by man. For a future Caithness to succeed technology does not mean big business. By creating a new paradigm for society through agriculture we can dissolve the dialectic of the big field, we can begin to address the essential contradiction within the organization of production. Most of the technology we need to achieve this structural re-setting already exists but new technology will have to be developed in order to ensure our continued existence. Like the 'Angel of History' we cannot go back, ever.

But we must draw on what has come before – for are we not the sum total of that? Our new technology cannot be at odds with our culture for it will have to give it sustenance. Without technology we have no culture and without culture there will be no technology. This is what Leon Trotsky has called 'a dialectical interaction'. Let us hail it as a counter-blast against the storm of progress which demands a continual catastrophe. Our present agricultural methods are leading us to catastrophe. We have a vast reservoir of culture deposited in our consciousness – everything learned, every skill achieved and ability acquired up to now – and it is this reservoir which ultimately will ensure our survival. Or it should, for there are no guarantees.

Farming methods and the land they are practiced on have to co-evolve as they have done, traditionally, over generations. In Caithness as in the rest of Scotland this has not been the case for too long. Mechanisation, chemicals and genetics have added to the pile of wreckage. It is salient here to remember that 'culture' originally meant a ploughed field, a cultivation, as contrasted with the primeval forest or un-opened ground: that is culture was what was achieved by human effort as compared to what was given by nature. In other words, settling as opposed to wandering. This antithesis is still at work on our subconscious to this day. This ancient tension is our modern conundrum.

Tradition does not mean being conservative. Nothing can be more conservative as field after field of genetically modified barley, or park after park of shivering big boned continental cattle. Tradition is radical because it is the continuity of change and the constancy of change. Agriculture, like art, has to reinvent itself continually and if it becomes complacent, over specialised, subject to money and markets rather than acknowledging the origins of its function which is feeding the people or celebrating the imagination then agriculture, like art, becomes something else entirely, something poisonous and decadent. As a result humanity suffers.

In order to create a matrix of localisms, to break up the big fields of landownership, of market and trade dominance by a handful of corporations, to create housing which is both affordable and environmentally vernacular, the big field of government also has to be dismantled. What would be the point if there was a local matrix of inter-dependent communities if they were dominated by a centralised state bureaucracy? The revolution necessary to keep a viable population on the ground in a future Caithness will, by its very nature, be unrecognisable to those who rule over us currently. However, Thordis who worked the ground behind the dunes of Dunnet over a thousand years ago, may see something in it he would recognise. Is this our conundrum, is this our contradiction? No, it is the reason it is necessary. We may be walking backwards into the future with the debris of 'progress', 'improvement' and 'enlightenment' piled up before our feet but we can, like Thordis, recognise it for what it is: a rehearsal, a prelude, the price humanity has had to pay for dominating the planet.

5.

> 'Death is the sanction of everything the storyteller can tell.
> He has borrowed his authority from death.' – Walter Benjamin

Whether existence is a wheel, a cycle or a spiral, death comes at some point: 'Death' is one of the two main characters in the lifelong struggle-drama of stubborn existence. In his great poem 'The Flyting o' Life and Death' Hamish Henderson states the uneasy, irresolvable stand-off in these terms:

Quo daith, the warld is mine.
I hae dug a grave, I hae dug it deep,
Fur war an' the pest will gar ye sleep.
Quo daith, the warld is mine.

Quo life, the warld is mine.
An open grave is a furrow syne.
Ye'll no keep my seed frae fa'in in.
Quo life, the warld is mine.

In Henderson's poem life and death could be imagined as two owls, or hoolets in a boor-tree. As Thordis, the old Norse farmer, proves – and as each hoolet's cry leads to another hoolet's cry, a call and response – continuity is a process which, however temporarily held in the cosmic scheme of things, lends a soil-fed permanence to human activity. "An open grave is a furrow syne." When it comes to fields and agriculture this is as much of a metaphysical conceit or as near a philosophical belief as the business of barley and cattle musters. When you look out over the broad acres of Caithness, out over the farmland, what you see is life and no matter how ill-formed or self-serving the intentions of those who have given us the set pattern of the enclosed fields, life and the sustaining of it is their purpose. The barley fields and the cattle parks cock a sneuk at 'Death' as he rides by on his black horse of 'the pest'. Beneath the fields lies another reality, another way of living, an older narrative born out of necessity, desire and the 'struggle-drama'.

War is the ultimate human fetish and it has left its whip marks on both the land and the people. The land can adapt and consume evidence but the people internalise every experience and those who, in the modern world, are driven to despair and attempt to set down the sequence of events, externalised in a history, are handicapped. The technology of the 21st century undermines these externalisations because everything that is significant or important has already been explored and explained so that the writing of history becomes mere reproduction. Prior to the mechanical and electronic age historians were storytellers in as much that the accuracy of what they related was relative to the available information but the interpretation of the events was left to the psychology of the reader. History was story. Now information is freely available and the explanation of everything bombards the reader, but knowledge does not always accompany information. The real story can sink beneath the messages received. A storyteller has no use for all this babble. The storyteller has to keep their narrative free of explanation in order for it to be memorable. For history to benefit humanity it has to be marvellous, it has to be free of psychology in order to be accurate and to communicate directly. This is how the narrative of history works and it is why the storyteller is the true historian and why myth and fable are accurate psychological interpretations of actual events.

One example of the 'marvellous' as 'history' is 'The Year of the Big Threshing', or *'Bliadhn' a Bhualadh Mhóir'*, which occurred in Reay either in the 17th or the 18th century depending on what folklore source you believe. This legend concerns one Donald Dhu Mackay who was a noted wizard and who had, reputedly, studied the 'black arts' in Rome under no less tutelage than that of the Devil. When he returned to the north of Scotland he met, one day, the Queen of the Fairies in Smoo Cave at Durness where he also frequently convened with his 'master'. In honour of his status as a distinguished member of the underworld The Queen of the Fairies presented Donald Dhu with a box which, she said, he must never open. Of course he did and out poured an endless tribe of the Shee demanding "Work! Work! Work!' He set them to draining Loch Clash Breac in Brubster in order to find the pot of gold hidden beneath it. They set to their task and soon two mounds of earth were thrown up as a result. These are now called Craig Mor and Craig Leath in the parish of Reay. The gold was secured but the Shee were still inexhaustible, still screaming for 'Work! Work! Work!'

It was the harvest time and coincidentally the district was awash with corn and barley, so much so that the people had no means to harvest such an unusual and quantitive bounty in time to save it from the imminent bad weather. Donald Dhu Mackay set his insatiable workers from the underworld to the task and in one day the enormous harvest of the entire parish was cut, gathered in and threshed which left the local people both astonished and grateful. 'The Year of the Big Threshing' has lived on in folk memory ever since. Unfortunately for Donald Dhu Mackay his unboxed Shee were not satisfied and still they screamed for tasks to perform. So he took them to Dunnet Beach and instructed them to construct ropes from the sand of the dunes in order to ferry him over to Orkney. Legend has it they are still there, diligently undertaking their impossible and eternal task. So Donald Dhu Mackay was free of the Queen of the Fairies' useful but impossible host.

The 'history' of this occult yarn concerns another Donald Mackay – the First Lord Reay who lived between 1591 and 1649. This Chief of the Mackays was a well-educated, connected and far travelled man who raised a regiment and fought for Gustavus Adolphus, the King of Sweden and champion of the Protestant cause in the Thirty Years War which ravaged much of central Europe between 1618 and 1648. Now although Mackay was a devout Protestant he was very much a royalist. King Charles I was always seen in Scotland as a Catholic sympathiser with a practising Catholic wife. Mackay was related to the Gordons who were in the 17th century still Catholics as were the Sinclairs to the north.

To merge Donald Mackay, the Chief of the Mackays, with the mythical Donald Dhu Mackay, pupil of the Devil and trained in Rome which was the heart of Papal power, was a neat piece of Protestant political propaganda. At a stroke it attached Catholicism to Satan and all his works with that of the culture of the Mackays. This was a rogue's gallery of mischievous free association which suited all the power elites in Scotland from King Charles I, who hated the Gaels, to the Gordon Earls of Sutherland, who had always coveted the Mackay lands of Strathnaver. Unlike Donald Dhu the First Lord Reay, historically, could not rid himself of the Gordons or the Stewart monarch as cunningly as Donald Dhu, the Devil's disciple, dispatched the Shee to the outer reaches of story. This is an example of where history breaks down into images and does not follow a linear narrative.

The poetry in this yarn is to be found in the 'marvellous' incidents which garnish the myth: a myth which as we have seen can illuminate history in a way information cannot. No storyteller, whether they hail from the famous Sutherland travellers or a blether in a bar, would ever contemplate 'explaining' the story of Donald Dhu Mackay. No real storyteller needs to force connections onto the listener or reader.

Where one useful connection to Donald Dhu can be found is in the sister mythology to the Gaels – that of the Greeks – and the idea of the box which should not be opened. This concerns the legend of Prometheus, the titan. Prometheus – meaning 'forethought' – made humankind out of clay and when Zeus oppressed humans and deprived them of fire Prometheus stole fire for them from Heaven and taught humanity many arts. To avenge himself Zeus made the fire-god Hephaestus fashion a woman, Pandora, out of clay. Athene breathed life into her and each of the other gods supplied her with every charm. Pandora means 'all gifts'. She was sent to Prometheus who seeing the trouble she would bring sent her to his brother Epimetheus – meaning 'after thought' – who readily accepted her. Pandora brought with her a box which when opened out poured all the ills and evils – the 'charms' – which have afflicted mankind ever since. Hope, according to the myth, was the only quality which remained at the bottom of the box to make humanity's existence less severe. For all of this, the stealing of fire and more, Zeus had Prometheus tied to a lonely rock in the Caucasus where an eagle daily fed on his liver which was miraculously restored each night.

In the earthly pantheon of history's players in the northern 'heaven' of the 'Province of the Cat' the Clan Mackay in particular and the Celt in general can be seen as being represented by Prometheus, chained to the Split Stone between the mountains of Strathnaver and the plateau of Caithness, their liver being consumed each day by the 'royal' Stewarts, the Gordons and the Sinclairs, to be restored at night by the common people. In the version of the story by Aeschylus, Zeus and Prometheus are reconciled but in 'Prometheus Unbound' by Shelley they are not. As he wrote of his own play from Italy in 1821:

> But, in truth, I was averse from a catastrophe so feeble as that of reconciling the Champion with the Oppressor of mankind. The moral interest of the fable, which is so powerfully sustained by the sufferings and endurance of Prometheus, would be annihilated if we could conceive of him as unsaying his high language and quailing before his successful and perfidious adversary.

Whether the Celt has yet un-said anything is debatable but the restoration of the Gaelic language to the civic and literary society of Scotland and Celtic music to the heart of the nation does suggest that the Mackay has begun to free himself, at last, from his rock. At this present time and to this particular writer it does not seem that the 'Champion' and the 'Oppressor' have been reconciled or are they likely to be while the estate system still prevails over the north of Scotland and too few people own and control too much land. Shelley's version of the myth is the one which holds true for the modern age. The days of 'quailing' before a 'perfidious adversary' are surely over. 'Death', like the horseman in Yeats' poem, can 'pass by'.

Poetry for the people of the 'Province of the Cat' has always been a vehicle for change and a storehouse of memory. It has provided both the subject of their history and given them the facility to re-imagine it. Poetry is the language of the theatre of memory. This can be best illustrated by citing the achievement of the last of the great bards of the

Clan Mackay – Rob Donn Mackay of *Ach na Cailliach* in Strathnaver. The sixty-four years of his life from 1714 to 1778 produced a volume and quality of work perhaps unsurpassed in the *bardachd* of the Gael up to the work of Sorley Maclean in the 20th century.

Of Rob Donn the Reverend Donald Sage of Achness in his classic memoir of life in Sutherland in the late 18th and early 19th century, *Memorabilia Domestica*, had this to say about the poetry, history, the people and the relationship between all these three things:

> His poetry is history – a history of everyone and everything with which he at any time came into contact in the country in which he lived. His descriptions do not merely let us know what these things or persons were, but identify us with them; we behold them not as things that were, but as things that are. They are all made to pass in review before us, in their characters, and language, and peculiarities, and habits. When he composed a song, he no sooner sang it than, with all the speed of the press, it circulated throughout the country. Then and for many years after his death, the only library in which his poems were to be found was the memory of the people.

The facility of the internet was not available to the people of the 'Province of the Cat' in the time of Rob Donn but what was common was the desire to survive – to go further, to live! This urge was strong. As it had to be for the Age of Improvement, the bastard child of the Enlightenment, was upon them. The poems and songs of Rob Donn and the tenacious act of necessary and beautiful reverence the people displayed in remembering them and handing them down to the following generations stands in direct opposition to the actions of the enclosing landlords and their agents and factors.

One was a creative instinct – the preservation of the *bardachd*, the continuity of culture. The other was a destructive impulse – the enclosure of land and the removal of the native people. Those who sang Rob Donn's songs were holding fast to the future even though all they could see was the wreckage at the feet of the Angel of History. A deep instinct informed them that they would get through this and that they would survive. On the other hand the agents of Dunrobin knew only what they were doing, which was making room for their master's money. Their primary and concentrated activity was clearing away those who stood in their way. This need for open space was far stronger than any hatred the burners of the thatch roofed houses had for the people who lived beneath them.

These instincts, these repeated actions, are connections through time and psychology 'not as things that were, but as things that are'. For example: a man sits in the cab of a modern super-tractor. His reversible super-plough turns over the wet sod in a large field. Is he aware of the archaeology beneath his wheels and of it being disturbed by the blades of his steel machine? The answer is probably 'no' – he will be unaware of anything other than the music coming out of the sound system in his cab or through his headphones. He will be shut off, internalised, cocooned in modernity and its tinny temporary now. But only an individual completely devoid of thought can deny that there is a correspondence between the technology of the super-tractor and the archaic underworld of symbols as represented by Donald Dhu Mackay, Prometheus and Rob Donn: the world of mythology.

The Reverend Donald Sage said of Rob Donn that not only does his poetry 'let us know what these things or persons were, but (that they) identify us with them': so it can be said that mythology allows us to identify ourselves as us. To understand what a field is and how it came into being – does this reduce our understanding of who we are or increase it? To say that the big fields of war have reduced farming to mere acreage and those who work the land as slaves to European Union subsidy – does this 'identify us with them'? But the man trapped by modernity in the cab of his uber-agro-machine has, latently, the archaeology of history in his memory. Within him are

Thordis and Prometheus. When he is released from modernity, from the big field of everything, from his rock of systems, he and those who come after him will be able to go further, to live.

That the world they will live in might have shrunk in field size will be as much the result of climate change as the determination of history. That cattle ranches and prairie style barley production suit the big field of government which is fashioned in Brussels then applied by degrees and shrinking decrees by London and then Edinburgh suit only statisticians and graph makers is evident by their hegemony in Caithness. This is the logical conclusion of Sir John Sinclair's 'agricultural improvements' and will empty the north more effectively than the Gordons of Dunrobin managed in the inner straths of Sutherland. A mixed arable farm as worked by Donald Gunn at West Greenland for most of the 20th century may appear to the bean counters of Brussels to be of as much relevance as a comic opera but as the climate becomes ever more damper due to the jet stream creeping further south each year, the physical nature of the agricultural tragedy which will unfold as a result will become ever more apparent across the big fields of Caithness.

It was not hunger which drove my grandfather to farm at West Greenland and it was not scarcity he created but these two spectres could return so easily if farming in Caithness is crucified on the cross of production knocked up by specialising in only one or two things. At the end of George Mackay Brown's seminal poem cycle *Fishermen with Ploughs* a group of futuristic refugees stand around drinking the last of their ale made from the last of their seed from a clay pot. It is their first – and maybe last – 'harvest home'. They have been driven from an un-named city to re-settle Rackwick after an undefined nuclear holocaust. They are hungry, prematurely aged, resigned. After the last mouthful of ale has ceremoniously been drunk the pot accidentally, portentously, falls to the floor and smashes into bits. One of the women, Trudi, looks on and she says:

We sit quiet in the midst of an enormous jerking masquerade. In silence and frenzy the shadows feast on us. They hollow out our skulls. We have returned, uncaring, into the keeping of the Dragon.

In the shorthand of myth the 'Dragon' is the oppression of old, the ancient threat which activates the events at the opening of Mackay Brown's masterpiece. The people have come full circle. History may be, like the ale pot, a heap of broken images on the floor of time but the human endeavour is to pick up those broken pieces and to recreate the pot, to re-imagine the story, to move on. The big field may also, in the end, prove to be just too big. The mixed arable farm undoubtedly is more sustainable and more productive because it depends upon diversity and not upon a single crop. In the future, however, it might too go the way of all things; it could conceivably not suit the human need of times to come in climate conditions we can only guess at. We might have to come to the sobering conclusion that in the future world of agriculture, in the 'Province of the Cat', that everything has to be crofting, eventually.

At Samhain now, as it passes, the shade of Donald Gunn walks these acres by my side. Between the living eloquence of the Dunnet Bay surf and the petrified silence of Dwarick Head he speaks kindly to me.

Chapter Five

ATOMIC CITY

In 1945 war ground to a halt across the planet with VE and VJ Day marking the end of hostilities in Europe and the Pacific and the world could begin to rebuild. In Thurso the activity of armed conflict and its related infrastructure went into suspended animation for ten years but come the mid-1950s it was reinstalled and re-activated once again. The metal dome of the nuclear reactor at Dounreay rose to the west of the town like a strange new temple. For many in Caithness who had made a good living from World Wars One and Two this seemed like a welcome return to normality and a logical continuation of business as usual. For others it was the beginning of a nightmare from which it would take over half a century to escape.

In Alistair MacLeod's novel *No Great Mischief* there is a scene of touching beauty when Calum Ruadh MacDonald, who in 1779 has crossed the Atlantic from the peninsula of Moidart in the West Highlands to Nova Scotia, gets off the ship after many weeks at sea and sets foot on the pier at Pictou. He breaks down and weeps. He weeps for two days and no-one knows what to do with him, so they just let him be to get it out of his system. When he left Scotland Calum Ruadh was a married man. When he arrives in Canada he his is both a widower and a grandfather. When he left Moidart he was a member of a community with a tightly knit culture shaped around a common language. In Nova Scotia he is a foreigner with a foreign tongue and from one end of the vast continent to the other he knows no-one. So he weeps. He acknowledges his weakness, his fate, his destiny, his history and he aches for the land and people he will never see again. He weeps for all of this, for his family who have survived and for his wife who has not. But mainly he weeps for himself because at that moment on the pier at Pictou he is the loneliest man in the world. Sometimes, when I look along the streets of Thurso, of Atomic City, the place of my birth, I feel like Calum Ruadh MacDonald.

Time passes. It is the beginning of February at the time of Imbolg and it is snowing. Imbolg in Gaelic means 'in the belly' and it is the time of celebrating the coming of spring and the pregnancy of the ewes. As I wander the pre-dawn streets of Thurso I see no signs of spring. According to the radio this morning inland districts are going to experience temperatures of −10. An easterly blows in from the Siberian Arctic, across the Baltic, over the North Sea and straight into my bones. There is no-one else about yet. Soon, however, the yellow jackets of the Dounreay day shift will illuminate fluorescently in the pale morning light and in the headlights of the busses and cars which flow as they do every morning from within Atomic City and without in a mechanical column along the A836. But now the snow dances like ghosts along Traill Street and into Olrig Street. The feckless streetlamps highlight this temporary haunting, allowing the wind to find an illuminated space to perform a twirl, a curtsey and a pirouette of blown snow to remind the few eyes who catch this moment that winter is not yet gone. This is the echo of a pre-industrial, pre-Christian candle-mass. Legend has it that if Imbolg is a bright and sunny day the White Cailleach of Winter will arise and leave her dwelling and gather firewood in order to prolong her season, but if Imbolg is a day of foul weather she will not venture out and is asleep and that winter will be nearly over.

It is still dark. I have risen early because not only is this the time of my birth this is the place of my birth and I am alone as is appropriate. As the Bard of Strathnaver, Rob Donn Mackay, wrote in 1771 of his own entry to the world:

Rugadh mis' anns a' gheamhradh
Measg nam beanntaidhnean gruamach
'S mo chiad sealladh den t-saoghal
Sneachd is gaoth mu mo chluasaibh;
On chaidh m'àrach ri aghaidh
Tir na deighe, gu tuathail,
Rinn mi luathaireach tuiteam
'S rinn mo chuislidhean fuaradh.

I was born in winter
among the lowering mountains
and my first sight of the world
snow and wind about my ears
since I grew up looking upon
a land of ice a northerly land
I declined early
and my veins chilled.

My mother always took great delight in telling me that when I was born two significant things happened: there was a great blizzard which resulted in her labour starting in the back of a car stuck in a snowdrift on the top of Clairdon Hill in the early hours of the morning and that after the birth all her teeth fell out. Also her hair turned white – to suit the weather no doubt. Whether my mother was the White Cailleach of Imbolg herself is a family secret and one she took with her to the grave. But my mother and her struggles and the challenges of her generation are firmly in my mind as I pull my collar up about my ears. I look up and a rook flies like a liquorice dart through the snow shower with a piece of twig in its beak. Is this a seasonal omen, a contradiction or a sign of not enough sleep? Or maybe it's the shape-changing Celtic goddess Brighid, whose time this also is, blessing the people with fertility as they sleep?

Another Gaelic Imbolg tradition is that:

> *Thig an nathair as an toll*
> *Là donn Brìde,*
> *Ged robh trì troighean dhen t-sneachd*
> *Air leac an làir.*

> The serpent will come from the hole
> On the brown Day of Bríde,
> Though there should be three feet of snow
> On the flat surface of the ground.

There is not quite 'three feet of snow' on the streets of Thurso as the dawn heaves itself over the cliff-ledge of the morning, in fact it is what we call a 'skifter', but in many ways my melancholy, my sense of sorrow, my '*coinniach*' or weeping, is a 'serpent' which walks beside me on the 'flat surface of the ground' as I navigate the rocky skerries of my memory. Atomic City, unlike Thurso, does not have a history because in many ways it is a work of fiction, so memory, however flawed and incomplete, will have to suffice for it. As the Czech novelist Milan Kundera has pointed out, 'The struggle of man against power is the struggle of memory against forgetting'.

It was not the United Kingdom Atomic Energy Authority, or before them the Ministry of War or the Ministry of Supply, or even the British post-war government who created the name 'Atomic City'. This was a mixture of the Co-operative Dairy and CB radio. In the late 1950s and early 60s when the housing estate at Pennyland and Castlegreen on the edge of Thurso was being built to provide accommodation for the legions of workers newly arrived to work at the Dounreay nuclear plant – and a period when the population of the town trebled – the 'Coapy', as it was known, had a problem in milk supply. Its operation had multiplied by two. So to keep matters of distribution simple some management genius stuck a sign bearing the legend 'Local' on one half of the fleet of milk carts and 'Atomics' on the other half. So those who lived in the brand new Authority houses to the south-west of the town became known as 'Atomicers' and their estate 'e Atomics'. Later when citizen band radios became normal in lorry cabs and taxis Thurso gained the handle of 'Atomic City'. Wick by contrast was known as 'The Big W' and the village of Keiss, for reasons I can only attach to deposits of seaweed at high tide, was called 'Smellytoon'.

Memory, of course, in relation to Atomic City, is a much more gregarious and entertaining beast than history and although the history of Thurso is long the written evidence of it is scarce. It is as though the town cannot bear to remember who or what it is. Now that Dounreay is being decommissioned and the future is a non-nuclear reality this search for identity has about it the peppery flavour of urgency.

This personal odyssey through the bending dimensional sea of time and space which is the 'Province of the Cat' has always been more in the way of testimony rather than history. History is confusingly specific and subjective, general and objective. It is also valuable. Sir Robert Gordon in the 17th century proved how much he valued the written historical record of Caithness – the 'muniments' according Iain Grimble – by destroying them. His mission to bring the earldom of the Sinclairs under the power of the Gordons in the same way as they has dispossessed the Sutherlands of Dunrobin and then the Mackays of Strathnaver was so threatened by the mere existence of a counter narrative that it had to be burned in 1623. No-one can argue for a history that does not exist. What happens then is that various myths, half-truths and assertions enter by the necessity of the state into the stream of remembered reality as the 'official' record: 'the' history. Unsatisfactorily history will always occupy that debatable land between subjectivity and objectivity and be used according to the needs and vicissitude of the times by whoever is likely to gain by the adoption of this narrative or that set of prejudices because that is how power is accrued, stored and administered. In this regard history can be no more trusted than my journey across the northern plateau of Caithness can be trusted – but a testimony, if it is anything, is a solemn attestation as to the truth of a matter. The word comes from the Latin 'testi' which refers to the notion of a third person, a disinterested witness. But I am not disinterested. Far from it. I am bound up in this place, with these people by blood and, yes, by history. This raises the question of whether 'truth' can be disinterested'. The truths – for there are more than one – I search for are psychological as well as political and as Herbert Marcuse has pointed out in *Eros and Civilisation* all 'Psychological categories have become political categories'. For a chronicler of impressions to give a testimony is as much a series of choices made and decisions taken as to what is to be remembered or recorded about who did what to whom, where, when and why because history is a set of impressions of the past equally as it is a construction of images of the present which, however they manage it, enter the human record. If I were to become the 'Angel of History' what I would see in front of me was my own people, struggling and dying on the threshing floor of time, caught up in the seemingly endless epic drama of human existence.

So in 1999 I wrote and staged a play called *Atomic City*. I had come back to Thurso to live a few years earlier, just after the Tory government of John Major had announced in 1994 that Dounreay would close and for good. The decommissioning deadline has now been set by the new site operators, Babcock International – or Babcock Cavendish as they have become – for the levelling of the site but in 1994 few in Caithness, certainly no-one I spoke to in Thurso, had an inkling of or an understanding about what decommissioning the nuclear reactors and associated plant at Dounreay meant. Later when the UKAEA gave way to the Nuclear Decommissioning Agency – both manifestations of the British government – the idea that the 'atomic dream' might be over had not sunk in. Even when Babcocks published their timescale in the John O Groat Journal stating the month and the year, March 2023, specifying when the site would be returned to nature as a 'green field site', the people of Atomic City could not accept or recognise the reality of closure. It was as if they were like the 18th century Australian aborigines in the dubious stories concerning Captain Cook, that the natives could not see his ship because it was too big when he anchored it in the bay and only noticed their presence when the crew took to the small-boats and rowed ashore – the notion being that Cook's ship was just too large and the native people had no visual memory by which they could 'see' it. The questions of scale and perception have always been both active and subterranean issues for the people of Caithness – and most directly of Thurso – when it has come to the reality of Dounreay, nuclear power and all that it means. As long as there was a job and the pay packet kept coming in then all was right with the world. For sixty years that was the narrative in Thurso. That is why it became Atomic City. That is why I wrote my play.

Dounreay has always been problematic due to the nuclear industry itself and its links to and origins in the military supply line have always been controversial, because they have been denied. Everyone who has ever looked at the history of nuclear energy in Britain knows that its primary purpose was to develop material for atomic weapons. It is the industrial child of Hiroshima and Nagasaki and the subsequent Cold War. What also makes it controversial is the implementation of the Official Secrets Act to every aspect of the nuclear industry, both civil and military. This makes it impossible and often illegal to have a rational and informed discussion about Dounreay or any other branch of the nuclear industry. By their insistence upon secrecy the British government have rendered that reality unreal by deeming it subjectively off-limits to those who have not been vetted by the state. This culture of state secrecy has had a strange nullifying effect on the majority of the people of Thurso. It is as if they live in two worlds – Dounreay/Thurso and that of the non-initiated. It also instils an unnatural passivity in the people. Their conversations and thought processes are stunted and shut down as a result. There are simply areas where conversation cannot venture. No-one can go into the Comm Bar on Traill Street and say, "How e ay night, Wullie. E hed a good day at yer work?" The Official Secrets Act demands that Wullie cannot tell you anything other than "Aye, fine." So the conversation goes somewhere else and in so doing the human-core, as opposed to reactor-core, existence of a man or a woman, of many men and many women since 1955, has become trivialised, deconstructed, compartmentalised and diminished. Psychologically they are constantly on guard, always ill at ease, as if half their life was an illusion. They become alienated and accept this alienation as normal. 'Psychological categories have become political categories'.

The Official Secrets Act cuts out a supply of information so there is no collective knowledge of what is actually going on. The people have been forced by legislation to live in a perennial now, where there is no past and there is no future, where there is, in fact, no history. So in the absence of information rumour fills that void, supplies the fuel for the reactor of energetic communication, of conversation, of community, of mutuality, which is the psychological and social benison of the human experience. Over the decades the people inhabit, through behaviour, a dream world where the central reality of everyday life is signified by the externals of the material world – by salary, by property and possessions, by holidays and leisure. Because meaning has been stripped from doing, in as much as on-site activity is a semi-mystery to the majority who work at Dounreay and a complete mystery to those outside the fence, so any chance of a cultural life has been denuded or redacted from the possible lived agenda of those who sign the Act. The politicisation of ordinary people in this way, without any expectation that they will engage in actual political activity and an unstated but nonetheless implied encouragement that they do not, is a denial of human rights and would be viewed if it happened in a pre-1989 Eastern European country as the expected repressive behaviour of a totalitarian state.

I did not want to write a play about Dounreay and I did not want, either, to write an ant-nuclear tract. What I desired to do was to write a pro-life drama which highlighted and showed to the audience, through the passions of a set of characters, the experience of the people of Caithness from the time when Dounreay first came to now, whenever that 'now' is. The theatre, also, lives in a constant 'now' so the beauty of the art form is that 'now' can be anytime because every time is 'now', both past and future. The difference between the 'now' of a state regulated secret society and the 'now' of the theatre is that in the theatre everyone is engaged in change, in a search for resolution in a highly charged, passionate arena which is totally open, where everything can be seen and secrecy banished, where a society can look at and debate with itself, where speech is free. Under the Official Secrets Act everything is ordained to stay the same and nothing can be said. This goes against nature. What transpired was that I wrote a portrait of – and a kind of love song to – Thurso. Like most honest love songs it was not recognised as such.

For most people who do not know the far north the idea of Dounreay, if it is anything, is some kind of big dome-like shop, or a power station, or a large, sinister building of some kind. What I would say is that there is the actuality of the Dounreay site and then there is a state of mind. The actual site is enormous and has on it not one but three reactors. There is the Dounreay Materials Test Reactor, the Dounreay Fast Reactor (the dome) and the Dounreay Prototype Fast Reactor, the PFR. Next door to all of this is HMS *Vulcan*, a Ministry of Defence establishment with two nuclear reactors, PWR1 and PWR2, which are used in the testing of nuclear submarine propulsion. It is operated on behalf of the MOD and the Royal Navy by Rolls Royce. It is due to be scaled down in 2015 and then for eventual closure. Like Dounreay it is prone to radiation leaks and secrecy and also like Dounreay it has been overtaken by computers and technology. HMS *Vulcan* lies to the immediate west of Dounreay. To the east, some three miles away, was sited the United States Navy Base at Forss. This was an acoustic telescope, one of the largest in Europe, used for tracking Soviet submarines in the Atlantic. It had a satellite station at Murkle which is three miles to the east of Thurso. The base at Forss closed after the Berlin Wall came down and Soviet bloc subsequently fell apart. This in Caithness was not seen as a triumph of capitalism over communism or as the success of freedom over totalitarianism: this was an economic disaster. When the US government shut its base with it into the sump of history went the actual purpose for Dounreay's existence, to the accompaniment of each hammer blow to the dividing edifice in Berlin.

But there we had, for the best part of fifty years, three of the horsemen of the apocalypse. This, the politicians kept telling us, was what kept us free in our democracy and allowed us to enjoy the benefits of consumer capitalism. We, in the words of Harold MacMillan, 'had never had it so good'. Harold Wilson followed on from this, declaring that the 'white hot heat of technology' would be what would drive our democracy, fuel our economy and develop our society. In Thurso it created a social, political and financial bubble which had little bearing on the real world and in fact was cocooned from it, which is why the population currently have no idea what is actually happening to them and have no inner psychological resources to deal with it. Change, that poetic language and constant impulse of the theatre, is a thing they have no real or immediate experience of and do not understand. Since 1955 everything has been the same. Now everything is different. The futuristic technology of the DFR and the PFR is now just so much rusting piping and nuclear junk. Half a century of developing a nuclear industry through vast amounts of tax payers' money has resulted in, when it comes to nuclear waste, burying it in the ground. Which is what will happen at Buldoo, a site just beside Dounreay, where several modern burial mounds – nuclear silos – will join the ancient Neolithic and Iron Age burial mounds which grace Caithness. Just south of Dounreay on the Hill of Shebster a recent survey involving laser scans from an aeroplane has detected some three hundred significant archaeological sites, some dating back over 3,000 years and these, on *Cnoc Freiceadain* – the hill of the watch or watching – are structures similar to the long grey cairns of Camster which are the finest examples of their kind found anywhere. The mounds at Buldoo, however, will not contain pottery or the charred remains of our ancestors but will house highly radioactive substances which no-one will be advised to go near for several thousand years. That is the legacy. That is how Dounreay will be remembered.

Far from making us secure in our safe North European home what in fact the siting of all that hardware on Caithness's north coast meant was that we were rendered vulnerable. In fact we were a second strike target for the Soviets in any nuclear war scenario, except we would not be counted as casualties – in the event of any nuclear proliferation the entire population would be considered as military personnel. Even in death we would be redacted. This concept was never taught to us at Thurso High School where everything nuclear was shown in a rosy light and where we were told that the electricity it – Dounreay – produced would be so cheap it would be free. Why on earth otherwise perfectly sensible teachers expected us to believe all this is a mystery? But then again the entire education I 'received' at Thurso High School was a mystery to me.

Although Thurso has a long and fascinating history my relationship with it has always been tangential as well as specific – I came here to be born. Not quite 'slouching to Bethlehem' to reference Yeats but, as

I've pointed out, rather dragged through a snow drift. I also came to the town to attend High School and this for me was earth shattering. I remember my first day at assembly. There were over a thousand pupils in attendance. I had just come from Dunnet Primary School where there were four in my class and around twenty in the whole school: I had never seen 1,000 people in one place before. I do not think, if I am honest, that I have ever recovered. It was also like going to another country. Yes, there were plenty of Caithness accents but there were also many English accents and of different hues, intonations and origins so that I found it hard to understand what was being said. Eventually, as children do, I adapted to this. But one thing I did not cope with, and it has been a subsequent problem for me all my life, was the alien culture the school operated and promoted. Learning here was functionary. You were encouraged to compete, to be good at sports, to join a 'house', to get a job at Dounreay or to go to university if you were lucky or bright. Looking back now, through the prism of forty years, I realised I was being designed to become something other. Everything local was looked down upon. We had no history, no literature, no culture. To be educated meant being educated out of your locality and into the amorphous soup of the nuclear world. I was instructed to abandon my language as it had no value, with the same result which my father's people had to learn to live without Gaelic. I, along with every other Caithness child, was expected to abandon their self, their life. Often I convince myself that I learned nothing whatsoever at Thurso High School. There were a couple of teachers who did try to connect but the history being taught wasn't my history and the literature on offer was somebody else's story. My reaction to all this, I realise now, is part of the 'weeping' of history. It is something that when I think on it still makes me very angry because I deserved better than that, as every child does, and it is true also to say that while education in Scotland now is not perfect it is better than the nothing I was given.

This, of course, is partly my own fault and I recognise that. I also recognise the strengths and weaknesses of the auto-didact which is so gracefully absent in my wife and I must confess I am jealous of her university education because her mind is trained whereas mine runs along a beach of a thread of thought like a great horse or lands clumsily on the roof of a problem like a giant drunk bird. The evidence is here, in the way this book is written which is scatological and random and enough to make any self-respecting editor pull their hair out. I could fantasise about doing something about it, becoming more academic, or studying for a degree in Scottish Literature or in Theatre at a university but that, I suspect, would be waste of everybody's time. In reality it is too late. I try to impress upon myself the need for humility but there is such a hole in Scottish literature and theatre which isn't being filled and the more they tell us how wonderful everything is in poetry, prose and drama the more I smell a rat and the bigger the hole gets. My arrogance is that I think I can fill that hole – every writer does I suppose – and it would be comical if it wasn't true. Just because something is true doesn't make it right. I am well equipped to see how ridiculous this is. I think it is better to contemplate an otter than it is to contemplate one's navel. The otter I see on the river bank, thank goodness, doesn't give a damn one way or the other.

At the end of my first day at Thurso High School I remember it was very hot as we trooped out in our columns to the various buses which would take us, the country bairns, home. Everyone was excited, confused and amongst the noise of the hundreds of young voices there were pockets of stillness as the more sensitive, delicately disposed or plain shy tried to make sense of what had just happened to them. These were generally the ones from the smaller country schools. As our bus left Thurso and pulled over Clairdon we could see the shimmering blue of Dunnet Bay in the distance. The sun was still high in the August sky and the barley crop baked in the fields. As we came through The Planting at Castletown and emerged from the trees to turn to take the links road to Dunnet the bay looked immense and a deep indigo-blue with the white of the thundering surf giving the scene an added grandeur. The beach curved yellow, north to the village. When the bus pulled up outside the shop we pupils eagerly hopped off. As if by some hidden, unsaid signal I found myself surrounded by the three other ones who had made up primary seven at Dunnet and who, like me, had undergone the same transitional, alienating, process. Without a word we walked down the road to the beach with the roaring of the surf drawing us on. Then we were running. Then we were on the sand with the sun on our backs and the four of us – two boys and two girls – were sprinting towards the water, articles of clothing flying off behind us as we tried to undress and run at the same time. Then we were in the water, in the friendly, reassuring surf, naked as far as I remember, in our own sea. We were home, almost beyond home, as if we were seeking, together, some comfort and protection from what we all knew so well, so instinctively. As the water washed over our bodies we were all laughing, crying almost, glad beyond expression to be back in the place of our origin, in our village, in the sea, somewhere we had all known from our first days of life.

Dounreay, *Dùrath* in Gaelic, means 'fort of the elongated place or mound'. The area is rich in Neolithic and Iron Age sites as I have mentioned and the recent surveying by wind farm companies proves. Since the 1950s there has been no fortification capable of stemming the tide of all things nuclear – Caithness is now going to be the 'home' of the 'National Nuclear Archive' – with all levels of local politicians queuing up to impersonate the three monkeys when Dounreay is discussed. The price paid is cultural as well as industrial. In a very perceptive article in the Scotsman in the mid-1960s, to mark the first ten years of Dounreay the nuclear plant, Magnus Magnusson interviewed the late Dr Donald Grant, the then recently retired rector of the newly built Thurso High School. Magnusson asked him what changes he had seen over this 'first atomic decade'? Dr Grant mentioned the increase in population, the economic impact, but mainly he said it had changed the education the children received at secondary school and how they behave culturally.

"We now have more of an English educational system," said Dr Grant, "with subject specialisation and the dropping of the generalist approach. Traditionally in Caithness education, knowledge was really the only way to better yourself and it was held in high regard because of this. Now there is more of an emphasis on competition, on team sports such as rugby – previously unknown in Caithness – and on identification with school 'houses' as opposed to community."

Light slowly grinds itself into existence to the north-east, bleeding into being over Weydale Hill. The snow corkscrews itself along Rotterdam Street. Some of the shops, the fish shop and the three bakers, have their lights on. Atomic City is waking up to Imbolg. I desperately need a cup of coffee but my house sits on top of Ormlie Hill and I find myself facing down the High Street towards the sea. I pass the Town Hall, now a ritzy, hi-tech, heritage centre called Caithness Horizons where extracts from some of my poems are displayed on the walls like messages from another world. In that building, when it was the old Thurso Town Hall, in 1999, my play *Atomic City* was performed for three nights. It was packed out every night with some 300 people at each performance desperate to see and hear just what it was all about. I was told later that practically all the middle and senior management of the United Kingdom Atomic Energy Authority had attended. Some in disguise, if the rumours are to be believed. At that time the *derigueur* weather protection for all on-site employees was a red waterproof jacket. There is a line in the play, 'And the process workers lined up at the bar like redcoats after Culloden'. Three months after the play was done and dusted the uniform of the redcoats had turned to yellow. The same yellow coats that I see now as the first shift bus passes. Everyone is asleep. Their heads nodding in rubbery unison as they turn the corner from Traill Street into Olrig Street. The same somnambulence will afflict them come five o'clock when the bus will turn the other way on its way to Castletown, or Halkirk or Wick, or somewhere deep in the atomic heart of the 'Province of the Cat'.

The early morning otter, fishing with the ease of Mephistopheles, is far from asleep. He has a trout by the head on the bank across from Seg Mackay's fish shop. Little wafts of snow blow around his sleek frame, highlighting him as though he were in a painting by Breughel. The river flows past in a peaty stream. Occasionally a piece of ice the size of a dinner plate floats past. This river is why Thurso is here. It is '*Skinandi*', or 'the shining one' as the first Norse raiders called it. The river gives the town its name. It is '*Thor sa*' or 'Thor's town' or more prosaically 'bull's crossing' as there must have been an ancient ford where the river is now crossed by the road bridge. The river gives Thurso its purpose. It gives it its beauty. If I were to worship anything it would be this river. The otter seems to agree. He has dispatched the trout and slides back into the icy flow like a small torpedo. If the river gives the town its character then the otter gives the river its poetry. The surf crashes in at Thurso East, the tons of water breaking on the flagstone shore, where the Vikings pulled up their longships, with the crescendo of some vast appreciative audience. I look along the deserted quays. The otter is gone. A pair of gormless Herring Gulls try to murder each other over a small mussel.

The Official Secrets Act fits perfectly into a society which does not know its past. History is what happened yesterday as well as what happened in 1623. History is the knowledge of the future even when that knowledge, strictly, is impossible. But how can any society have a conversation with itself or anyone else when it does not know what it is because it does not know where it came from? This 'alienation effect' as Brecht would have it is strange in Caithness because the place is all about history, even if, as I have said, my version of it is more of a testimony. Of course, this is the same for anyone in any place if they care about that place and acknowledge that their sources are limited. Or it should be. The theatre, I have found, is the presented history of everything because it is about people coming together, of which history is the record. Rumour, on the other hand, is the gossip of history. Rumour was not there, it did not turn up, the events are un-acted, unseen and its story is third hand. For many people in Thurso the State has insisted that they cannot inhabit their own lives, that they cannot act out the events of their recent or immediate past, let alone their 'history'. This is what tragedy is. It is an internal alienation. Unlike the Roman poet Ovid exiled in 8 AD to the shores of the Black Sea by the Emperor Augustus, the citizens of Atomic City are exiled within themselves. Ovid died nine years later, still in exile at Tomis in Romania, but the internal reality of a human being is where life is to be realised and enjoyed, not endured because the new 'Empire' has channelled your consciousness in a certain direction or decreed what you can and cannot say. We have to be free to be alive and to act now or the future is impossible. For we are all characters in the dramas of our own lives. When we enter onto the stage of the 'now' we come from memory, from the past. When we are here, in the 'now', we inhabit the present through our primary emotions which are happiness, sadness, fear, anger, surprise, disgust and the unknown or subjective emotions which originate in dream or instinct. When we exit the stage of this brief experience we go into the future which is the imagination – not ours, but of others. If we cannot live fully now and engage all our primary emotions without external restraint then we will diminish the future generations ability to trust memory, to understand the past and therefore limit their imagination, hem in their future. As Walter Benjamin wrote: 'Memory is not an instrument for exploring the past but its theatre. It is the medium of past experience, as the ground is the medium in which dead cities lie interred.'

To walk through Thurso as the snow is falling is to walk out of the past and into memory, but the 'now' I see around me as the morning progresses is somehow unknown. I have come from Thurso into Atomic City and I am returning to Thurso, to the future, to the imagination. This theatre, the memory, is a strange performance.

The otter has popped his head out of the water. He has something. A small crab. He munches it, shell and all, lying on his back, swimming. Otters have such high metabolisms that they must eat all the time. With the flick of a crab claw and a shake of his whiskers, he slips beneath the surface of the water. Little spots of snow fall on the ever moving crown of the river. The otter is heading out to sea and it is only when you are on the sea, or on top of Dunnet Head looking west on a clear day, do you really get a sense of what Thurso actually is: a Highland town at the mouth of a Highland river sitting on a bay between two headlands. The rolling hills of West Caithness merge into the mountains of Sutherland. Klibreck, Ben Loyal and Ben Hope loom over the top of Thurso like giants and you can see that the water flows from them through the straths and down to the sea and that the people follow them, from the hills and from the sea, and the logical place both topographically and culturally for them to land up is Thurso. Dunnet Head stands like a sandstone wall to the east and the breakwater of Holborn Head shelters Thurso bay from the West. Scrabster – '*Skarabólstaðr*' in Norse or '*Sgrabastal*' in Gaelic – sits snug in the lee of Holborn and has become, over the many centuries, the principal port for Caithness, supplanting the old harbour at the river mouth from which Thurso grew.

There has been human activity around the mouth of the Thurso River from the beginnings of recorded time and the fertile land of the strath which follows the river to its source beyond Loch More has yielded evidence of agriculture dating back to Neolithic times. This increased greatly as technology evolved and the Stone Age made the transition to the Bronze Age. To the east and west of Thurso lie, undiscovered, some of the most ancient and significant cultural sites such as burial barrows, cairns and mounds, settlements and artefacts. Is it just indifference that allows the heather to grow over our history? In Caithness, literally, the people do 'come out of the ground'. If we could begin to liberate our past from the prison of neglect and the enclosed acres of landowners then some of the unanswered questions and unconnected threads, when it comes to cultural tourism and economics, might be answered and joined together, for Thurso is exactly that point within Caithness where the unrecorded and recorded history, where the Gaelic and the Norse cultures, come together and where the 'dead cities lie interred'.

Just as the early Neolithic people who built the long grey cairns and raised the stone circles gave way to the Beaker People who left us their burial mounds and field systems, the Iron Age civilisation who constructed the impressive brochs gave way to the first arrivals of the Brythonic Picts who established a sturdy Celtic culture in the Far North. Such are the human waves which roll up on the beach of history. At the western edge of the Pentland Firth, with a fresh water river and a natural harbour, Thurso was always, will always be, a prime site for settlement. The town grew out of the sea like a stone flower and since 1125 its main architectural bloom has been the magnificent St Peter's Kirk, which in actual fact became a cathedral when it was rebuilt and extended by Bishop Gilbert Murray in 1223 after his predecessor, Bishop Adam, was boiled alive by an angry mob in Halkirk in 1222 for raising taxes. The stark grey ruin with its padlocked gate which greets me as I shuffle past, as countless other sets of feet have done over the centuries, is a reminder of this denuding business of not having access, literally, to our past. For the 'cathedral' is the centre of the old Viking town of Thurso which stretches from the river mouth up through the litany of ancient, forgotten names of closes and wynds, long levelled by one 'improving' local authority after the other: The Auld Howe, the Hossag and the Hossag Peel, Stripag, the Ellan, Coogait, Booragtoon and the Black Gutter. This lost music, these names which lie under the footprint of town planners and shape-changing cultural distortionists, I hear it in the wind as it blows in off the sea and over the roof of the old Marine Hotel. I see the people in their home-spun hoddan grey clothes and their rillens, their rough leather boots, on their feet. They are beside me now. It was for the benefit of these people that Bishop Gilbert translated the Psalms and the Gospels into Gaelic which, as Calder in his *History of Caithness* grudgingly admits, 'it may be inferred that in this time the Gaelic was the common dialect of the both Sutherland and Caithness'. The same people who, in the mid-18th century, would take their cattle up to the shielings in the hills behind the town in June and at milking time would sing to the cows in their native tongue which was Gaelic – the Gaelic 'which was never spoken in Caithness' – and according to Dr John Henderson in his *Agricultural View of the County (of Caithness)* published in 1812, 'the cows listened (to) with apparent attention and pleasure'.

The Fisherbiggins, which shivers beneath its Highland Council harling, at least bears the shape and form of the early medieval town in which many Haralds, Thorfinns, Hakons and Magnuses would have recognised as they leaped from their longboats to love, eat, drink to the point of fighting so that sometimes these heroes would be dispatched to Valhalla by a blade or a club in one of the many ale houses for which Thurso was famous. The *Orkneyinga Saga* may be a chronicle of the Earls of Orkney and it might proclaim its regal intent by beginning with a description of the creation of the world but it also displays its humanity through its sketches of the less aristocratic habits of the ordinary people. Many a Norseman came to grief in a Thurso alehouse.

If Caithness, as I have claimed and as is obvious to those except the most Anglo-prejudiced, is the place in Scotland which can justly claim to be where the Norse and the Celtic cultures meld, then within that claim it is physically here, where the River Thurso meets the Pentland Firth and in Thurso where that melding is culturally and physically made manifest. Nowhere else can you cross from the Gaelic west to the Viking east by crossing a river. Thurso or '*Thirsa*' as it is in Caithness Scots, or '*Inbhir Theòrsa*' in Gaelic – all these names and more, the old town 'holds them all. Atomic City is a late arrived bird and nervously sits a-top the stone flower of the town. The newly created sump-estate of High Ormlie shakes her dowdy feathers of cheap housing with impatience. Few of the residents of Thurso's latest expansion are there by choice. It is as if the inhabitants of the saga-town have trekked through time and camped at the beginning of a new century like so many refugees from history. Their language, as it radiates around them from the cultural hub of their satellite TVs, has become strange and unknown even to themselves. When your language, as well as your economic power, has been taken from you then you are truly 'decommissioned'.

I have gone now as far as I can go. I stand at the end of the pier at the river mouth. The light is flooding into the February sky from the great estuary of the north-east where the sun rises. Reds and purples cup the undulating tops of the Clairdon and Olrig hills and everything becomes more apparent, as if history comes to life in the Imbolg dawn which, of course, it does. The dark towering cliffs of Hoy, north across the firth with the hills which bestride Rackwick, turn from a deep claret colour to a bright orange as the sandstone drinks in and holds the light. The thin snow still dances on the easterly wind and as I look west I see the ocean heave itself against the buttress of Holborn Head. Scrabster shelters beneath its braes. Floodlights shine down as the construction of the new pier approaches completion. This is part of the general hope that Caithness will, somehow, 'benefit' from the oil fields west of Shetland and from the development of the Pentland Firth as a tidal energy producer, the much vaunted 'Saudia Arabia of renewable energy' as proclaimed by Alex Salmond, Scotland's ebullient ex-First Minister.

The quest to replace the two thousand jobs 'lost' at Dounreay is the constant obsession of the politicians and business leaders. They have developed retrospective planning into a cross between an art form and an exercise in civic panic. For Caithness the oilfield aspiration has come twenty years too late and as far as the renewable energy business is concerned a mixture of self-serving by the Crown Estate and a lack of actual political foresight and of investment form both the Scottish and UK governments means that, so far, the only real beneficiaries from tidal stream energy will be the usual suspects of big utility companies and, of course, the Crown Estate and the Exchequer in London. As to how this is all going to manifest itself no-one seems to know. Just as the little shards of ice flow down the river impersonating icebergs this mixture of hot air and incompetence is what passes for politics and economics in the modern world of the 'Province of the Cat'.

The importance of the 'Scrabster roads' to Thurso is a constant throughout its history. The sea-road for centuries was the only 'road' in and out of the Far North. It is from the sea where the hardy voyagers of history first saw Thurso. What they saw was a town which has one of the most beautiful settings in Europe. Most modern visitors either come by road or rail and what they first see is the back of the town. They are, literally, coming to Thurso from the wrong direction. The impression of the place is therefore diminished. The grandeur of the setting is not perceived and this business of perception is so vital to our progression into the future, into the imagination. The ongoing tragedy for Thurso is that from the beginning of the 20th century the place has been repeatedly seen the wrong way round. From the end of the 18th and throughout the 19th century the view, for many, was of a Scotland receding into the distance as yet another vessel crammed with Highland *émigrés* left Scrabster for Canada or the Carolinas. Seen from Holborn or Dunnet Head their white sails would slowly disappear over the horizon into the north-west Atlantic.

It's almost daylight now as I walk along from the Fisherbiggins and west towards the Salvation Army building. Several dog-walkers parade their pride and joy along the esplanade above the beach. A braver few combat the elements on the sand itself. I remember once a few years ago, before the Town Hall was converted into Caithness Horizons, I had occasion to be in the rooms which were once occupied by the old Thurso Town Council and the County Court. On the wall was a large black and white photograph taken, I guessed, before World War One. It was taken from Thurso East looking west over the town and towards Scrabster. The place in the photograph was made entirely from stone. What light there was reflected off slate and flagstone roofs. The town I was looking at was a smaller, tidier version of Thurso than is extant now. The town was almost entirely west of the river. Around the old harbour, where several sloops leaning against the harbour wall because of the low tide, the buildings rose up and fell away around St Peters like chickens around a mother hen. Streets spanned west and south in an easy line of solid masonry punctuated by spires. This indeed was Thurso but the town I was looking at in the photograph was very beautiful. It possessed none of the romantic appeal of French or Italian villages of similar sizes. Here was a place that contained practicality of purpose as well as humility in design. It also perhaps lacked the drama of similar Scandinavian settlements but it looked back at me for what it was: a market town, a port and a place where people lived and worked and if the photograph had been in colour then the various shades of stone and their infinite varieties of reflected light would have been a marvel to the eye and an easy compliment to the painted colours of sister harbour towns across the North Sea in Norway. It certainly had an equal aesthetic claim to beauty as the quite rightly admired port of Stromness in Orkney with its stone nousts and narrow wynds and closes. It was an exquisite moment of a magnificent place captured at a particular time. Ninety-eight percent of what I was looking at, from the Fisherbiggins to the corner of Olrig Street and Traill Street, is gone. It has been destroyed.

As I walk along Rotterdam Street the snow has turned to hailstones. The shops are now almost all open. The fierce tiny balls of hail in their short lived anarchic frenzy rattle along the carefully laid paving-stones of the pedestrian precinct. Early morning shoppers or people going to their work pass each other in half-recognised urgency and for all that the electrical shop has a window full of flat screen TVs and the occasional passer-by is talking into a mobile phone this could easily be the early 1960s when the most sophisticated thing Liptons could sell you was an avocado pear. On the corner of Rotterdam Street beside the traffic lights Dounreay Site Restoration Limited – or 'Dounreay dot com' as they are known – has an office. Like almost everything attached to the nuclear industry the interior of the office is very smart and corporate looking. As I press my nose briefly against the large double glazed window the lights shine brightly and I can see desks, plants, leather seats, computers, phones but no sign of human life. There is a poster on the notice board informing anyone who reads it about the Dounreay Social Fund and how you or your community group can apply for cash for a project. What it doesn't tell you is that Babcocks have closed the fund down last October just as the company have withdrawn from anything which is concerned with 'social and economic benefit'. For the lead contractor in the decommissioning of Dounreay everything is about price. It is not their business, they would say, to 'replace' the two thousand 'lost' jobs at Dounreay.

I walk on a little further and as I look up at my old theatre company office which sat like an insurrectionary cell on the top third story of the building. I see four individual posters which occupy most of a window on the ground floor looking out on Traill Street. One by one they read 'Down', 'Devoured', 'Dismantled', 'Demolished'. These then must be four of the dimensions of 'Decommissioning'. I think of Walter Benjamin, the German Marxist philosopher, pursued from Paris by Nazis at the beginning of World War Two and dead by his own hand in an obscure hotel room in a Catalonian mountain town. I think of Calum Ruadh in Alistair MacLeod's novel, alone and weeping on a Nova Scotia pier in 1779. One a reality the other a fiction but both instruments 'for exploring the past', each a kind of ending and beginning, an exit and an entrance, like the never ending circle of Celtic mythology – two patterns forever crossing over. Beside the posters of the 'four Ds' there is a smaller one from an amateur group advertising a performance of Handel's *Messiah*. How fitting that a nuclear congregation which has lost its religion is waiting for the employment miracle which will never come. If a new Jesus of energy walked the streets of 21st century Thurso, passing on parables of wind, wave and tide he would be crucified on Druimhollistan, as the old Mackay cattle thieves used to be, quicker than Babcocks can whisper 'plutonium'. Alternative energy is a fatal heresy in this nuclear Vatican town.

Here in Atomic City is the theatre of my memory. Sixty years of living off a false dream has resulted in four posters on a wall declaring their alliterating termination of the present set of circumstances, that the certainties are no more. Here is a town which is awakening from the ground of its own earth-bed to find that, in fact, it is its own ruin.

When you look along Traill Street, past Sir John's Square, with its sycophantic statues, to Sinclair Street and the classic facade of the public library and the Millar Academy primary school beyond you are looking along the spine of Sir John Sinclair of Ulbster's stone dream. This, it is claimed, is the jewel in the crown of north Highland architecture, a mini Edinburgh New Town in the north. This development was on-going from the late18th century and throughout the 19th. This then is the Enlightenment in Caithness, rationalism in street dimensions and reason in the grid-like layout which speaks of the modern world. Gone are the medieval confusions of Shore Street and Booragtoon. Here is achievement, confidence, sophistication and it speaks of the benefits of aristocratic patronage, of the liberal *laisser faire* capitalism, of empire and the Queen and all that is good with the world.

Thurso, however, was never as well dimensioned as that. From the 13th century when King William the Lion of Scotland marched an army to Scrabster where he destroyed the castle as part of his campaign against Earl Harald of Orkney, who had cut out the tongue and put out the eyes of the then Bishop John (popular legend relates that Harald nailed the Bishop's tongue to a plank as well as slicing off both his ears), to the various clan raids and skirmishes, to Cromwell's troopers watering their horses in the river in the middle of the 17th century, Thurso has always been a town of rough edges and dangerous corners. This is because it has always been a market town, a place where men from all the airts and pairts have come to buy and sell cattle and with many ale-houses for them to quench their thirst or let off steam. By the late 18th century over 3,000 head of cattle a year would pass through the town. With the constant availability of cash and with plenty of places to spend it Thurso, throughout time, has always been home to a population who, on whatever provocation or sensed injustice, could, as their ancestors had done in 1222, easily rise up and boil a bishop.

The harbour was also a busy place and while white fishing was always a thriving if subsistence occupation in Thurso the main industry around the river mouth concerned itself with the export of grain and as early as 1700 around 864 tonnes is recorded to have left the quay. This productivity of grain – bere and barley – eventually brought to boil the constant tension between the pastoral, cattle culture of the majority who were cottars and the landed minority who, as the 18th century turned into the 19th, increasingly desired to extend their interests and maximise their wealth.

The Sinclairs of Thurso East, Sir George Sinclair and his son, the 'improving' Sir John, were classic examples of feudal overseers turned respectable squires in the English model. Or at least on the surface that is what they presented to the world. Beneath the leather gloves and the cotton and silk shirts was the same old iron fist of centuries of entitlement and the beating robber-baron heart of the Normans.

The payment of rent by the peasant to the laird was generally in kind. The grain exported, however, belonged solely to the landowners. As the 17th century turned into the 18th the cottars were expected to till, sow and harrow Lord Thurso's land as well as cut his peats and to provide the castle at Thurso East with poultry, lamb, butter, cheese and any other produce the proprietor demanded from the tenant. The population of Thurso were also expected to harvest the crops of their 'superiors'. If they did not do so they could be punished by the medieval application of 'poinding of the tongs or best blanket'. This was a form of torture quite common to the state of 'vassalage' the people 'enjoyed'. Sir John's mother Lady Janet was very keen on this practice and a drummer was sent around the town to 'tuck' the vassals to their feudal tasks. Even Calder, the great respecter of the Victorian status quo, remarked in his cap doffing 'History':

> How the poor people contrived to live under all these burdens is not a little surprising to us at the present day (1863). The conditions of the slaves in America and the West Indies was infinitely preferable. And yet, as the balance of happiness is pretty nearly equal in all conditions of society, we have no reason to think that they were without their own share of comforts and enjoyments of life.

Happiness is a relative concept when you are near to starvation and as far as a 'share' is concerned 'the poor people' would recognise King Lear's reproach to his daughter Cordelia – 'Nothing comes from nothing – think again!'

Despite the recent half century of conformity Thurso has never been a place which housed a people who were shy to express their grievances. These were the people who thought it only fair to remind a bishop as to iniquities of over taxation so the hectoring demands of a Sinclair aristocrat with a drummer could only be tolerated up to a point. From Dr Henderson's most revealing history we learn that 'the rigidly enforced vassalage' met with a singular revolution when 'at length a sturdy citizen named Sandy Murray put an end to it by driving his staff through the drum and daring the drummer to tell Lady Janet that he had done so.'

Towards the end of the 18th century the gulf between the cottars and the landlords had grown proportionally as the value and concept of property increased. These tensions heightened as land enclosure inevitably led to destitution becoming common. The herring boom of Wick throughout the 19th century cushioned much of Caithness, especially the eastern districts, against the poverty and unemployment which was bleeding the Highlands of its population but as Thurso was in the west of the county and was, essentially, a Highland town, hunger and emigration was experienced much more acutely in the old 'Thirsa' than in the newly forming herring metropolis of Pulteneytown. The 1820s and 30s saw many ships leave the Scrabster roads with their ragged and gaunt human cargoes preparing themselves as best they could for the unknown as they tried to escape the unbearable.

In 1846 the potato crop succumbed to disease and by 1847 the atmosphere in Thurso was highly charged as hungry eyes watched shipment after shipment of grain leave for the south. The grain carts were brought to the quay at Thurso harbour under the armed guard of soldiers from two companies of the 76th Regiment and later by the 27th Foot – the Inniskillens. The British Empire yet again implemented the divide and rule principle it employed throughout the world – to get peasants of a similar culture with weapons to oppress their brother and sister peasants who have none. In Thurso the soldiers were attacked and the mob driven off at bayonet point and in Wick some squaddies from the 76th opened fire on a crowd, wounding a man and a girl. The Thurso river estuary-mouth was blockaded by small boats and a crowd 'invaded' a Leith grain-ship. There were marches and demonstrations around the town and people even assembled on Dunnet Sands to protest against the iniquity.

The Corn Laws, which these desperate events were the result of were implemented in 1812 and consolidated as the Importation Act of 1815 and were not repealed until 1849. The Act was designed to maximise the profits of the landowners who were the principal grain producers and to increase their representation in the House of Commons. In Caithness there was not the same constituency of opposition to the Corn Laws from a rising industrial class as there was in the south of Scotland and in England. Artificially high grain prices meant that the industrialist could not maximise their profits as they had to keep wages high in order that their workers could afford bread. The new capitalists of industry, it should be emphasised, were not primarily concerned with the welfare of the poor in their clamour to change the law. The subsequent unemployment and mass emigration from country to town which followed the repeal of the Corn Laws did not overly concern them. Indeed they benefited as there was more available and cheap labour for their factories. After 1850 they became champions of a brand new concept – the free market. Never was an idea so crammed with irony.

It is a measure of the great distance real political change still has to travel to reach the shores of the Pentland Firth that the patterns set by the Corn Laws continue to shape contemporary society in the 'Province of the Cat'. It is an indictment of modern Scottish politics that a hereditary peer can represent the Far North of Scotland as an MP, despite the fact that he has claimed to have renounced his title of Viscount Thurso and given up his seat in the Lords and changed his name, in somewhat comic fashion, from Lord John Sinclair to 'John Thurso'. He has not given over his vast estates to community ownership or redistributed his considerable wealth and shows no signs of doing so, or that he has considered the contradiction his position represents. The relationship between wealth and power is a child of the Corn Laws and the seed of all subsequent and future discontents which will only increase and grow until that corrupting umbilical cord is cut. The fact that John 'Thurso' Sinclair lost his seat in the SNP tsunami the General Election of 2015 does not redesign this paradigm.

Sir John Sinclair of Ulbster had no industrial barons to combat so instead he turned his attention, through a series of mad-cap schemes, to turning Caithness into a model community, the ideal of which remained firmly in his imagination. In reality his Malthusian enterprises resulted in emigration and hunger for many powerless people and the enclosure of the common lands delivered an increase of arable acreage of which he claimed title. As Walter Benjamin noted in an essay in 1931, 'The destructive character knows only one watchword – make room. And only one activity: clearing away. His need for fresh air and open space is stronger than any hatred.'

From the profits of the Corn Laws, through the upheavals of World Wars One and Two, the organisation, socialisation and the political pacification of the people led directly to the imposition of Dounreay on a community that had no political structures in place or psychological stamina left to resist. Modernity had robbed them of their spontaneity and their tradition of direct action. Political parties had emerged from the Machiavellian shape-changing at the beginning of the 19th century to absorb the potential but dormant power of the majority. From Viking times, through the Middle Ages and the various raids of the feuding clans, to the press gangs of the Napoleonic War, the people of the Far North had always nurtured a spirit of resistance and maintained a necessary and cultural mutuality. Now, come the middle of the 20th century, they were left exposed, urbanised and exploited in a way they had never encountered before and were, above all else, vulnerable.

—

I move towards the rising sun and cross the bridge from the *Gàidhealtachd* to the *Ghalltachd*. Before the bridge was constructed the river was crossed by a series of stepping stones. This seems fitting. This is where the bulls crossed. This is where the dead also cross on their way from the kirk to the graveyard: from life to death – from memory to history. So I cross this morning as the old town fills with new life. The snow has persisted and now that the sun is as fully up as it is likely to rise in a northern February the sky has swallowed it and turned to a low grey; the snow is beginning to lie on the ground. I look back and see my footprints follow me from one side to the other. I stand, momentarily, on the eastern side and watch as the evidence of my crossing slowly disappears under a thin layer of snow. I fantasise that I am like Leo Tolstoy plotting out the Battle of Austerlitz in his head for his novel *War and Peace*, but in actual fact I am just a poor storyteller who cannot sleep, wandering the early morning streets of his own little town is search of significance, looking for a purpose and a pattern to it all. Such existential indulgence tends to get you nowhere but so far it has got me across the river, cold and wet, realising that history is actually nothing at all, or if not that then just a series of images, yet without a story what use is a set of images? History may be a jigsaw but it is one with a discernible narrative – fickle, malleable, deceptive and sometimes even invisible but the storyteller must tell the story, the testimony has to be given and the pieces have to fit some pattern.

The vision of Tolstoy is blown away in the snow as it dusts the parapets of the bridge and drifts like a ghost down into the river. Again it is Walter Benjamin who comes into my mind, 'Death is the sanction of everything the storyteller can tell. He has borrowed his authority from death.'

I make my way along by the boating pond and tip my head in reverence to the cemetery, my 'sanction' and my 'authority'. I cross over by the 'new' footbridge which replaced the one washed away in a flood a few years ago. When the Thurso River bursts she does so spectacularly and the low lying districts at the river mouth are often submerged by the peaty dhu-loch water from the heart of Caithness.

I walk up Lovers Lane to the railway station. Where once hundreds of sheep pens housed the thousands of lambs which passed through the mart every autumn there is now a rubble strewn wasteland. This is what 'land banking' courtesy of Tesco looks like. The mart is half demolished. A local outlet for a national builder's merchant sits in sublime and defiant contrast across the railway tracks. I look down the broad avenue of Princes Street. The snow half obscures the kirky outline and clock tower of the new St Peter's kirk. School buses pass in a short lived convoy full of country faces with their usual mixture of eagerness and dread. A young loon stares briefly out from a window. It could have been myself.

After the flurry of buses has past I cross the road and lean against the high drystane dyke in front of the fringe of sycamore and boor trees which surrounds Ormlie Lodge. At home I have a picture of my mother and father standing in the gothic archway after their wedding in 1952. Again the snow provides a shape for the ghosts as they stand there happy in the photograph of my memory. This house once belonged to George Gunn, my great grandfather. The mystery of how he made his 'fortune' is a story I will never unravel. His father and his father before him came out of the Strath of Kildonan with the smoke of 'the burnings' in their collective memories. In truth the Gunns were by necessity and cultural habit renowned cattle rustlers and whisky makers. 'A lawless set of thieves' as Angus Mackay put it plainly in his history. It is interesting to note that this was not necessarily a condemnation. George Gunn, to add to the mystery, had two uncles, both doctors, called Sigurd and Kildonan Gunn but what actually happened to them no-one ventured to tell although I did hear New Zealand and South Africa mentioned, so one can only assume they trod the broad sea-road of exile. Quite how a descendant of cattle thieves and whisky makers came to inhabit such a pile as Ormlie Lodge was never illuminated or dwelt upon. The UKAEA used the place as a hostel up until the 1980s and a funeral director has – fittingly or not, I cannot decide – opened a parlour on the west wing of the building and as I stand and look at it now the entire picture has a certain unloved quality to it.

A pile of broken branches stands in the middle of one of the two lawns which flank the pathway which runs up to the arched doorway. In one of these lawns my great-grandmother, Johanna Mackay, used to sit out and take her ease, "Looking for all the world," my uncle Jimmy used to say, "like Queen Victoria." Seemingly she had a stick and if you displeased her or got too close she would hold it up to you to tell you, wordlessly, that you were liable to receive a nasty dunt. She wore black, as was the custom of the age and kept her hair in a severe bun. She was a proud member of the Clan Mackay from Durness and her tongue was Gaelic and her eye was steely and if ever there was a picture of a '*feach*' then Johanna Mackay holding court to the world on her stool in the garden of Ormlie Lodge would be it.

My great-grandmother was a matriarch of the 'Province of the Cat' and it would not be difficult to imagine her to be a shape-changer or to be the leader of some dark, alternative sisterhood. In 1719, which is quite recent for these sorts of affairs, Margaret MacGilbert was arrested and imprisoned in Thurso on suspicion of witchcraft. The story goes that Hugh Montgomery, a carpenter of Scrabster, was a great hater of cats. He was also a well-known producer of good quality ale. So it came to pass that Montgomery was driven to distraction by a pride of cats that assembled in his backyard each night and proceeded to go about their 'caterwaulings' and to drink his ale.

One night he could stand it no longer and ran out and attacked the assembled felines with a sword and cut the leg off one creature and wounded two more. A few days later two old women died and were found to have severe wounds on their bodies. A third, Margaret MacGilbert, was said to be in 'ill in bed and without a leg'. She was unceremoniously carted off and presented to the sheriff. She was tortured, as was normal, to extract her 'confession'. In Edinburgh the Lord Advocate, Robert Dundas, when he heard of the case ordered all proceedings to be dropped immediately. Unfortunately for Margaret MacGilbert 'the immediate' in the 18th century took quite a long time to come to pass and the poor woman died in prison, the loss of a leg and the subsequent torture proving too much for her to bear. Thomas Pennant, who wrote of this extraordinary story when he was on tour in the north, asked, "what part of the old lady would have been wanting had the cat's tail been cut off?" Robert Mackay, the historian of the Clan Mackay, had an answer. "Both the enquiry itself, and the question whether or not it was witty, might have been suspended until it was ascertained that such cats had tails!"

I walk up the hill. School pupils swarm out of 'the Atomics' and from the buses and move in a black uniformed column into the rectangular assemblage of Thurso High School. This was the architectural creation of Sir Basil Spence and won many awards in the early 1960s when it was constructed. Just why someone with any aesthetic taste whatsoever would choose to place a set of concrete and steel boxes on the top of Ormlie Hill is beyond me when the landscape all around is both parallel and undulating. Ian Begg, the distinguished Scottish architect, once described to me how architects 'enclose space with form' and how playwrights 'liberate space through action'. The 'space' of my childhood was certainly enclosed within Spence's boxes and was only 'liberated' when I escaped, aged sixteen, to find the 'action' of the rest of my life. If Sir Basil had to endure a few years schooling within the enclosed space of his 'award winning' creation he might have built fewer brutal buildings.

I look out to Dunnet Head and behind it the sky moves through the firth in a curtain of snow, its filigree fingers trailing over Dwarick and the lighthouse like the tendrils of some huge spectral jellyfish. Or perhaps it is the 'Angel of History', a vision of which came to Paul Klee so intensely that he had to paint it and so obsessed Walter Benjamin until it caught up with him in the Pyrenees. Patches of darkness and light, yellow and faint blue, surround the moving snow shower so that it becomes more like the Valkyrie as seen by Dorrud all those centuries ago when the Battle of Clontarf raged in Ireland and the Raven Banner went down into the blood-earth with Sigurd. Through the thin snow I can see the fields of Caithness open out towards the eastern light and my mind drifts with the weather as I think of all the human struggle which lies beneath these deceptively tidied acres. The politics of the 'Province of the Cat' is etched on the landscape by countless hands and these fences, these parks and fields and all the choices and conflicts, crisis and resolutions which they represent, bear witness through the shapes and colours of this agriculture to the mark of the human on the face of the world.

And the questions blow by me as I walk towards the Dunbar Hospital, the place where I was officially 'born', and I think about the patterns of my great-grandfather's stone wall: can a society truly be said to exist in harmony with the environment when it makes so many material demands on nature and what kind of society would exist if these demands were fewer? Is it only poverty which conditions equality? Is scarcity the only guarantee of peace? I know that my great-grandfather and all who came after him accepted neither poverty nor scarcity because they worked hard to overcome them and my life, if it is anything, is evidence of that. But their generations were enveloped in war and where, exactly, have equality and peace been apportioned in our historic journey? Have we forgotten them in our desire to survive? How long can this land, so beautiful, so stark in the Imbolg snow, support our demands and ourselves? The diurnal ceremony of the plough and the harvest has brought us to this point in time.

Last year, at this time, the sun shone in the sky for weeks and the farmers took advantage of the early spring to plough their fields. Dust blew from their furrows in the west wind. Our weather is quixotic. In the spring of 1999 the north of Scotland was hit by a series of equinoctial storms. One of these highlighted the vulnerability of which I spoke earlier.

The *SS Multibank Ascania*, a Cypriot registered chemical tanker, was making her way through the Pentland Firth from Liverpool *en route* to Teesside. Some miles west of Dunnet Head she developed a fire in the engine room and lost all power. There was a Force 8 gale blowing and the *Ascania* started to drift, at first – alarmingly – towards Dounreay. The prevailing wind took her closer to Thurso. On board the *Ascania* was 1,800 tonnes of vinyl acetate monomer, a highly flammable gas. With an out of control fire on board the ship was a potential bomb which, if it exploded, would have flattened half of Thurso – this was the stuff of nightmares. The coastguard was alerted and the rescue services sprang into action. The crew were air lifted off – Fijians and Croatians – and only the German skipper remained aboard in a desperate attempt to avert disaster. It was never very clear what he thought he could do it all by himself but as the *Ascania* drifted towards Dunnet Head and its potential date with doom he did eventually manage to drop one of the anchors, but the ship still drifted menacingly towards the sandstone cliffs.

The authorities correctly deduced that this was potentially a real disaster scenario which could have major human consequences so the police closed the road at the Castletown Planting end of Dunnet Beach, with a similar road-block east of Mey. Six hundred people were evacuated from their homes and crammed into various village halls for the night. Meanwhile at sea the Longhope and Scrabster lifeboats were on the scene and a tug was dispatched from Scapa Flow. One of the problems was that the captain of the *Ascania* had mistaken the radar echo from Dunnet Head as that of Stroma so he had no real idea where he was. Fortunately the crew of the Scrabster lifeboat knew the Firth intimately and they managed to pick up the tow line which had been put aboard the *Ascania* by the Scapa tug but which had snapped. They managed to ease the stricken tanker round the headland to the Brough side of Dunnet Head and into more relatively sheltered waters. If they had not done so one wonders what the consequences would have been. As luck would have it the storm subsided a little and the Scapa tug managed to get another line onto the *Ascania* and towed her into Scapa Flow where the fire was put out and the cargo of vinyl acetate pumped to another vessel. Eventually the *Multibank Ascania* was towed to Rotterdam.

As dramatic as this incident was it was, in the history of the Pentland Firth, not unusual and no-one was killed. What made it potentially disastrous was the mixture of fire, highly inflammable and explosive industrial chemicals and all of this drifting towards a nuclear complex, a relatively populous town and, eventually, a coastline of crofts and residential houses. In March 1999 the people of Caithness and the government of Britain were lucky. They may not be so lucky in the future. Ironically the Minister for Shipping, John Reid was in Caithness on some other business. One of the cost saving schemes his Labour government were proposing was to move the centre for coastguard control to Aberdeen and to scrap the safety tug based in Scapa Flow and to have its correspondent based in Stornoway. The tug in Stornoway was detailed to go to the assistance of the *Ascania*. It took sixteen hours to get on location. Mr Reid went around the village halls to meet and greet the evacuated people of the Coast of Widows, no doubt reassuring them that they would be even safer under these new proposals to remove their local coastal defences entirely from the Pentland Firth.

That was not the only comedy attached to the *Ascania* incident. A boat builder from Skarfskerry, let's call him Willie Paterson, was in Thurso drinking himself into a stupor. Things were not going well.

His business was failing. His wife had left him. So, as the alcohol removed all sense form his body, he decided the best thing to do was to kill himself. Unfortunately he was too drunk to notice the news being flashed up on every TV screen in every pub in Thurso about the drama unfolding in the Pentland Firth. Every available TV news team and camera crew were located around the lighthouse wall on Dunnet Head urging on the longed for explosion. The interests of the media then, just as they are now, are not the same as the interests of the people. Willie Paterson was far too caught up in his own personal tragedy to register any of that. So eventually he lurched out of the bar he was in, found his old landrover wherever he left it, got in and set off for Skarfskerry to end it all.

His plans were frustrated, however, by the police road block at the Planting in Castletown, which he did not see. He drove straight through it, oblivious. Needless to say the Northern Constabulary's finest took great exception to this and gave chase thinking, perhaps, that Willie was a terrorist or a suicide bomber. If they did then they were only half right. Two police vehicles gave chase. Maybe Willie, drunk as he was, might have thought it strange that there were no other cars of any description on an otherwise busy road. His mind was too focused, no doubt, on his own terrible mission of self-destruction. Willie never managed to commit suicide by driving his landrover off the Skarfskerry pier as he intended. As he hurtled towards his final destination some old netting and mooring lines got tangled up in his crankshaft and Willie's chariot of deliverance staggered to a stop some yards from its destination and when he half fell out the door to see what had gone wrong two hefty Highland police sergeants wrestled him to the ground, slapped a set of cuffs on him, bundled him into a police helicopter which was handily sitting in a nearby field and flew him to Inverness where he was duly sectioned. Some months later, when he was released, Willie Paterson wrote a letter to the John O Groat Journal to assure people that the rumours of his intending suicide were entirely false and that he was only returning home to get some oxy-acetylene cutting gear to assist in the rescue. As one of the lifeboat crew remarked later, that with 1,800 tonnes of highly flammable vinyl acetate gas on board, this was one item the rescuers of the *Ascania* did not need.

But the comedy surrounding this potential tragedy grows. In the very same edition of the John O Groat Journal in which Willie Paterson's letter appeared there was another letter of complaint about the *Ascania* episode, this time from a well-known musician and convicted drug dealer called Johnny Fats who, fantastically, actually lived in one of the lighthouse keepers' cottages on Dunnet Head. Johnny, in my mind, because he is now dead, was a cross between Jimi Hendrix and Albert Steptoe and was at the helm of many a northern musical combo, of which he was the electric axe-wielding hero, playing endless and self-possessed guitar solos at ear splitting decibels. He was not an attractive character and had an unduly negative influence over many impressionable young would-be guitar heros and budding rockers. Johnny's relationship with the Drug Squad of the Northern Constabulary was long and clandestine, involving midnight raids, arrests, 'confessions' and time spent in Inverness's Porterfield prison. All this over cannabis either shipped in or grown up at the lighthouse. No-one in their right mind would ever trust Johnny Fats. The police, however, used him as bait to entrap harmless musos whose only real concern was their instrument.

As has been previously relayed, at the time of the *Ascania*, the authorities evacuated everyone in a five kilometre radius of the incident – some 600 souls. Everyone, that is, except Johnny Fats. He alone was left in his Dunnet Head cliff top domicile, unaware of the potential maritime catastrophe unfolding, literally, beneath his feet and oblivious of the various media crews beaming the action around the world via TV satellite dishes just yards from his door. Johnny, famously, never watched TV or listened to the radio. What he did do was to play his guitar morning, noon and night and it was highly likely that he was doing so as the Scapa tug was attempting to get a tow line onto the powerless tanker and while the Scrabster lifeboat crew were risking their lives easing it around the headland. All this while, no doubt, Johnny's guitar gently wept.

When he eventually found out what had happened he, like Willie Paterson, wrote a long and indignant letter to the John O Groat Journal complaining about being left to his fate. There they were, side by side, two testaments to the comedy of human folly. Both letters were passionate, deeply felt defences of two differing experiences of a particular emergency. Neither letter made any sense. Shortly after all of this I met an off-duty bobby, a local lad whom I knew and who was on Dunnet Head that night in 1999. I asked him why the police had not evacuated Johnny Fats with all the rest of the people. He said that they knew where his wife was and they knew where his children were and that they were safe. "And, quite frankly, George," he continued, "if we had gone to his door we'd have had to bust him and, you know, we had enough on our plate that night!"

From the top of Ormlie Hill Dunnet Head emerges from the snow shower like a huge stone ship. Its rugged geos and battered cliffs represent the solid geology of time as much as they are signatures of rock. It is hard to imagine anything more permanent than this headland or that a boat load of chemicals, a drunken boat builder or a demented guitarist would make any difference to it. The headland has seen the sails of Roman galleys and Viking longships pass. A crippled tanker, a botched suicide and a stoned musician are just a few more stitches in the sandstone tapestry.

I think the beginning of the unravelling of whatever tapestry I had woven of Atomic City happened in 1977. Other than it being the year I turned twenty-one, three significant events took place. The first was the Queen's Jubilee which seemed to me, as I 'came of age', to be ridiculous; the second was the release of 'Never Mind The Bollocks' by the Sex Pistols which I thought was revolutionary; and the third was the explosion down the waste disposal shaft at Dounreay which put an end to any slight faith I had in the nuclear 'project'. Pageantry, punk rock and bad chemistry; privilege, nihilism and lies; royalty, rebellion and pollution – these then the unholy trinities of 1977. The first instinct of the UKAEA was to deny that anything had happened to the waste shaft at all, despite the fact that a solid steel lid had been blown twenty feet into the air and the sound could be heard several miles away. Then they admitted that a 'minor incident' had occurred. After that they began to describe it in the media and press releases as 'a controlled explosion'. Over the following years the full story about the real extent of the nuclear release has emerged, not in any fleshed out narrative but in the usual dribs and drabs, bits and pieces which are the orphaned truth-children of a secret state. Denial is not a fallback position which offers much in the way of progress. Denial about the 1977 waste shaft explosion has shape-changed into denial about decommissioning and about any past radiation leaks. The UKAEA may have surrounded itself with a velvet wall of misinformation but in actual fact it is the people of Atomic City themselves who put up the soft fences against reality. The Official Secrets Act is both the hammer and the fence-post. So corralled the people are difficult to reach.

To reach them was exactly why I wrote the play *Atomic City* which Grey Coast Theatre Company, in association with Eden Court, toured around Scotland in 1999. A new millennium was approaching and I wanted to tell the truth as I saw it about the place I came from. The theatre and opera director Johnathan Miller has said that 'a play must be a witness of where it comes from'. That was my wish for *Atomic City*, the play. As has been the proven norm with my theatre work the majority of the people loved *Atomic City*, seeing in it a portrait of a time and a place and with characters which they could recognise and sympathise with and which made them laugh. On the other hand the central belt critics hated the play, one even ended his review with this magisterial conclusion 'and the ultimate weakness of this play is its improbability'. This I found hilarious as I had, actually, made very little up. Critics are free to dismiss my work, this I accept. Dismissing history is another thing.

In the ancient drama of classical Greece tragedy was portrayed as a loss of life. In modern drama tragedy is loss of purpose. This is what has befallen Thurso in the second decade of the 21st century. A loss of history – including a dismissal of it because of ignorance – leads inevitably to a loss of purpose. Theatre at least brings people together to look at their society. The pity is that there is not a constant forum for this discussion to take place in Atomic City. Thurso has to evolve out of rumour and denial into harbouring the prospect of responsible citizens taking control over their own lives, of being able to make choices, take decisions and plan.

The art critic Murdo MacDonald has invented the term 'metroparochialism' to describe the exclusivity of the concerns of the urban centres, whether these be in London, Edinburgh, Glasgow or Inverness, at the expense of the interests and experiences of the periphery. It has been my experience that the arts managers in the central belt and in the 'capital of the Highlands' always considered it ludicrous that Thurso, or Caithness more generally, could (or should) support a theatre company dedicated to new writing about the north of Scotland. The Grey Coast Theatre Company took its lead from the history of Thurso itself: we were dedicatedly local but passionately international: we had a specific locus but we had a global focus. Where Thurso sits on the map of Europe informs you that if there was to be a theatre company in the old Viking town then it would have to adopt such a world view if it were to survive. The cultural trade routes of the Grey Coast Company were to Norway, Iceland, Ireland and Canada and wherever the Scandinavian and Highland diaspora were to be found. We succeeded for the best part of nineteen years and eventually were closed down by a few, powerful arts managers and ambivalent politicians who never believed in it and were hostile to the concept from the start. That the theatre company raised and spent over £1.25 million in that period never seemed to be important to them.

But this saga is not about a theatre company, even if it is part of the reality. The ability and facility to take control of your own destiny is a daunting prospect for a country's entire population of millions and even more so for a town of a few thousand. In 2013 the Highland Council, with funding and direction from the Scottish government conducted a series of 'charrettes', or design led planning workshops in Thurso. Over a period of a week the public, from school children to pensioners were invited to come to a series of 'brainstorming' sessions at which they could raise issues or contribute ideas for the betterment of Thurso, some of which probably would be incorporated into the council's 'local plan'. It has to be noted that the Highland Council's record as far as Thurso's 'local plan' is concerned – and local planning in general – is not good. Nonetheless scores of people participated in the 'charrette' process and many sensible things were said and many good ideas mooted. Except for several retired 'Atomicers' who all said they 'felt threatened' by the process, the general mood after the consultation week was over was one of positivity.

Unlike a play a Highland Council/Scottish government consultation exercise does not necessarily translate dialogue into action, or nouns into verbs. Also what is one actually to make of the Dounreay retirees who said they felt threatened? I suppose being asked to think for yourself – and act locally – after a lifetime of cultural, social, professional and political paternalism is probably a behaviour pattern and a state of consciousness for which they are not programmed. But can Thurso afford to say, "Well, they are old and soon they will die?" If we think that then we really do have a town with no soul and I am fully aware that there are a considerable amount of people who already believe Thurso is beyond redemption. I am not one of them. Even if, from time to time, it makes me weep.

The snow continues to fall, but gently, as the wind has dropped and the unexpected stillness seems to fatten out the snowflakes into tiny drifts of cotton. Neil Gunn Drive, named after the greatest writer Caithness produced in the 20th century, runs in a useless u-bend around Petrie's paint shed and a car auto-parts warehouse. Such do our civic leaders so value the blessings of literature that they have named a road in an industrial estate after the author of *The Silver Darlings*. Behind me lies the whippet training ground of High Ormlie where Atomic City most decidedly stops and where the 'learned helplessness', so beloved of American sociologists, takes everybody for a walk.

I have lived on the edge of High Ormlie, on the cusp of this 'learned helplessness', for fifteen years and in that time the estate has risen, fallen, risen again and is now falling back into the unloved sump it became almost at once when it was built in the early 1980s. The unemployed and unemployable, single mothers, drug addicts, socially inept and sometimes dangerous, the lost, the lonely, the elderly, the disabled, immigrants, emigrants and migrants, people with mental health issues, the homeless and the gormless – all manner of refugees were packed into the loveless streets, some with houses so close together the buildings look as if they have been concertinaed, some are supposed to look like traditional Caithness croft houses but were so rushed up and covered in grey harling they look like brick hen houses and all looking in the way, across at each other, on top of each other, surrounded by a fence, with one road in and one road out: this is the ghetto of the 'Province of the Cat'. In High Ormlie people learn helplessness between giros or the current equivalent. Or so the popular myth goes.

Because property has no intrinsic value, because the land is value's real measure, the houses in High Ormlie are packed together, as I've said, but even in the terms of the estate agent many of the 'properties' on the estate are literally valueless and only a very few residents own their own homes. So if ever a group of people were absolutely not responsible in any shape or form for the financial crash of 2007/8 it is the people of High Ormlie. The money system's collapse was predicated upon a banking sector which was driven by debt and who measured wealth in the weight of their mortgage folios in an over inflated property market where house prices were sheer fantasy and only matched by the delusional method of paying for them. Yet it is the people of High Ormlie, many of whom are turning on their morning lights to begin their day, who are the ones being made to pay, not the bankers. The so called 'bedroom tax' will take away a significant part of their weekly income. Their rents, whether housing association or Highland Council, only go up. The price of food, fuel, electricity, clothing and of sending their children to school increases monthly. So, in effect, High Ormlie drifts further away from the 'normality' of the nuclear narrative like some island from Celtic mythology which only rises out of the sea every seven years, or like the moon which leaves the gravitational influence of the earth at a quarter of an inch a year.

The snow seems to be falling more heavily as I look up Henderson Street and the road is a more consolidated shade of white. Prior to 2008 the Highland Council hatched a plan to sell off their entire housing stock to an independent housing association on the premise that this new housing association would be able, somehow, to raise more money to invest in the existing housing stock and to build more new houses. Because of government restrictions on borrowing the council, it claimed, could do neither. The Highland Council did spend, however, a lot of money and used a lot of resources and staff hours trying to convince their tenants during the propaganda campaign in the run up to the referendum on the issue that they should 'vote for change'. Throughout Caithness and the rest of the

Highlands, but specifically in High Ormlie, the people instinctively knew that a 'vote for change' was a vote for a leap into the dark with all the security of tenure a council lease offers becoming so much fuel, potentially, for the housing association shredder. The people knew, although not one of the council employees who handed them glossy leaflets on their doorsteps would tell them, that housing associations can be bought up, sold off or go bankrupt as happened in Glasgow when the biggest housing stock transfer in Scotland resulted in the new association going to the financial wall.

When the majority of the tenants resoundingly voted to stay with the Highland Council several councillors and Jamie Stone, the Liberal Democrat MSP, told the press that they were 'disappointed with the choice' and that 'the tenants had voted the wrong way'. Suddenly in High Ormlie we were transported back to East Germany in 1953, when the poet is not George Gunn but Bertolt Brecht, who wrote of the suppressed uprising of the people against the communist government:

> After the uprising of the 17th of June
> The Secretary of the Writers Union
> Had leaflets distributed in the Stalinallee
> Stating that the people
> Had forfeited the confidence of the government
> And could win it back only
> By redoubled efforts. Would it not be easier
> In that case for the government
> To dissolve the people
> And elect another?

When it comes to the poor and the disadvantaged our elected representatives often find it too easy to discover their totalitarian tendencies. The reason that Atomic City, the nuclear burgh, ends in High Ormlie is that it is in High Ormlie where the poor have been placed: out of sight from the main thoroughfares of Thurso, safe on their hill where no tourist or enterprise wonk may embarrassingly run into them. With their one shop, their one take-away, their one bus and their one road in and out they are at perfect liberty to live out their stressful lives striving and always failing to meet the exacting demands of the consumer credo and the aspirational social standards of those who live elsewhere and for whom such things are considered normal. In High Ormlie poverty is normal. As you walk through the estate you can cut the stress with a knife. What is dissolving is the 'learned helplessness' the state offers the majority of the residents of High Ormlie. When there is nothing left for most of the people they may well move off their hill and enter into Atomic City to explore what has been denied to them and to participate in their share and when that happens all the middle class plays and novels about the 'limits of empathy' will have been staged and read for naught. A new theatre will be needed then and a new literature because Atomic City will have a new history.

The snow has stopped now, the Imbolg sun is in the sky and I walk to the light. By the time I get to Buckies Hill it is mid-morning. Just over two miles south-east of the town this hill is a good place to come to survey the landscape. The cloud has blown back and sits moodily on the horizon, forever drifting west. The sky is a pale egg-shell blue. The snow covered hills of Hoy hump whale-like to the north. In the Pentland Firth a huge container ship noses around Dunnet Head on its way to Rotterdam or the Baltic. The cold has eased a little but the easterly wind still cuts like a knife. I coorie-doon for shelter behind a dry-stane wall. To the south-east, beyond Loch Calder, Morven and the Scarabens take on the mountainous attributes of the Alps as the sunlight bounces blue and yellow off their snowy mantle. The Flow Country disappears into an icy idea of itself, mile after mile of imagination, dream and frozen bog with names such as *Bog na Gaoithe* (the bog of the winds) and *Blàr nam Faoileag* (the plain of the gulls), names which pepper the mind. To the west, even more impressive than the Morven range, rising out of the bog is the dorsal tipped lyric poem in rock which is Ben Loyal and its massive sister, Ben More, a white wall of ice at the root of Loch Eriboll. To the south-west the long rocky spine of Klibreck appears to dig itself into the whiteness of the earth.

From Buckies Hill it is easy to discern the triangular shape of Caithness. From the west she emerges from beneath the bog-blanket of Sutherland her sister. The Atlantic sweeps out far north-west to Iceland and beyond and funnels her colossal energy into the tiny aperture of the Pentland Firth. There, each side of Stroma, she battles twice daily with her own smaller but violently petulant sister, the North Sea. Diurnally, perennially, they clash and boil. The February cliffs will be quiet now from the lack of seabirds. A few fulmars will squat between fishing expeditions and storms in the camp of the flagstone ledges and on the sandstone fractures. They are seldom away for long now as climate changes and habits adapt accordingly. Some of the croft parks on the Coast of Widows will have already tasted the plough but, for now, they lie dormant under their snow cover. Duncansby Head shades into a shadow behind a swirling curtain of cloud. From Wick down to The Ord the Grey Coast is a faint impression but I know it is there, skirting the Moray Firth, licking her frosted lips to taste the legends of salt and the dreams of history, our perfect literature.

My eye follows the course of Wick River backwards from east to west, out past the shieling hill of Dorrery, into Munsary and the shared dhu loch beginnings of Thurso River in the head waters of Loch More where Dirlot Castle hugs its crag of ice. As my eye searches west and follows ‘*Skinandi*’, the shining one, the contours of the land open out as the river flows towards Thurso through the ferm-toons of Westerdale and Harpsdale. Here we see the transition from the pastoral cattle country of the Celtic world into the enclosed, squared and fenced planned economy of the 19th century, the generator of war. The atmosphere of Atomic City somehow blows away from the reality of Thurso as the old Viking town sits at the mouth of her river like an open purse of wet stones. The faint trace of a snow shower passes over the upturned boats of her morning roofs only to be blown out into the green sulking bay sacrificing its ballet to the storehouse of the sea.

The provider of the land stares back at me, shyly, because she is not really the provider for the people in the way she could be. Vast tonnages of barley and ample beef provide the top-earning Caithness farmers with a comfortable quota of European Union cash, specialising the land into indolence and tying the people to the retail tyranny of Tesco and the myth of the global market. Equally insincerely the wind farm on the Cassiemire summons the breeze with its two dozen slow signalling turbines. The blades circle in the false promise of green energy and community wealth which the landowner and the power-utility company pocket between them. I think of the young men marching over the hill and out of their strath, The *Riasgan*, to go to war in *Butcher's Broom*, the novel by Neil Gunn, followed as far as they dared by the young children who thought that this was a grand game and a memorable day and how that actual story must've been played out in countless straths and glens throughout the north. I think of Donald Sutherland who died at Waterloo and the cold stony reality of his name carved into the memorial in the clearance village of Badbea where the children – the same children as in Gunn's novel, for the children are always there, laughing, playing – had to be tethered to the ground along with the animals to stop them from being blown over the cliffs. Because it is land enclosure and human displacement which pave the pathways to war for the young men of The *Riasgan* to follow and how it bleeds the land as well as the sea; and again it is Neil Gunn who provides the dramatic scene of Tormod and his two fellow fishermen press ganged by an English man of war just off the

Grey Coast during the Napoleonic War. That scene, too, a common occurrence as the British Empire expanded and the navy needed men. I look north-west towards Dounreay and HMS *Vulcan* and see another kind of press gang at work keeping alive the corrupting narrative of another ship of war.

What hope for the people when their labour is stolen and misspent? The residents of High Ormlie, the poor of our community, are not criminals but they do live in a camp. The UK government have decided, because it is the opposite of truth, to criminalise the poor by insisting that living on benefits is a lifestyle choice and therefore a fraud. The rich have managed to placate their guilt at such a false judgement by compounding it and putting the poor in jail where there 'unoccupied' cells can be taxed. The 'bedroom tax' is a low point in British governance. It is in High Ormlie where the damage will be done. 'Nothing comes from nothing. Think again!' Cars hiss by me on the road down to Glen Golly.

This transference of wealth from the poor to the rich is the most blatant exploitative one-way traffic of recent times. The neat rectangular fields which fan out in every direction below remind me that this transference has equally exploitative historical precedents. What will it take to redirect and undo this injustice? Will the politicians have to run naked through the streets of Atomic City in search of the elusive 2,000 jobs needed to repair the flag of their tattered fiction? Will a contemporary of Sandy Murray have to put their foot through the expecting drum of privilege? Will the evicted of High Ormlie have to live in shelters by the side of the road?

Why must it remain a dream that the process of wealth creation cannot be a two-way affair, where everything is linked and in which humankind can be endlessly creative – instead of war-like – through combining ideas and where money can be exchanged equitably when labour, material and intellectual property are used? Instead the people of High Ormlie are trapped on the sea-ledge of powerlessness by the receding high tide of the Cold War, which in Atomic City has metamorphosed their town into a 'technopoly', a place or condition which the writer Neil Postman has described in his 1992 book *Technopoly: The Surrender of Culture to Technology* as a living hell where a society believes that, 'the primary, if not the only, goal of human labour and thought is efficiency, that technical calculation is in all respects superior to human judgment … and that the affairs of citizens are best guided and conducted by experts.'

The people of High Ormlie are trapped in a traveller's camp of permanent temporality. As automation increases we will all become the prisoners of 'technopoly' as employment, as we understand it, will be in a terminal crisis. 'Experts' already run governments. Sir John Sinclair of Ulbster was an 'expert'. The nuclear scientists who plied 'the locals' with 'whisky and biscuits' in Thurso in the early 1950s were 'experts'.

What sleeps beneath the croft parks and enclosed farm fields of Caithness is the seed of a lengthier and altogether more deliberate political dialogue, which we desperately need to grow because the system I see laid out before me is so locked-in to its own structure it has not even the slightest sense that it is unsustainable. It has no room for the poor. The belief that everything will continue on as before is as much of an orthodoxy for the internet generation as it was for the 'improvers' of the 'Enlightenment'. As the ghettoisation of people of High Ormlie indicates the paradigm which has emerged is of a society hollowed out, where there is officially no longer a working class. Whether it is on the World Wide Web or in monitoring the Caithness beaches for radiation we are all in thrall to the 'Songs of the Sirens' of the cadres of utility providers and corporations which currently control us. They bleed and collect the wealth that we create without sharing that wealth. This is how the one-way street operates, so if we desire to return to our home port we will have to learn from Odysseus to stuff our ears against the 'Songs of the Sirens' with the philosophical and economical equivalents of beeswax, or we will be consumed and all the dynamic links to an alternative reality will be wrecked on the rocks. This is what happens when economic theories atrophy and the orthodoxies become 'locked-in'. Like machines they will beat themselves to death. But human beings are not machines.

On Buckies Hill I see that the White Cailleach of Winter has gone back into her house. The prospects for the coming spring look good. The rising blood of life is ever-optimistic. I watch the windmills turn. Now Walter Benjamin becomes the White Cailleach. On the shimmering snow of a Caithness field he writes, 'Only a thoughtless observer can deny that correspondences come into play between the world of modern technology and the archaic symbol world of mythology.'

In my ear I hear the soft yet forceful voice of Hamish Henderson singing 'Roch the wind in the clear day's dawin...' and it does and it is as it blows over Buckies Hill, over this raised rocky plateau of flagstone, this stage where giants act, where the stories are broken down into images and then put back together again into the great play of our history, our choreography disappearing behind us as we dance across the performance space of time and the applause of the sea swallowing itself and our meaning.

From that sea of memory, passed on, remembered, distilled, mythologised, I see my Nana More at the gutting pool in Wick between the wars, her cooper husband Alastair dead barely a year; her youngest of four, her daughter, my mother, a bairn in a creel; all five of them packed like the herring she gutted, into a single-end in Lower Pulteneytown. I see my grandfather and grandmother in 1924 winding up the gently sloping track to their new home at West Greenland, everything they owned in the cart on which they sit, the parks they are to farm spread out around them like bleaching sheets.

Two languages then, Caithness Scots and Gaelic; two realities, the sea and the land. The cultural dichotomy which is Caithness is caught in those four people. Out of their lives flows the 'carrying stream' of Norse and Celt, of fisher and farmer. Like the Wick and Thurso rivers they have a common source and the sea they flow into is the sea of world culture, that thing for which the Russian poet Osip Mandelstam expressed a deep, impossible nostalgia. All drift with the snow showers through the Pentland Firth.

I walk back down from Buckies Hill. I can faintly hear the dull throbbing sound of Atomic City as the traffic increases. The faint sunlight reflects off various transit vans and articulated lorries as they pass through the town from Scrabster to the A9 and south or in the other direction out to Dounreay. The snow which lies so beautiful and cold on the fields will melt and come August the parks will be yellow with barley. As the year progresses the sea will warm and become blue once again. I go down to Atomic City which sits beneath me. The 'Province of the Cat' is all around me. The wheel of the ages will turn and more memory and history will swim up the river like so many salmon and like the salmon they will spawn and die and be reborn. Maybe they will become poems? Perhaps they will enjoy their new life in songs? I open up my jacket collar and loosen my scarf and the cold air catches my throat. At the side of the road the wind whistles through the branches of the boor trees which in Caithness shoulder the burden of the prevailing blast. I hear the music of a brand new day.